SPORTS IN AFRICA, PAST AND PRESENT

SPORTS IN AFRICA, PAST AND PRESENT

EDITED BY TODD CLEVELAND, TARMINDER KAUR,
AND GERARD AKINDES

OHIO UNIVERSITY PRESS, ATHENS

Ohio University Press, Athens, Ohio 45701
ohioswallow.com
© 2020 by Ohio University Press

First paperback printing 2021
Paperback ISBN 978-0-8214-2451-3

To obtain permission to quote, reprint, or otherwise reproduce or distribute material from
Ohio University Press publications, please contact our rights and permissions department
at (740) 593-1154 or (740) 593-4536 (fax).

Printed in the United States of America
Ohio University Press books are printed on acid-free paper ⊗ ™

Library of Congress Cataloging-in-Publication Data

Names: Cleveland, Todd, editor. | Kaur, Tarminder, editor. |
Akindes, Gerard, editor.
Title: Sports in Africa, past and present / edited by Todd Cleveland,
Tarminder Kaur, Gerard Akindes.
Description: Athens : Ohio University Press, 2020. |
Includes bibliographical references and index.
Identifiers: LCCN 2020020309 | ISBN 9780821424254 (hardcover) |
ISBN 9780821446966 (pdf)
Subjects: LCSH: Sports—Social aspects—Africa. | Sports—Africa—History. |
Sports—Sociological aspects.
Classification: LCC GV655 .S65 2020 | DDC 796.096—dc23
LC record available at https://lccn.loc.gov/2020020309

*To everyone who participates in making sports
such an important part of Africa.*

CONTENTS

Contents

Contents

ACKNOWLEDGMENTS

We would like to thank all the authors for their contributions and, more broadly, for rigorously engaging with the topic of sports in Africa, which is still in the process of garnering serious consideration within the academy. At Ohio University, we would like to thank the Center of International Studies, the College of Health and Human Services (now the College of Health Sciences and Professions), The Multicultural Center, The Center for Sports Administration, and The Patton College of Education for their foundational support of the conferences from which this volume emerged. We also greatly benefited from the various forms of assistance provided by the following individuals: Charles Higgins, Andrew Kreutzer, Matthew A. Adeyanju, Steve Howard, and Chase Barney. We would also like to thank the anonymous reviewers, whose comments appreciably enhanced the content of this volume. Finally, we would like to express our enduring gratitude to Gill Berchowitz for her faith in this project from the onset, as well as the incomparable staff at Ohio University Press for their prodigious efforts in transforming an assortment of files and images into the polished product that you are currently reading.

Introduction

More Than Just Games

TODD CLEVELAND, TARMINDER KAUR,
AND GERARD AKINDES

In February 2004, Ohio University hosted the first Sport in Africa Conference. The event quickly gained both traction and momentum, and in the spring of 2019 the thirteenth conference was hosted by the Université Cheikh Anta Diop in Dakar, Senegal, marking the third time the gathering was held on the African continent.[1] In the years since the inaugural conference, a sizable—and ever-expanding—group of scholars, including myriad conference participants, has continued to legitimize the study of sports in the academy. Correspondingly, both academic and commercial presses have been increasingly receptive to publishing the diverse range of high-quality research that this collection of scholars, housed in an array of disciplines, has generated. Although the pioneers of sports studies focused their research and teaching efforts on subjects and topics related to the Global North, more recently the study of sports-related processes and developments elsewhere in the world, including Africa, has been gaining momentum, tangibly evinced by the enthusiastic and expanding participation in this series of conferences.[2] This volume, which grew out of these gatherings, aims to contribute to this steady procession toward mainstream academic recognition of

African sports studies by generating an instructive text that engages with the core themes that have emerged from these conferences since the initial gathering in 2004.

With papers from these conferences constituting both the impetus and, ultimately, the core content of this volume, we initially reached out to the hundreds of participants who had presented at one (or more) of these events to invite them to submit a chapter for this book. The result of an enthusiastic response from scholars based in Africa, Europe, and North America, the chapters in this volume examine an array of sports across multiple eras and revolve around themes that transcend individual sports: athletic migration, crossing racial boundaries, sports pedagogy, the sporting periphery, sports as resistance, sports and identity, sports heritage, the impact of political legacies on sports, and sporting biography.

Collectively, through the prism of sports this scholarship offers significant insight into the varying and shifting experiences of African athletes, fans, communities, and states. At the most basic level, the chapters explore Africans' reception and subsequent appropriation of an assortment of "modern sports" that European colonizers introduced, including but not limited to soccer, cricket, and rugby; the roles that these sports played both during and after the process of decolonization in shaping local and national identities in the newly independent African states; and the diverse ways that African individuals, communities, and governments utilize sports and sporting activities in contemporary Africa for varying social and political ends.

Since their introduction, modern sports in Africa have reflected cultural, social, political, economic, generational, and gendered relations on the continent but have also precipitated significant change in this array of interconnected facets of everyday life. The chapters in this volume examine these processes and consider the ways that broader historiographical and political developments and emphases have shaped the production of African sports knowledge. In particular, in the first chapter, Albert Grundlingh and Sebastian Potgieter trace this process as it has unfolded across South Africa in different periods. The subsequent section on pedagogy explicitly engages with the ways that sports material can be effectively delivered in the classroom to enhance various learning processes and is intended to assist the growing number of instructors who are interested in incorporating various African sports topics into their curriculum.

In 1987, William Baker and J. A. Mangan, in their pioneering volume *Sport in Africa: Essays in Social History*, presciently proclaimed, "The future of African sport history is rich in promise."[3] In continuing to mine these bountiful sporting veins, this volume strives to provide for scholars, instructors, and students alike an array of "sporting windows" through which to view and comprehend key developments in Africans' engagements and experiences with leisure and professional sporting activities since their inception on the continent.

The History of Sports in Africa

As John Bale has argued, the development of the "modern sports movement" during the early nineteenth century "paralleled (and was often part of) the colonial policies of the great powers of the Western world."[4] Thus, the European introduction of so-called modern sports—the sports that we reflexively identify, such as soccer, basketball, and rugby—into Africa in the nineteenth century constitutes but one dimension of a series of increasingly violent intrusions on the continent. Following the Berlin Conference in 1884–85, during which European imperial nations carved up Africa into colonial territories, missionaries, administrators, merchants, corporate officials, soldiers, and settlers—the standard agents of colonialism—began to introduce various sports to indigenous residents. These athletic endeavors spread from port cities to the hinterlands, often along roads and railway lines but also through rural missionary schools. In explaining Africans' initial receptiveness toward these sports, scholars have emphasized the strong relationships and linkages between these new activities and precolonial martial and athletic traditions.[5] John Bale and Joe Sang have even argued that local customs and notions of masculinity provided the "soil into which the seeds of European sport would be later planted."[6] Even in these arguably unlikely sporting incubators, these games steadily took hold.

Although Africans throughout the continent generally embraced these sports, their introduction was anything but innocent. Colonial regimes intended these sports to "civilize" indigenous populations as part of a broader program of "muscular Christianity," intertwined with physical education, that aimed to improve the bodies of the colonized masses. These sports were also intended, in turns, to subdue, discipline, inculcate, and even demean local populations.[7] Indeed, these sports were introduced into a series of oppressive, exploitative environments that characterized African imperial space. The constituent colonial settings featured institutionalized racism, segregation, and pervasive inequity. As such, sports constituted more than just games; Europeans used them to establish and deepen both physical and psychological control of their colonized subjects. Sports served as key components in the colonial powers' campaigns of cultural imperialism, important pillars in the broader processes of empire. As Nuno Domingos has argued in relation to the Lusophone African colonial context, the games themselves were "instruments of socialization, infusing discipline ... [and] respect for hierarches and rituals."[8] If Europeans colonized Africa, as the maxim goes, with a gun in one hand and the Bible in the other, they were also equipped with soccer, rugby, and cricket balls, a third hegemonic tool.

Notwithstanding the intentions of the colonial powers, scholars of the history of sports in Africa have cogently established that although Europeans introduced these games, indigenous practitioners were hardly passive consumers; they contested various aspects and fashioned new meanings of these sports. For Africans, sporting endeavors were "more than just games." For example, pioneering work by Phyllis M. Martin and Laura Fair, among others, has astutely identified the nationalist and protonationalist dimensions of soccer in British and French colonial Africa, insightfully reconstructed the contention over leisure time and the limits of European control, and rightfully analyzed football (soccer) as a "terrain of struggle."[9] Elsewhere, scholars have examined the ways that indigenous practitioners essentially appropriated these games, attributing meanings to them unintended by those who had originally introduced the sports.[10] As part of this process, Africans produced unique, often "creolized," styles that reflected local aesthetic values.[11]

Because they were typically banned from White settlers' sports clubs and associations, African players and coordinators often responded by forming teams and leagues of their own that helped foster the development of distinct identities and, concomitantly, political consciousness.[12] The chapters in this volume by Trishula Patel and Mark Fredericks adroitly illuminate these processes in Zimbabwe and South Africa, respectively. In certain cases, these autonomous endeavors of sporting organizations even simulated the process of institution building in an imagined postcolonial state.

Following the gusting of the "winds of change" that marked the independence of African nations, beginning with Ghana in 1957, sports continued to play an important role on the continent. Inheriting populations that had been artificially bound by the arbitrary borders the European imperial powers had established at Berlin decades earlier, the first generation of African leaders eyed sports as a means to forge unity among the disparate subpopulations that resided within their states. National stadiums were constructed (often with Chinese money), national teams were formed, and these fledging nations entered both continental and international sporting competitions. Michelle Sikes's chapter on long-distance running takes the reader through this process in Kenya.

In the decades following independence, many African nations experienced devastating violence. Although these civil conflicts were almost always fueled by competing Cold War interests, the divisions ran along local fault lines. These domestic clashes suggest that the prospective unifying capacity of sports was either overestimated or simply overwhelmed by deeper social, often ethnic, divisions that had been suppressed by the respective colonial regimes.

Following this period of seemingly endless coups d'état, rebellions, and other forms of conflict, which uncoincidentally subsided after the conclusion of the Cold War in the 1990s, African leaders and civil society members once again began eyeing sports as a unifying force. Perhaps most famously, the efficacious exhortation in 2005 by Ivorian soccer star Didier Drogba and his teammates to end the conflict in Côte d'Ivoire is exemplary of the coalescent power that sports may, indeed, possess, even if only temporarily. A more cynical observer might remind us, however, of the periodic meddling of national governments in national soccer federations, often along ethnic lines, or of the contentious, racially based quota system in effect in South African sports, to demonstrate that sporting environments not only reflect social divisions but may even exacerbate them. It is our hope that sports in Africa can continue to help precipitate positive change on the continent while enabling practitioners, supporters, and observers to better understand the lifeworlds in which these sports are played and take on meaning.

Why Study Sports in Africa?

If you've read this far, you can most likely already provide a number of cogent answers to this question.[13] Moreover, there are currently fewer individuals posing this question, at least with any tinge of skepticism or hostility. But it is worth addressing for readers who may not have considered this query or who remain dubious. There are, of course, countless possible answers to this question, but perhaps the most obvious is that sports and athletic endeavors feature in the daily lives and attention, in some form or another, of millions of Africans throughout the continent. As among supporters and practitioners worldwide, sporting activity generates excitement, pleasure, and despair and can also forge community. Chapters in this volume by Tarminder Kaur, Solomon Waliaula, Todd Leedy, and Marizanne Grundlingh consider the roles that various sports play in the formation of communities of different types and sizes. Moreover, as John Nauright and Mahfoud Amara have contended, sports are woven into the "social, political, cultural, and economic dynamics and fabrics of African nations."[14] And perhaps most important, as anthropologist Bea Vidics has argued, studying sports activity can provide "insights into social, cultural, political, and historical processes that transcend the sporting arena."[15] In this volume, for example, Christian Ungruhe and Sine Agergaard follow former soccer players from West Africa in northern Europe into their postsporting lives and thus beyond the formal "sporting arena," though their plights and decisions are, as the authors demonstrate, deeply informed by their athletic experiences.

We wholeheartedly concur with Nauright, Amara, and Vidics, and we add that sports activity on the continent at both local and national levels highlights a range of enduring and novel power dynamics between various actors and entities. Often these constitutive interactions and relations reflect broader social imbalances that generally run along gender, generational, ethnic, racial, and religious lines, but explorations of these sites of engagement also reveal the ways that marginalized groups utilize sports to contest these inequities and struggle to narrow various gaps. For example, Chuka Onwumechili and Jasmin M. Goodman's chapter in this volume showcases efforts by women footballers in Nigeria to challenge the sports patriarchy in the country. Studies such as this one also serve to highlight the continuities—in this case, male dominance in the sports realm—that persist across the colonial-independence divide, a conventional periodization narrowly characterized through a primarily political prism. Derek Catsam's chapter addresses how the legacy of apartheid-era policies and concomitant perceptions continue to limit opportunities in rugby for Black South Africans.

Finally, we propose that Baker and Mangan's prescient statement regarding the promise of African sports studies remains as relevant now as it was when they first penned the passage more than four decades ago. With sports studies now legitimized in the academy, generations of younger scholars from across Africa and beyond its borders are examining the histories of sports on the continent. But much work remains to be done. Studies of African sports need to further diversify beyond soccer, for some time and to a great extent the scholarly favorite; indeed, even long-distance running, one of the continent's highest-profile sports, remains puzzlingly understudied.[16] Matt Carotenuto's pedagogical chapter outlines the innovative ways he works around the predominance of soccer in African sports studies while in the classroom. Moreover, scholars continue to neglect women's sports and the ways that children engage with sports in Africa, both informally and, increasingly, formally.[17] Indicative of this inattention is that only rarely do these demographic groups feature in this volume. In addition, although scholars have focused on African athletes who have migrated to Europe to ply their skills, significantly less research has followed these athletes to other world regions.[18] Again, this volume reflects this topical emphasis. We would also welcome more transnational and continent-wide research, as much African sports scholarship continues to be bound by national borders artificially established over a century ago, even if they retain analytical utility for certain areas of inquiry. In the diaspora, research on the countless numbers of Africans who play on National Collegiate Athletic Association (NCAA) and American professional basketball and football teams awaits its scholar. Of course this litany of prospective topics is hardly exhaustive, but significant progress has undoubtedly been made; the epistemological foundation is now laid. Indeed, the diversification and overall expansion of research on sports in Africa are extremely encouraging. Baker and Mangan would surely be satisfied.

A Note Regarding the Predominance of South African Sports Scholarship

Even before we began to gather chapters for this volume, we anticipated that scholarship related to South Africa would be well represented. Indeed, South Africa holds an unrivaled place in the scholarship on sports in Africa, for a number of reasons. Even as far back as 1987, in the infancy of African sports studies, Baker and Mangan alerted readers in the introduction to *Sport in Africa* that they had "decided not to include an essay on South Africa and apartheid per se because that issue is already well covered in the literature; it is, in fact, the only topic sufficiently documented in the history of African sport."[19] Even before African sports studies was a viable and cohesive, if still fluid, scholarly area of inquiry, research related to South African sports dominated.[20] This scenario is partially attributable to the intense global focus on the country's racist apartheid system, which stretched from 1949 until the early 1990s and naturally led scholars to examine various aspects of South African society under this durable regime. As part of this investigative process, researchers, journalists, and other observers quickly identified the centrality of sports in the struggle for the nation and the important political and social roles that sports played across the spectrum of racial communities in the country. Moreover, as a long-standing dominion of the British Empire, South Africa already featured in the history of sports as a founding member of the international governing bodies of cricket and rugby.[21]

In many respects this focus simply reflects broader trends related to scholarship pertaining to the continent, in which South Africa continues to play an outsized role. In addition to attracting innumerable international researchers to the country to investigate an interminable number of topics, unlike most other African nations, South Africa features a series of established institutions that house faculty actively generating knowledge about their homeland. Although long-standing inequities among these institutions of higher learning have persisted since the dismantlement of apartheid in the early 1990s, the partial democratization of funding and support has opened up opportunities for increasing numbers of South African–based scholars to contribute to this corpus.

Also contributing to the discrepancy in scholarly output between South Africa and other settings on the continent is that the country admittedly does possess a remarkable sports history, with which even casual observers may have some familiarity. Perhaps the most prominent way that a portion of this history was mainstreamed was via Clint Eastwood's 2009 film *Invictus*, starring Hollywood heavyweights Morgan Freeman and Matt Damon, which re-created the postapartheid ascendance and transcendence of the South African national rugby team, the Springboks. In his pedagogical piece in this volume, Peter Alegi explains how he incorporates and discusses this well-known film in his "Sports, Race, and Power in South African History" seminar. Well before the Springboks' improbable capture of the 1995 Rugby World Cup on home soil, the global sports boycotts of South Africa's various national teams, prompted by the country's racist apartheid system, had made international headlines. Scholars have examined at length these sensational sporting proscriptions, as well as non-Whites' courageous efforts to pursue nonracialized sports in the country and, more broadly, to use sports as a weapon to topple the apartheid regime. Scholarship on these two topics alone constitutes a substantial body of work, perhaps rivaling the entirety of publications related to sports studies of all topics for the rest of the continent.[22]

Of the seventeen chapters in this volume, South Africa is the setting for almost half. This preponderance may well exemplify accusations of South African exceptionalism, which scholars have long warned against on both epistemological and experiential grounds.[23] Yet Robert Archer and Antoine Bouillon remind us that sports were (and continue to be) an important component of both Black and White identity in South Africa, thereby differentiating the country from other settings that lack such sizable White populations or such deep socioracial divisions.[24] Although we acknowledge the predominance of South African sports scholarship in this volume, we have placed some of these chapters in different thematic sections, deliberately grouping them with work that focuses on settings elsewhere on the continent. And where the thematic links were too logical to separate them, they have been mixed with chapters that consider different sports. It is our intention that the synergies generated by these thematic clusters and the epistemological contributions that these chapters are collectively poised to make will transcend South Africa's borders, while still deepening and expanding knowledge of sports in that country.

Organization and Composition

After the chapter on historiography, the book is organized into thematic sections, each featuring at least two chapters, that examine an assortment of sports and sports-related themes across a range of settings. The chapters consider how these sports have profoundly shaped Africans' lives, but also how the continent's residents have utilized sports to various ends to improve their own plights. Each section illuminates a variety of social, cultural, political, and economic processes in ways that more traditional analyses of the continent often neglect. Collectively, the chapters familiarize readers with the history of the introduction and reception of so-called modern sports on the continent, tracing these initial sporting encounters during the colonial period, through the end of the imperial era, and on into contemporary Africa, including in the diaspora.

Part I features Albert Grundlingh and Sebastian Potgieter's meditations on South African sports historiography and the close relationship between social history and sports history, while also featuring a critical examination of the much-utilized phrase "sports and society." The chapter highlights the inextricability of sports and politics, while also considering political and social influences on the production of (sports) knowledge. Although the authors examine the particular case of South Africa, the chapter's lessons apply to scholarly trends that transcend the country's borders, while its conclusions, in conjunction with the introduction, effectively frame this volume.

Part 2 considers what may be considered the "final frontier" of African sports: the classroom. Indeed, even as research on sports in Africa has gained considerable traction, the introduction of this topic into the classroom lags behind. The well-attended workshop on African sports pedagogy, held at the 2017 Sport in Africa Conference in Bloemfontein, South Africa, suggests that there are, however, many scholars throughout the world interested in introducing this topic into their courses and classrooms. To this end, three scholars have contributed pedagogical chapters to this book. Todd Cleveland draws upon his experiences teaching his History of Sports in Africa course to offer both lessons and insights. Matt Carotenuto's chapter brings the reader into the environment of a liberal arts institution and offers pedagogical advice based on his experiences teaching African Athletes and Global Sport in a sophomores-only classroom. Peter Alegi's chapter examines his experiences teaching an upper-level undergraduate seminar that examines the intertwined relationships between sports, race, and power in South Africa. All three chapters address course design, approaches, and learning outcomes, while also considering how African sports content can hone students' critical analysis capabilities, digital research methods, and intercultural learning skills.

Part 3 features chapters that consider the ways communities of different types and sizes have utilized sports to forge and deepen particular identities and counter various forms of discrimination. Trishula Patel's chapter on cricket in Rhodesia (Zimbabwe) examines the ways the game helped reinforce various identities of the resident Indian community as members struggled to negotiate racial discrimination experienced at the hands of the White settler regime. Similarly, Chuka Onwumechili and Jasmin M. Goodman examine the ways that the Nigerian women's national soccer team has both faced gender discrimination in a deeply patriarchal society and employed a series of sports-related strategies to push back against a range of sexist structures and entities, including the Nigerian Football Federation.

Part 4 features two chapters that consider sports history in South Africa, though the sporting activities—surfing and bicycle racing—are far removed from the sporting mainstream. Both David Drengk's chapter on surfing along the Transkei's Wild Coast and Todd Leedy's chapter on the history of bicycle racing throughout the country complicate reductive analyses of interracial interactions during the apartheid era. Both authors acknowledge the proscribed nature of this type of contact during this period but also describe the ways and contexts in which meaningful interactions could and did occur, which were often marked by amity or at least basic tolerance and respect.

Part 5 brings us to the very edges of the sports periphery, but in both of its chapters the margins are often, in practice, more properly understood as the core for those individuals who are examined in these studies. Solomon Waliaula's chapter offers significant insight into the pay-to-watch football kiosks that are ubiquitous throughout the continent, though his particular focus is on Kenya. He refutes the notion that because participants pay to watch European soccer, Western cultural hegemony dictates the dynamics in these settings, instead arguing that these spaces function based on local realities, cultural norms, and social relations. Similarly, Tarminder Kaur's chapter is set far from the manicured European soccer pitches, instead considering the unofficial "gambling games" that comprise the world of semiformal soccerdom in the farmlands of the Western Cape. Exploring working-class leisure pursuits at the intersection of soccer and gambling, Kaur demonstrates how they take on much larger and more impactful meanings, propelled by the aspirations of these practitioners, thereby inadvertently sustaining the official structures of the sport.

Part 6 expands the focus of the volume to include the African sporting diaspora, exploring examples of migrant athletes' experiences and broader impacts. Ernest Acheampong, Michel Raspaud, and Malek Bouhaouala consider the ways that African soccer players' labor migration strategies have shifted due to changing perceptions of the European soccer market over the course of a distinct series of periods following political independence. In their chapter, Christian Ungruhe and Sine Agergaard retain the focus on West African football migrants but consider the acute challenges that players based in northern Europe face upon retirement, highlighting the "precarity" that these athletes experience following their careers, devoid of social networks and lacking sufficient nonsoccer occupational training.

Part 7 features chapters that use personal biographies to illustrate broader social and political trends in twentieth-century Africa. The chapter by Francois Cleophas reconstructs the experiences of Milo Pillay, a South African–born, ethnic Indian physical culturalist, to illustrate the racial challenges that athletes faced, and at times surmounted, during the apartheid era, even in "fringe" sports such as weightlifting. Michelle Sikes turns our attention to East Africa, using the example of elite sprinter Seraphino Antao to highlight both the challenges and opportunities that sports generated in the concluding years of the British colonial project in Kenya and on into the dawn of the independent nation. In an attempt to cultivate a common identity and purpose for the country's residents, the initial leaders of the fledging nation opportunistically trumpeted Antao's successes; in practice, politicians throughout the continent similarly used sports as a means to build national unity in the aftermath of imperial overrule.

Part 8 considers how sporting and political legacies continue to shape the ways and conditions in which contemporary Africans engage with sports, while also examining how sporting exploits and accomplishments are remembered going forward. All three of the constituent chapters are set in South Africa, with chapters by Derek Catsam and Mark Fredericks both exploring the postapartheid rugby landscape in the country. In both cases, the authors lament a series of developments in the new era of South African rugby following the dismantlement of apartheid. Catsam dissects and condemns the litany of "alibis," or excuses, that rugby officials continue to offer when pressed about the persistent lack of racial diversity on the national rugby team, the roots of which can be identified much earlier on in the development, or lack thereof, of a rugby player.

Fredericks demonstrates how the end of apartheid and the attendant unification of rugby (and other sports) leagues, which were previously fractured along racial lines, ironically signaled the death knell for community sports and, in practice, any mass-based sports within Black communities. With the formal racial barriers between rugby leagues and associations dissolved (though we need to be mindful of Catsam's arguments here), "Black rugby" endeavors were obviated, leaving a conspicuous absence of sports in many communities. Finally, Marizanne Grundlingh examines the museum associated with the Comrades Marathon, the world's oldest and largest ultramarathon event. In particular, she considers the ways that the race is remembered through gift-giving, a practice in which former participants donate various items for display, thereby adding to the emerging subfield of sports as heritage.

Notes

1. The 2017 conference, held in Bloemfontein, South Africa, was the first to be convened on the continent, and the subsequent year's gathering was in Lusaka, Zambia.

2. The initial collection of African sports research articles appeared in *Sport in Africa: Essays in Social History*, edited by William A. Baker and J. A. Mangan, in 1987 (London: Africana Publishing Company).

3. Baker and Mangan, *Sport in Africa*, ix.

4. John Bale, *Imagined Olympians: Body Culture and Colonial Representation in Rwanda* (Minneapolis: University of Minnesota Press, 2002), xvii–xxx.

5. See, for example, Sigrid Paul, "The Wrestling Tradition and Its Social Functions," in Baker and Mangan, *Sport in Africa*, 23–46; and Peter Alegi, *African Soccerscapes: How the Continent Changed the World's Game* (Athens: Ohio University Press, 2010), 15.

6. John Bale and Joe Sang, *Kenyan Running: Movement Culture, Geography and Global Change* (London: Frank Cass, 1996), 49–50.

7. Todd Cleveland, "Following the Ball: African Soccer Players, Labor Strategies and Emigration across the Portuguese Colonial Empire, 1945–75," *Cadernos de estudos africanos* 26 (July–December 2013): 19.

8. Nuno Domingos, "Football and Colonialism, Domination and Appropriation: The Mozambican Case," *Soccer and Society* 8, no. 4 (October 2007): 480.

9. Phyllis M. Martin, "Colonialism, Youth and Football in French Equatorial Africa," *International Journal of the History of Sport* 8, no. 1 (1991): 56–71;

and Laura Fair, "Kickin' It: Leisure, Politics and Football in Colonial Zanzibar, 1900s–1950s," *Africa* 67, no. 2 (1997): 224–51. The terms *football* and *soccer* are used interchangeably throughout this volume.

10. See, for example, Terence Ranger, "Pugilism and Pathology: African Boxing and the Black Urban Experience in Southern Rhodesia," in Baker and Mangan, *Sport in Africa*, 196–213. Ranger reconstructs the African appropriation of the sport, as well as the ways that colonial authorities reasserted control, essentially by reappropriating it.

11. See, for example, Fair, "Kickin' It"; Domingos, "Football and Colonialism," 478–82; and Alegi, *African Soccerscapes*.

12. Fair, "Kickin' It," 244; Marissa J. Moorman, *Intonations: A Social History of Music and Nation in Luanda, Angola, from 1945 to Recent Times* (Athens: Ohio University Press, 2008); Peter Alegi, *Laduma! Soccer, Politics and Society* (Durban, South Africa: University of Natal Press, 2004); and Alegi, *African Soccerscapes*.

13. Bea Vidics posed a similar question in the title of his 2006 article, "Through the Prism of Sports: Why Should Africanists Study Sports?," *Afrika Spectrum* 41, no. 3 (2006): 331–49.

14. John Nauright and Mahfoud Amara, eds., *Sport in the African World* (New York: Routledge, 2018), 4.

15. Vidics, "Through the Prism of Sports," 331.

16. Exceptions include Aswin Desai and Ahmed Veriava, "Creepy Crawlies, Portapools and the Dam(n)s of Swimming Transformation," in *The Race to Transform: Sport in Post-apartheid South Africa*, ed. Aswin Desai (Cape Town: HSRC, 2010), 14–55; and Marizanne Grundlingh, "South Africa: The Battle for Baseball," in *Baseball beyond Our Borders: An International Pastime*, ed. George Gmelch and Daniel A. Nathan (Lincoln: University of Nebraska Press, 2017), 337–48. Note that both essays consider South Africa.

17. Exceptions to this durable pattern include Martha Saavedra, "Football Feminine—Development of the African Game: Senegal, Nigeria and South Africa," *Soccer and Society* 4, nos. 2–3 (2003): 225–53; and Sasha Sutherland and John Nauright, "Women and Race in African and African Diaspora Sport," in Nauright and Amara, *Sport in the African World*, 205–22.

18. Paul Darby has been particularly active in this research area. For more recent work, see Paul Darby and Nienke Van Der Meij, "Africa, Migration and Football," in Nauright and Amara, *Sport in the African World*, 94–109. See also, for example, John Bale, "Three Geographies of African Footballer Migration: Patterns, Problems and Postcoloniality," in *Football in Africa: Conflict, Conciliation and Community*, ed. Gary Armstrong and Richard Giulianotti (New York: Palgrave Macmillan, 2004), 229–46.

19. Baker and Mangan, *Sport in Africa*, ix. Remarkably, they also declared that they "regrettably, were unable to provide essays on . . . the universally popular modern game of soccer." It's unfathomable that a volume on sports, irrespective of geographic focus, wouldn't include at least one piece on the world's most popular game.

20. For example, even a quick glance at the scholarship that focuses exclusively on South Africa reveals a literature that spans almost four decades and includes the following: Robert Archer and Antoine Bouillon, *The South African Game: Sport and Racism* (London: Zed, 1982); Douglas Booth, *The Race Game: Sport and Politics in South Africa* (London: Cass, 1998); John Nauright, *Sport, Cultures, and Identities in South Africa* (London: Leicester University Press, 1998); André Odendaal, *The Story of an African Game* (Cape Town: New Africa Books, 2003); Desai, *The Race to Transform*; Scarlett Cornelissen and Albert Grundlingh, eds., *Sport Past and Present in South Africa: (Trans)forming the Nation* (London: Routledge, 2013); and Tarminder Kaur and Gerard Akindes, "Sports Africa: Sporting Subalternities and Social Justice: Rethinking South African Sports Studies," *ACTA Academica* 50, no. 2 (2018): 51–75.

21. See, for example, Roger Hutchinson, *Empire Games: The British Invention of Twentieth-Century Sport* (Edinburgh: Mainstream, 1996).

22. See, for example, Douglas Booth, "Hitting Apartheid for Six? The Politics of the South African Sports Boycott," *Journal of Contemporary History* 38, no. 3 (July 2003): 477–93; and Alegi, *Laduma!*

23. Mahmood Mamdani's cautions as they appeared in his 1996 book, *Citizen and Subject*, are arguably among the most compelling and prescient. Mahmood Mamdani, *Citizen and Subject: Contemporary Africa and the Legacy of Late Colonialism* (Princeton, NJ: Princeton University Press, 1996).

24. Archer and Bouillon, *South African Game*. See also, for example, Albert Grundlingh, "Playing for Power? Rugby, Afrikaner Nationalism and Masculinity in South Africa, c. 1900–1970," *International Journal of the History of Sport* 11, no. 3 (1994): 408–30; Nauright, *Sport, Cultures, and Identities in South Africa*; John Nauright, *Long Run to Freedom: Sport, Cultures and Identities in South Africa* (Morgantown: Fitness Information Technology, West Virginia University, 2010); and Albert Grundlingh, *Potent Pastimes: Sport and Leisure Practices in Modern Afrikaner History* (Pretoria: Protea Boekhuis, 2014).

ONE

Historiography of South African Sports

ONE

Reflections on Pathways to the Writing of South African Sports History

ALBERT GRUNDLINGH AND SEBASTIAN POTGIETER

This chapter focuses on the historiographical trajectory of sports history in South Africa and the academic frame through which empirical material has been refracted, as well as possible future directions. The quest for academic relevance and for the recognition of embedded meanings in sports is outlined. Central to this analysis is an assessment of the salience and durability of a flexible social history paradigm. The implications of more recent challenges are noted with a view of broadening the overall scope of sports history without sacrificing its core components. While fully recognizing the early activist antiapartheid writings that highlighted the many discrepancies and contradictions of South African sports at the time, the emphasis here is on academic historical work as such.

Pioneering Days and Wider Meanings

In trying to establish an academic foothold in the last decades of the twentieth century, the history of sports in South Africa had to contend with other areas of research that dominated the historiographical landscape: Afrikaner politics and its historical antecedents, Black resistance movements and their origins, and of course apartheid itself and its many ramifications. Moreover, besides jostling for position in the marketplace of thematic preferences, sports history also had to differentiate itself sharply from popular books about the history of sports, particularly of the biographical kind, and those focusing on specific teams, sports tours, and clubs.

It fell to early academic pioneers to demonstrate how their work intersected with the fault lines of South African society and to carve out a niche in order to elevate sports history to a respectable level of scholarly inquiry.[1] Underlying the skepticism was the almost unspoken assumption, given South Africa's turbulent history and the dramatic way in which opposing political forces squared up against one another, that sports and leisure are rather trivial phenomena, best left to amateurs and not the kind of topics to be taken seriously by guild historians. As also happened in other countries, to some the field even appeared frivolous, outside the domain of serious intellectual endeavor, and sports historians seemed to be hardly more than "fans with typewriters practising their esoteric craft with little contact with the historical mainstream."[2] One of the authors of this piece experienced such disdain at first hand when he was bluntly told in the early 1990s that sports history is simply something one does at one's leisure after watching rugby at Loftus Versfeld stadium in Pretoria on Saturdays. Such an attitude can be misleading, "for it is in the fertile loam of the marginal that we may find the structures of power revealed in peculiarly fascinating ways."[3]

That point is nowhere more apparent than in dealing with the issue of sports and politics. Only those who do not wish to probe any deeper can believe the assumption that sports and politics are completely separate domains. In South Africa, even more so than in most other countries, despite the best protestations of some, this was never the case, as the sporting boycotts during apartheid strikingly revealed.

Apart from formalized sports politics, as played out for instance by antiapartheid and pro-apartheid forces in the previous South African dispensation, the study of sports history can also be conceived of as a form of "deep politics" in which "social traditions and attitudes are expressed through recreational practises." Tony Collins, a British author of rugby history, has reminded us that all "sports that have mass appeal reflect the preferences and prejudices of those sections of society that nurture them."[4] It is for the sports historian to ferret out the precise significance and meanings of a particular sport over time in a changing context and to establish how these interconnect with other relevant forces in the rest of society. These linkages, of course, must be proven and cannot simply be assumed or assigned. Nor can their outcome be considered preordained. Jeremy MacClancy has made the salutary point that any "particular sport is not intrinsically associated with a particular set of meanings or social values. What it is meant to represent is not laid down like some commandment etched in stone." Accordingly, sports are rather "an embodied practice, in which meanings are generated, and whose representation and interpretation are open to negotiation and contest."[5]

The Social History Project and Sports History

For the academic historian of sports and leisure, it is important to be constantly aware of his or her moorings in the wider historiographical landscape. South African historiography over the past forty years or more has exhibited certain distinct traits: from an Afrikaner interpretation of history that foregrounded White nationalistic interests; to a liberal version usually emanating from White English speakers who emphasized "wrong turnings," premised on notions of individual agency within a free-market economy; to an oppositional neo-Marxist frame that included a strong social history tradition and an emphasis on the material underpinnings of society. Within such a stark characterization there are of course many overlaps and nuances.

Until recently, social history as an analytical frame had a proven record as a fertile point of departure to pursue the wider connections between sports, leisure, and society. Writing in 2007, Tony Collins had little doubt about its salience in the United Kingdom: "It remains the case today that the most interesting work published on sport and leisure history is produced by historians working with the methods of and asking the questions originally posed by social historians."[6] The situation has been the same in South Africa, where early pioneers all had some exposure to the development of social history, which emanated primarily from the History Workshop at the University of the Witwatersrand during the 1980s and which in turn was influenced by "history-from-below" intellectual currents at certain universities in the United Kingdom. Significantly, it was at the History Workshop conference in 1981 that historians who had made their names working on other historical topics prized open the field of modern sports history. At that conference, Jeff Peires presented a paper on Black rugby in the Eastern Cape, and Tim Couzens presented one on soccer in South Africa.[7] These were modest beginnings, but locating sports history within the social history genre gave it a certain respectability and academic legitimacy.

Although the term *social* in social history has not always been defined with precision, three main aspects can be discerned. First, it can be seen as a synthetic notion, interrogating spheres that at first glance may appear as distinct but may actually be intricately interwoven. Second, as opposed to focusing only on individual agency, it foregrounds systemic forces usually rooted in, but not necessarily axiomatically defined by material considerations as, the encapsulation of the "social." Third, social history declared a strong focus on the everyday lives of "ordinary people."[8] Overall, the main thrust is to grasp, often simultaneously, the manifestations of large and abstract structures as well as the small details of life; recapturing people's experiences and understanding the multiple grids that mediate these.

These elements of social history were sufficiently flexible to incorporate a cultural practice such as sports or leisure. Culture in this respect was loosely defined as an awareness and expression of how phenomena were perceived and how they were represented and internalized.[9] At the same time, the notion was infused with an understanding that the "cultural" cannot operate in isolation. Writing on these developments in a Western context, Nancy Struna has emphasized that in the phrase "sports *and* society" the conjunctive indicates equal attention. Therefore, "one of the goals of this kind of social history is the telling of a 'large' story about the nature, fit and meanings of sporting practices as these were embedded in society; hence the common focus on the making of sporting life as an inextricably linked dimension of the making of a nation, a people or a sub-period."[10]

Though all of this is valid, it is also necessary to enter a caveat. Ideas, meanings, and representations that help to constitute the "larger" story about sports and society do not exist in a vacuum but are more often than not grounded in the prevailing realities of life. In contemporary South Africa, professionalization of sports has helped to shape a reality in which class considerations as much as race help to shape the sporting environment.[11]

This fact is equally important historically, where class and material conditions largely determined the growth of a sporting code such as cricket among Afrikaner as well as Black communities. It was only once Afrikaners had become financially relatively prosperous during the 1960s that they took to cricket in greater numbers and began to assert themselves on the pitch during the ensuing decades.[12] Historically, Black cricketers, with some exceptions, are likewise the products of a class-oriented system. During the late nineteenth century and for most of the twentieth, a tiny sliver of an emerging Black middle class slowly moved up the slippery class ladder, with cricket being a culturally constituent expression as part of a patient quest for wider recognition.[13] The postapartheid dispensation generally provided ample new opportunities for a purposeful class scramble to the top to compensate for the long and lean years of the past. Moreover, as far as cricket is concerned, Black administrators who moved to the higher echelons of the game were inclined to adopt a class outlook similar to those of their White predecessors.[14]

Although there may be varying emphases in a social history approach to sports history, at the core of it the omission or neglect of material conditions is likely to have an overall attenuating analytical effect. There are also some other related challenges. When using class as an analytical tool, it cannot be restricted, for example, only to the aspiring Black middle classes who took to cricket, as it leaves the great swathe of underclasses untouched and marooned, far removed from organized mainline sports.[15] Focusing on the acculturated class and foregrounding that segment of Black sportspeople by writing them back into history can of course fill important gaps in coming to a fuller understanding of South African sports and society. Yet there are also limitations; as far as

Black communities at large are concerned, this can only be a partial recovery, as too much is left unaccounted for in terms of explaining preferences, apathy, or rejection of certain sporting codes. Ideally, such silences should also be interrogated.

Moreover, there are also problems as far as decolonial thinking is concerned. As S. M. Clevenger has recently asked: "[C]an a historical field dedicated to a modern concept like sport represent physical cultural pasts without presuming or imposing the epistemology and constructs of Western modernity as a proclaimed universal means of representing the past?"[16] In this respect a more sensitive anthropological approach, dealing for instance with sports outside the charmed circle of certain sporting codes and their customs, may still yield rich insights.[17] Historians would also do well to emulate anthropologists, who have a penchant for working narrow and deep and have been attuned to the "internal properties" of sports as well as the rituals that accompany sporting practice.[18] Otherwise, as has been observed, the implication is that "Black sport differed little in its social and cultural context from White sport in late nineteenth-century Europe."[19]

It may also be useful to alert academics that despite all the seismographic changes in South Africa, the ingrained style and nature of sports codes have overall remained remarkably intact. There has been, for instance, no significant evidence of hybridization of a sporting code as happened in Trobriand cricket in the previous century. Whereas English elites regarded values and attitudes such as strict discipline and control coupled with clearly demarcated hierarchies as part and parcel of cricket, in the Trobriand Islands cricket was substantially adapted to fit local customs. Dozens of players freely changed sides, the rules were amended to tie in with local preferences and tribal dances were part of the proceedings. "Trobriand *cricket*, it has been noted, has become *Trobriand* cricket."[20] Such creolization in South Africa is most likely to be met with folded arms by the administrators, as established notions of elitist competitive participation on the international circuit will have to be abandoned to allow a newly adapted game to become a priority throughout the entire structure.

Conceptual Challenges and the Road Ahead

The discourse of sports, it has often been argued in fairly homogenous ethnic societies, "has heroic and mythical dimensions and can be viewed as a story we tell ourselves about ourselves."[21] In South Africa, with so many contending factions, it is particularly difficult to construct a narrative of "ourselves." Well aware of this, the social history paradigm has attempted to locate its subject at the juncture of crosscutting influences. As indicated, the paradigm's imprint can be traced back to the dominant points of departure during the 1980s, when it converged with the emergence of scholars who sought to pursue sports history as a serious academic objective. This does not imply, however, that all researchers bought into the paradigm in equal measure, while there are also those who followed a more explicitly political and empirical approach.[22]

From a different perspective, one cannot ignore shots across the bow aimed at some of the assumptions of the social history and sports paradigm. There has been an undercurrent of criticism that the social history lens at times fails to do justice to the variegated nature of the sporting experience. A fixation on antagonisms generated by class, race, and gender can reduce historical actors to abstract categories with no or little regard for them as living agents and affective beings.[23]

This criticism relates to a shift toward the aesthetic, linguistic, and discursive elements of historical evidence that has occurred under postmodernism. "Historical knowledge and understanding are not acquired exclusively as an empiricist enterprise," Alan Munslow contends, "but rather are generated by the nature of representation and the aesthetic decisions of the historian."[24] Likewise, for historian Hayden White, the narrative used to emplot the past is not a detached vehicle for transmitting past realities, and the way in which the historian chooses to convey his or her work is at least as important.[25]

Some of the assumptions pertaining to postmodernism and sports history have not gone unchallenged, primarily on the basis that postmodernists tend to read false dichotomies into more traditional histories.[26] It is not our task here to arbitrate in this debate. Without necessarily subscribing to all the points of departure of postmodernism, our concern is to briefly tease out how this debate can impact the writing of sports history in South Africa.

Conceptually, the debate may imply that existing histories can be rewritten with a view of re-emplotting the narrative by interrogating the linguistic and standard historical devices that underpinned these interpretations. This means that the social history approach would come under scrutiny, but it may also suggest that social history, which through a certain flexibility has been a durable vehicle, is capable of incorporating new dimensions without severely destabilizing the whole project. It is a compromise position, which like all such approaches is a tightrope act with attendant risks.

Besides these broader implications, the debate can also alert historians to relatively novel themes, such as representation of sporting experiences in the fractured South African society and the way this has changed over time. What comes to mind here is the experience of the "coloured" Springbok rugby player Errol Tobias, who in the 1980s played in what was seen by the antiapartheid activists as establishment structures; a fresh interpretative departure may highlight not only the experiential aspects of his participation as such but also the kind of political discourse this decision generated.[27] Of similar interest, though on a different order, is the experience of defectors during the amateur era from rugby union to paid rugby league abroad. Taking leave of the amateur code, they were excommunicated from the "pure" rugby playing fraternity in South Africa, and their involvement in paid rugby was characterized as "unpatriotic" conduct.[28] In the professional era of rugby union after 1995, the floodgates opened, with an exodus of South African rugby players to the more financially lucrative playing fields of Europe and the United Kingdom. The way in which these players, with some exceptions, adapted in a new habitat, as well as the wider ramifications for the overall structure of top-flight rugby and individual player loyalty, should cast light on issues of representation and cultural dynamics.[29]

The variety and changing emotional dimensions of fandom and how different groups expressed their sentiments in South Africa are equally pertinent. Loyalty to the national team cannot necessarily be taken for granted. For example, the persistent tendency among some "coloured" rugby fans, particularly in but not confined to the Western Cape, to support the New Zealand rugby team, the All Blacks, as opposed to the national Springbok team is one apparent anomaly that calls for elucidation. Closely related to the affective turn is the number of popular sports books that often unwittingly document sports as a form of nostalgic expression, encouraging a yearning for yesteryear among the public, as well as being paper monuments in biographical form testifying to individual achievements.[30] Explaining the nature and appeal of these writings may yield a novel understanding of the predilections of particular sporting communities. Equally underresearched is the visual representation of sports in South Africa, from which attitudes and predilections can be gleaned in the composition of sporting photographs (of which there are of course more than enough).[31] In general, it would appear that there is a rich vein to be tapped, and interpretations and reinterpretations of these themes can draw from postmodernist impulses, but at the same time they do not necessarily have to be restricted by them.

Overall, serious sports history writing in South Africa is firmly established. While the number of practitioners in the country is more limited than one would ideally wish for, they are certainly enthusiastic and well supported by some influential trendsetters from abroad. The genre still awaits, as has happened elsewhere, the kind of clashes sparked in part by generational tensions as a younger cohort of scholars take the field.[32] Whether this will take the form of a full-blown Africanist attack on existing paradigms and/or incorporate gender dimensions to a greater extent remains to be seen.

Notes

1. Over the past thirty-five years or so, the academics who have been consistent in producing work on sports history in South Africa have been André Odendaal, John Nauright, Douglas Booth, Christopher Merrett, Bruce Murray, Chris Bolsman, Peter Alegi, and Floris van der Merwe. Recently, scholars such as Ashwin Desai, Goolam Vahed, Dean Allen, Hendrik Snyders, and Gustav Venter have come into the frame. For a full historiographical overview, see André Odendaal, "Sport and Liberation: The Unfinished Business

of the Past," in *Sport and Liberation in South Africa: Reflections and Sugges-tions*, ed. Cornelius Thomas (Alice, South Africa: University of Fort Hare Press, 2006), 11–38. See also the appraisal by John Nauright, "Epilogue: Mak-ing New Histories of Sport in South Africa," in *Sport, Past and Present in South Africa: (Trans)forming the Nation*, ed. Scarlett Cornelissien and Albert Grundlingh (London: Routledge, 2012),180–84; and John Nauright, "Africa (Sub-Saharan)," in *Routledge Companion to Sports History*, ed. S. W. Pope and John Nauright (New York: Routledge, 2010), 319–29. In compiling this chap-ter, Albert Grundlingh has also drawn in part upon his book, *Potent Pastimes: Sport and Leisure Practices in Modern Afrikaner History* (Pretoria: Protea Books, 2013).

2. Quoted in Douglas Booth, "Escaping the Past? The Cultural Turn and Language in Sport History," *Rethinking History* 8, no. 1 (2004): 103.

3. Rita Barnard, "Contesting Beauty," in *Senses of Culture: South African Cultural Studies*, ed. Sarah Nuttal and Cheryl Ann Michael (Cape Town: Uni-versity of Cape Town Press, 2000), 347.

4. Tony Collins, *A Social History of English Rugby Union* (London: Rout-ledge, 2009), 213 (both quotes).

5. Jeremy MacClancy, "Sport, Identity and Ethnicity," in *Sport, Identity and Ethnicity*, ed. Jeremy MacClancy (Oxford: Berg, 1996), 4.

6. Tony Collins: "Work, Rest and Play: Recent Trends in the History of Sport and Leisure," *Journal of Contemporary History* 42, no. 397 (2007): 399.

7. J. B. Peires, "Facta non Verba: Towards a History of Black Rugby in the Eastern Cape" (paper presented at History Workshop conference, Univer-sity of the Witwatersrand, 1981); and Tim Couzens, "An Introduction to the History of Football in South Africa" (paper presented at History Workshop conference, University of the Witwatersrand, 1981). See also John Nauright, *Sport, Cultures and Identities in South Africa* (Cape Town: David Philip, 1997), 17–18.

8. Compare D. Posel, "Social History and the Wits History Workshop," *African Studies* 69, no. 1 (2010): 30.

9. Jeffrey Hill, *Sport in History: An Introduction* (London: Macmillan), 3.

10. Nancy Struna, "Social History and Sport," in *Handbook of Sport Stud-ies*, ed. Jay Coakley and Eric Dunning (London, Sage, 2000), 3.

11. Nauright, "Epilogue: Making New Histories," 182.

12. Albert Grundlingh, *Potent Pastimes: Sport and Leisure Practices in Mod-ern Afrikaner history* (Pretoria: Protea Books, 2013), 192–218.

13. See, for example, André Odendaal, "South Africa's Black Victorians: Sport and Society in South Africa in the Nineteenth Century," in *Pleasure, Profit and Proselytism: British Culture and Sport at Home and Abroad, 1700–1914*, ed. J. A. Mangan (London: Frank Cass, 1988); André Odendaal, *The Story of an*

African Game: Black Cricketers and the Unmasking of One of Cricket's Greatest Myths, South Africa, 1850–2003 (Cape Town: David Philip, 2003); and Andrè Odendaal et al., *Cricket and Conquest: The History of South African Cricket Retold, 1795–1914* (Pretoria: HSRC Press, 2017).

14. Ashwin Desai, *Reverse Sweep: A Story of South African Cricket since Apartheid* (Johannesburg: Fanele, 2016), 202–9.

15. For work on the mining compounds, see, for example, Cecile Badenhorst and Charles Mather, "Tribal Recreation and Recreating Tribalism: Culture, Leisure and Social Control on South Africa's Goldmines, 1940–1950," *Journal of Southern African Studies* 23, no. 3 (1997), 473–89.

16. Samuel M. Clevenger, "Sport History, Modernity and the Logic of Coloniality: A Case for Decoloniality," *Rethinking History: The Journal of Theory and Practise* 3 (May 2017): 2.

17. Compare, for example, John Blacking, "Games and Sport in Pre-colonial African Societies," in *Sport in Africa: Essays in Social History*, ed. William J. Baker and J. A. Mangan (London: Africana, 1987), 3–22.

18. Richard Holt, "Historians and the History of Sport," *Sport and History* 10 (November 2013): 19.

19 David Black and J. Nauright, *Rugby and the South African Nation: Sport, Cultures, Politics and Power in the Old and New South Africa* (Manchester, UK: Manchester University Press, 1998), 11.

20. Richard Giulionotti, *Sport: A Critical Sociology* (London: Polity, 2005), 204.

21 Richard Holt, *Sport and the British: A Modern History* (Oxford: Oxford University Press, 1990), 3.

22. For example, P. A. H. Labuschagne, "An Analytical Perspective of Afrikaner Ideological Hegemony (1961–1980): The Role of Politics and Rugby," *Journal for Contemporary History* 40, no. 1 (2015): 125–43.

23. See, for example, Douglas Booth," Invitation to Historians: The Historiographical Turn of a Practicing (Sport) Historian," *Rethinking History* 18, no. 4 (2014): 595n1.

24. A. Munslow, ed., *The Routledge Companion to Historical Studies* (London: Routledge, 2005), 242.

25. A. Munslow, *Deconstructing History* (London: Taylor and Francis, 2006), 149.

26. For example, John Hughson, "The Postmodernist Always Rings Twice: Reflections on the 'New' Cultural Turn in Sports History," *International Journal of the History of Sport* 30, no. 1 (2013): 35–45.

27. For rich primary material on this see Errol Tobias, *Errol Tobias: Pure Gold* (Cape Town: Tafelberg, 2015); and Heindrich Wyngaard, *Bursting through the Half-gap: The Story of Errol Tobias* (Cape Town: DB Press, 2017).

28. For details on this see, for example, Peter Lush and Hendrik Snyders, *Tries and Conversions: South African Rugby League Players* (London: London League, 2015).

29. See, for instance, Bernard Cros, "From the Transvaal to the Cantal: The Exodus of South African Rugby Union Players to France," *Cultures of the Commonwealth* 18 (Autumn 2012): 89–102.

30. Compare Wouter de Wet, "Tendense en tematologie in populêre werke oor Suid-Afrikaanse rugby, 1984–1995" (MA thesis, Stellenbosch University, 2013), 14–30, 74–107. On the way in which sports nostalgia can function in a wider context, see Sheranne Fairley and Sean Gammon, "Something Lived, Something Learned: Nostalgia's Expanding Role in Sport Tourism," *Sport in Society: Cultures, Commerce, Media, Politics* 8, no. 2 (2005): 182–97.

31. For some tentative but suggestive forays into this field, see Christopher Thurman, ed., *Sport Versus Art: A South African Contest* (Johannesburg: University of the Witwatersrand Press, 2001); and Pieter A. Labuschagne, "Nonverbal and Paralinguistic Political Communication in Sport: An Analysis of Images of Springbok Rugby," *Communicato: South African Journal of Communication Theory and Research* (June 2017): 80–102.

32. See, for example, John Nauright, "From Looking Back to Moving Forward: The Evolving Scope of Sports History in the 21st Century," in *Making Sport History: Disciplines, Identities and Historiography of Sport*, ed. Pascal Delheye (London: Routledge, 2014), 229–36.

TWO

African Sports Pedagogy

TWO

The Final Frontier

African Sports Studies in the Classroom

TODD CLEVELAND

This chapter examines a course that I teach, History of Sports in Africa, which focuses on the history of sporting and athletic traditions and competitions on the continent. As outlined in the introduction, as Europeans violently colonized Africa over the course of the nineteenth century, they introduced "modern sports" to the continent as part of their so-called civilizing missions, intended to deepen their hegemonic control. In general, Africans responded enthusiastically to these alien sporting introductions, including soccer and rugby, as many of these athletic endeavors built upon precolonial, indigenous traditions. However, Africans quickly appropriated these athletic pastimes, "indigenizing" them and using sports as a vehicle through which to express and organize themselves and, often, to challenge or undermine colonial rule. Following political independence, newly formed governments of African countries used sports to unite their diverse populations, encouraging nationalism in an effort to create national identities where none had previously existed. My course explores this recent history of Africa through the prism of sports, examining Africans' shifting relationships with athletics, the ways that sports have helped to develop—or conversely, impeded development on—the continent, and the ways that sporting practices in Africa have both shaped and been shaped by international developments, including globalization.

The course, offered at the University of Arkansas, where I am based, is intended to generate interest in African history and, more broadly, African studies and Africa in general, for majors and nonmajors alike.[1] I have designed the course in a deliberately accessible manner, centered on what is a very familiar topic for many students—sports—to enable them to more comfortably engage with subject matter with which they are most likely unfamiliar. In practice, most students who enroll in the class do so for the following reasons, in the following order: (1) its sports theme, (2) its focus on Africa, or (3) the opportunity to earn credit toward a History or African American and African Studies (AAST) major or minor. Given these demonstrated motivations, I take it as my charge to inspire my students to marry their existing penchant for sports with what I hope will be newfound interests in Africa and history.[2] Ultimately, if students conclude the class with a deeper comprehension of the continent's past and corresponding present, I consider the undertaking to have been an unmitigated success.

Outcomes, Objectives, and Challenges

As someone actively involved in the production of knowledge about Africa's past, I take my responsibility to teach my students what I know—and continue to learn—very seriously. Given that most American college students perceive the continent's residents as largely passive, forlorn individuals mired in intractable political, martial, and epidemiological crises, this task is formidable. Yet although misconceptions about Africa are legion, a thorough exploration of the rich and complex histories of Africans reliably prompts students to revise their typically narrow impressions of the continent and, moreover, to begin to understand how their sentiments became so firmly entrenched. Thus, the classroom constitutes an ideal setting in which to both raise awareness about the continent's past (and present) and help students move beyond durable perceptions of African ineptitude, stagnation, and hopelessness.

Sports provides these students a recognizable point of entry into Africa, which is for most of them an "alien" world. Our focus on Africans' strategic responses to oppressive conditions both within sporting realms and beyond during the colonial and postcolonial periods is one way to underscore indigenous vibrancy and dynamism and thereby help dispel reductive notions of Africans as (helpless) victims. In the class, I consistently center the shifting strategies that Africans have employed over time to creatively respond to a range of sporting-related challenges—historical and contemporary, organic and external—that highlight the active roles Africans have taken in shaping their own histories, as well as community-level, national, and international histories. I believe that this pedagogical approach constitutes a powerful explicatory and corrective process for my students.

To explicitly link Africa's past and present, in this case via sports, the course features assignments that require students to connect contemporary challenges in Africa to the continent's colonial past. These identifiable connections render Africa's past analytically relevant and enhance students' understandings of how it continues to shape the present. These exercises also draw students' attention to the long historical trajectories of the inequitable global structures and asymmetrical power relationships in today's world and help dispel myths they may hold about Western hegemony being predicated solely on hard work and dedication. These sports-themed exercises and explorations bring into sharp relief the long histories of exploitation that have marked—and continue to mark—our world, and in turn hopefully make my students more aware, and thus better, "global citizens." Ultimately, it is my hope that the course will encourage each of them to think critically about the position of Africa and Africans—and in the process, their own position—in our increasingly interconnected world.

Genesis of the Course: Cautiously Entering the Final Frontier

This course was born out of a combination of personal interests: sports, Africa, and history (not necessarily in that order), and a broader, prolonged struggle in academia in which I have only participated rather recently. As many readers will know, and as outlined in this volume's introduction, for some time a small but steadily expanding group of scholars has been striving, increasingly successfully, to legitimize the study of sports in the academy. Indeed, even if there remain academic holdouts who (still) do not take the study of sports seriously, academic publishers have been increasingly receptive, which in turn has effectively countered these more cynical, dismissive voices. Yet even as scholars engaged in sports studies declare victory on the publishing front, the classroom remains the next, and arguably "final," frontier, the ultimate challenge. While there are now innumerable scholars conducting research on a remarkable array of sports-related topics across a range of disciplines, there are far fewer who offer sports-themed classes at their respective institutions. And even fewer focus on Africa. Although a growing number of sports-themed classes include Africa, such as a variety of "global soccer" courses, these classes typically offer minimal or only peripheral coverage of Africa. I therefore decided to confront this challenge head on. My course, History of Sports in Africa, is the product of this decision.

As a trained historian of Africa whose initial research endeavors were related to the continent's diamond history, I was admittedly not an ideal candidate for this undertaking. However, as a labor and social historian and an avid sports fan, I strove to meld these interests, all of which are manifested in a book of mine published by Ohio University Press that examines African soccer migrants to Portugal during the colonial period.[3] In general, I treat the Lusophone African footballers who appear in *Following the Ball* as economic migrants rather than soccer superstars. Meanwhile, the social historian in me sought to reconstruct their daily lives, challenges, and successes, while the labor historian in me considered the occupational strategies they employed to navigate their exacting existences in Portugal's colonies and, eventually, the metropole following their relocation to Europe. While conducting the research for the book, I was fortunate to meet a great number of African and European scholars at conferences, archives, and other venues who were actively conducting sports-related research and generating impressive publications. Collectively, their sheer numbers and enthusiasm—in the face of an array of formidable challenges—helped to convince me that a course on African sports merited my attention and efforts.

Constituent Parts: The Anatomy of the Course

Facilitating the process by which American college and university students gain an enhanced appreciation for the complexity of Africa's past and present constitutes an extremely challenging endeavor, even through a prism as familiar as sports. Yet if they are going to be able to comprehend the nature and range of the continent's contemporary challenges—which are often manifested in the realm of sports—students' (mis)perceptions and limited knowledge should be addressed, and quickly. To this end, initial lectures that offer them both foundation and context are imperative, while in-class discussions predicated on assigned readings serve to complement and deepen students' understandings of the topics covered in the lectures. In addition, more in-depth research assignments prompt students to familiarize themselves with their chosen topics as part of the discovery-comprehension-prescription process. Finally, I incorporate relevant films into the curriculum to enhance the lectures, as well as to provide visual images of life on the continent.

The course is divided into a number of units, many of which revolve around the introduction and development of various sports. Beyond the initial foundational unit on Africa's recent history, we explore precolonial athletic traditions on the continent, many of which proved to be fertile ground for the European introduction and African cultivation of "modern sports." Our first engagement with a specific sport following the arrival of Europeans is, naturally, soccer—by far the most universal and popular sport on the continent. We segue from that undertaking to an exploration of the African dominance of long-distance running, with which most students already have at least a passing familiarity. We next explore the history of "mega-sporting events" on the continent, which includes the 2010 World Cup in South Africa but also some of its predecessors, including the "Rumble in the Jungle" boxing match in 1974 between George Foreman and Muhammed Ali in Mobutu's Zaire (Congo), and "Sport Aid" in 1986. We close these focused examinations with a unit that traces the introduction and spread of cricket and rugby, two sports that have historically been characterized by racial exclusion and tension on the continent, though primarily in South Africa. Although the Fédération Internationale de Football Association (FIFA) banned the South African Football Association prior to the imposition of bans on the country's national cricket and rugby teams, the latter were more controversial, as South Africans of European descent were, and remain, deeply passionate about these sports. The class concludes with students presenting the research they conducted to satisfy two large assignments (see "Out-of-Class Learning: Research Assignments").

CLASSROOM LEARNING:
LECTURES AND DISCUSSIONS

To begin to build the historical foundations that the students need to proceed and, ultimately, succeed in the course, we spend the first three weeks examining Africa's history since roughly 1500. During this exploration, we move through different eras on the continent in order to highlight Africans' increasing contact with Europeans and Asians and, subsequently, the processes of colonization and independence, the shifting postcolonial environment, and the ways that Africans have creatively navigated these different periods. The classroom is an ideal setting in which to both raise students' awareness about the continent's past (and present) and help them move beyond durable perceptions of African ahistoricity and hopelessness. Note that we do not discuss sports at all until *after* we complete the third week of the class. This sequencing is deliberate, as I need the students to be able to situate sporting developments into a broader history of the continent, and this approach also reminds them that the course is, first and foremost, an African history class. Besides, some twelve weeks remain, during which sports will feature prominently.

Our initial engagement with sports comes via an exploration of long-standing precolonial athletic traditions and pastimes. Because the course subsequently considers the engagement between Europeans and Africans and the effects of these interactions on sports and society, it is imperative that students explore precolonial African cultural traditions and social practices in order to understand how these dimensions changed over time owing to these intercultural encounters. To this end, students examine political, economic, social, and religious systems, as well as sporting practices and traditions, and gauge the significant impact of Western encroachment, but they also learn how Africans creatively negotiated this advance. I assign an article coauthored by Emmanuel Akyeampong and Charles Ambler that examines the history of sports and leisure in Africa and a chapter crafted by Sigrid Paul that considers the continent-wide tradition of wrestling to illuminate the core thematic lessons of this unit.[4]

Our next unit constitutes the course's longest: soccer. It is facile to make the argument that football should receive our most thorough engagement owing to its extreme popularity throughout the continent. Indeed, the sport enjoys an immense following, and its already significant fandom continues to expand. But Africans have also engaged with the game in other, much more consequential ways, especially during the colonial period, when soccer often constituted a contested site between European authorities and African practitioners. To explore these dynamics, I assign Nuno Domingos's article "Football and Colonialism, Domination and Appropriation" in conjunction with Laura Fair's "Kickin' It: Leisure, Politics and Football in Colonial Zanzibar."[5] Both pieces demonstrate that Africans actively engaged with the game, mixing politics and dissent and challenging an array of local and imperial power structures via this otherwise seemingly innocuous pastime.

We conclude this unit with an examination of African football migration and an assignment linked to Peter Alegi's *Soccerscapes*, a sweeping examination of the history of African football.[6] Alegi's highly accessible book reinforces a core theme of the course: rather than passively receiving an imported game, Africans have been actively shaping the soccer landscape not only on the continent but also globally. Students who follow the game even casually are aware of the large number of African players plying their skills abroad, though they are generally unaware of the deep roots of this outmigration. Beyond our classroom discussion of this long-standing phenomenon, I juxtapose Paul Darby's work, which highlights the ongoing exploitation of these migratory athletes, with my work—either in book or article form—which treats these (temporary or permanent) exoduses as calculated labor strategies. The contrast between our analyses highlights the various, often contrasting, ways that migration can be interpreted, but in both cases Africans' strategic engagement with a shifting global landscape and attendant opportunities is featured.

We next explore the world of African long-distance running, long an area of dominance for athletes hailing from the continent, though primarily from Kenya and Ethiopia. Central to this weeks-long examination is the question: What makes these runners so dominant? Articles from popular media sources help fuel this debate, as does the documentary film *Town of Runners*, which examines girls' long-distance running in Ethiopia.[7] Adharanand Finn's *Running with the Kenyans* takes the students to the neighboring epicenter of African long-distance running, where he embedded himself with these world-class athletes for an extended period while he interrogated each of the array of theories about why they are so dominant.[8] As part of this unit, I ask each student to search the internet for an article that attempts to explain this dominance and bring it to class. The resultant discussion is student generated and student led, as each participant explains the content of his or her respective piece and how it pertains to the broader debate.

We follow these sports-specific topics with a unit on so-called mega-sporting events on the continent. Naturally this examination features the 2010 Men's Soccer World Cup in South Africa, and I assign articles by Dean Allen, and Ashwin Desai and Goolam Vahed that consider the buildup to the event and its aftermath.[9] This discussion revolves around a simple question: Is/was it worth it? Of course the answer to that question is extremely complex, as the subject of the question—worth it *for whom*—needs to be identified before it can be entertained. And of course it's impossible to measure some of the core motivations that organizers cited in seeking to host the tournament, such as generating pride not only among South Africans but among Africans across the continent or proving to the world that Africa was capable of effectively hosting an event of this magnitude. These discussions engender lively debate among students, as many of them link the issues to similar phenomena in the United States, including the construction of taxpayer-funded stadiums and municipal outlays to host a range of sports tournaments. Many students have already concluded that these sorts of endeavors are only "worth it" for billionaire owners and deep-pocketed leagues, while others promote the nonfinancial, less tangible benefits of these types of undertakings. Among other topics that we examine in this unit is the 1974 heavyweight bout between Muhammed Ali and George Foreman held in Kinshasa, Zaire (Congo), widely known as the "Rumble in the Jungle." We watch the 1996 documentary film *When We Were Kings*, which provides a deeply interior perspective of this global spectacle.[10] This match arguably constituted the first mega-sporting event held in Africa and drew considerable international attention to the continent.

We conclude our examination of Africa's sports history with an extended unit entitled "Racism, Sports, and South Africa." As part of this exploration, students learn about apartheid and the protests against racialized sports in the country, which eventually precipitated international boycotts and bans of South African sports, namely rugby and cricket. Articles by Douglas Booth and Elizabeth Rankin and the film *Fair Play* illustrate the creative ways that protestors demonstrated against touring South African teams and the effects of these efforts.[11] The documentary film *Branded a Rebel* examines the ways that the apartheid regime used to attract cricketers—in this case, West Indians—to tour the country by offering large sums of money, as well as the severe consequences for these athletes upon their return home.[12]

IMAGES OF THE CONTINENT: THE INCLUSION OF FILMS IN THE CURRICULUM

In my estimation, film constitutes a vital pedagogical tool when teaching American college students about Africa. These students typically have very few visuals of the continent, beyond what they see on the news and, perhaps, the ubiquitous wildlife programs. Even mundane scenes of African urban life often surprise students, who either passively or firmly believe that the continent's residents live exclusively in rural areas in makeshift homes. Beyond the images themselves, I also design assignments around the films we watch so that students critically engage with the medium itself. For example, when we screen a film, students are required to determine what insights the film provides that a text could not, and vice versa. In this way, they are not only learning from a film's content but are also assessing its evidentiary value by determining both what it reveals and what it conceals.

OUT-OF-CLASS LEARNING: RESEARCH ASSIGNMENTS

Our classroom discussions are intended to prepare students to engage in two research projects, for which the majority of work is conducted beyond the classroom walls. Although quite divergent in their nature and learning objectives, both the "Media" and "Development and Diaspora" assignments offer students opportunities to access African voices in order to better understand the continent and its peoples. Another benefit that both assignments help to deliver is the generation of information literacy, as students learn how to access foreign newspapers, African-themed websites, and academic journals. In order to assist them in this process, I schedule sessions with library staff at our on-campus facility, Mullins Library, prior to the deadline for identifying a topic. The librarian who conducts these training sessions is familiar with both the syllabus and the attendant assignment tasks and thus can guide students on exercises that, for example, explain how to access newspapers based on the continent through various portals to which the University of Arkansas subscribes. These research endeavors often constitute students' initial forays into these digital repositories and thus help them not only with the assignments for this course but also with other classes going forward.

The "Development and Diaspora" research assignment requires that students identify an African athlete (active or retired) who has played professionally beyond the continent's borders but who has retained active connections to his or her home country and has played a role in the development of that nation. Students are charged with crafting a medium-length (six- to seven-page) paper that demonstrates their knowledge of the individual, his or her home country, the history of the issue(s) this player is addressing, and the changes he or she is trying to effect through his or her ongoing involvement. As many of these athletes are involved with charitable foundations, students are strongly encouraged to make contact with these organizations and, potentially, the athletes themselves. Students typically select male and female soccer players—including, most famously, George Weah, who starred in Europe and is now the president of Liberia—but also a number of basketball players, including Congolese women's basketball player Mwadi Mabika. This assignment prompts students to engage with primary source materials via interviews with foundation employees and ensures that students deepen their understanding of not only the continent's past and present but also the ways that Africans in the diaspora stay positively connected to the continent via sports.

The other major project that students complete in the course is the "Media" assignment. For this endeavor, students select a sports-related development within a particular country, for example, Ghana, or a continent-wide sporting event, for example, the African Cup of Nations, and follow this topic over the course of the semester, compiling articles from African newspapers (and/or other African media sources). Students are charged with exploring the history and social, political, and economic importance of the entity chosen and constructing a medium-length (seven- to eight-page) paper based on the coverage of the topic. Students present their completed work to the class and submit both a list of the articles collected and the final paper. The assignment prompts students to deepen their knowledge of African events, peoples, and places, and also to understand historical developments and corresponding responses from an array of African perspectives.

Just as the course prompts my students to engage in various research undertakings, teaching the course has also shaped my own research endeavors. On a tangible level, my students' engagement in both research papers and class discussion with recreational activities, such as sailing, fishing, hunting, and swimming, that are on the periphery of the African sports core, informed my most recent book project, which examines the history of tourism in colonial Mozambique. In practice, for many South African tourists to the colony, these activities constituted the primary impetus for their visits. As such, my comprehension of sporting activity was meaningfully expanded via the inclusion of these sporting under-takings. More transcendently, weekly discussions in the classroom about the ways that Africans creatively engaged with European-introduced sports have opened up new ways of thinking about colonial encounters across the continent that are manifest in my scholarship, which, irre-spective of the specific topic, considers the array of interactions between Europeans and Africans over the course of the colonial period.

After teaching this class a number of times over the years, I had the opportunity to query other scholars from a number of continents at the Sports Africa conference held in Bloemfontein, South Africa, in April 2017, to gauge their interest or mine their experience in teaching African sports–themed classes. As part of this inquiry, and in conjunc-tion with the conference, I organized a "Teaching African Sports" work-shop, which sought to explore the various ways that sports in Africa are employed in the classroom—either as stand-alone courses or as part of broader, more topically varied courses—pedagogical strategies and ap-proaches, and challenges to further incorporation. The workshop pro-vided a forum in which scholars who are actively teaching African sports in the classroom could exchange ideas, approaches, and experiences. To maximize the fruits of this session, I solicited syllabi and short peda-gogical essays from participants and precirculated these items. Perhaps even more importantly, a number of scholars attended the workshop who weren't currently teaching African sports but sought advice from those of us who were. Upon review, the workshop provided an opportu-nity for a fruitful, face-to-face exchange flowing out of these pieces and the attendant discussion, with the ultimate aim of growing the presence of African sports in the classroom. Consequently, the organizers of the annual Sports Africa conference have expressed a desire to offer similar pedagogical workshops going forward. Ultimately, it is my hope that, propelled onward by these efforts and myriad other initiatives, African sports studies can successfully breach the walls of what seemingly con-stitutes the final frontier: the higher education classroom.

Notes

1. Other texts that assist instructors in designing African history classes are Brandon D. Lundy and Solomon Negash, eds., *Teaching Africa: A Guide for the 21st Century Classroom* (Bloomington: Indiana University Press, 2013); and Trevor R. Getz, *A Primer for Teaching African History: Ten Design Principles* (Durham, NC: Duke University Press, 2018).

2. I share the pedagogical design and delivery related to an interdisciplinary class on African studies that I teach in Todd Cleveland, "Africa: Which Way Forward? An Interdisciplinary Approach," in *Teaching Africa: A Guide for the 21st Century Classroom*, ed. Brandon D. Lundy and Solomon Negash (Bloomington: Indiana University Press, 2013), 27–37.

3. Todd Cleveland, *Following the Ball: The Migration of African Soccer Players across the Portuguese Colonial Empire, 1949–1975* (Athens: Ohio University Press, 2017).

4. Sigrid Paul, "The Wrestling Tradition and Its Social Functions," in *Sport in Africa: Essays in Social History*, ed. William J. Baker and James A. Mangan (New York: Holmes & Meier, 1987), 23–46; and Emmanuel Akyeampong and Charles Ambler, "Leisure in African History," *International Journal of African Historical Studies* 35, no. 1 (2002): 1–16.

5. Laura Fair, "Kickin' It: Leisure, Politics and Football in Colonial Zanzibar, 1900s–1950s," *Africa* 67, no. 2 (1997): 224–51; and Nuno Domingos, "Football and Colonialism, Domination and Appropriation: The Mozambican Case," *Soccer and Society* 8, no. 4 (2007): 478–94.

6. Peter Alegi, *Soccerscapes: How a Continent Changed the World's Game* (Athens: Ohio University Press, 2010).

7. *Town of Runners*, directed by Jerry Rothwell (London: Met Films Productions/Klikk, 2012).

8. Adharanand Finn, *Running with the Kenyans: Discovering the Secrets of the Fastest People on Earth* (New York: Ballantine Books, 2013).

9. Ashwin Desai and Goolam Vahed, "World Cup 2010: Africa's Turn or the Turn on Africa?," *Soccer & Society* 11, nos. 1–2 (January–March, 2010): 154–67; and Dean Allen, "The Successes and Challenges of Hosting the 2010 FIFA World Cup: The Case of Cape Town, South Africa," *Soccer & Society* 14, no. 3 (2013): 404–15.

10. *When We Were Kings*, directed by Leon Gast (Los Angeles: PolyGram/Gramercy, 1996).

11. *Fair Play*, part 4 of *Have You Heard from Johannesburg? Seven Stories of the Global Anti-apartheid Movement*, directed by Connie Field (Franklin Lakes, NJ: Clarity Educational Productions, 2014).

12. *Branded a Rebel*, directed by Jenny Stevens (Atlanta: CNN/CNN, 2013); Douglas Booth, "Hitting Apartheid for Six? The Politics of the South African Sports Boycott," *Journal of Contemporary History* 38, no. 3 (2003): 477–93; and Elizabeth Rankin, "Banners, Batons and Barbed Wire: Anti-apartheid Images of the Springbok Rugby Tour Protests in New Zealand," *Journal de arte* 42, no. 76 (2007): 21–32.

THREE

African Sports in the Liberal Arts Classroom

MATT CAROTENUTO

At the start of a recent semester, fifteen eager students joined me in a pedagogical experiment. With no background in African studies but a wealth of personal experience as athletes and fans, these American students and I embarked on an introductory seminar titled "African Athletes and Global Sport." The goal of the class was twofold. First, from an analytical standpoint, I challenged students to use the lens of global sports to examine the broader social and political world of Africa and the wider African diaspora. And as it was a course in contemporary African history, I wanted students to learn how historians use sports to connect Africa's past with the present. Second, in this course designed only for sophomores, students had a chance think about their broader academic trajectory within a research seminar format usually reserved for more advanced students.

These lofty pedagogical goals aside, the experiment taught me a lot about approaching sports history in the classroom and how American students first need to turn their analytical lens inward before venturing into the more unfamiliar terrain of African history. This chapter analyzes the role African sports history can play within a liberal arts curriculum. Through an examination of the course design, pedagogy, and outcomes of a semester-long class, I argue that an interdisciplinary course based on sports in an African context provides an ideal framework for teaching undergraduate students broad historical lessons as well as important analytical and communication skills. The course also gave me, as a scholar of African sports history, an important chance to reflect on my own research methodology and positionality in balancing American sporting experiences with an empathetic African historical perspective.

St Lawrence University: Sports and Sophomore Transitions

St. Lawrence University (SLU) is a private, residential liberal arts college of twenty-five hundred students, located in northern New York State. Despite its rural US location, SLU has a long tradition in African studies. Beginning with a robust study abroad program in Kenya founded in 1974, the university built a broader African studies program around this tradition of off-campus engagement.[1] With faculty drawn from several departments and programs across the social/natural sciences, arts, and humanities, the university regularly offers more than twenty cross-listed African studies courses each semester. This results in around twenty graduates each year who complete five or six courses to fulfill the requirements for a combined major or minor in African studies.[2]

As at many US colleges, sports is embedded in campus life. St. Lawrence fields thirty-two varsity teams. With the exception of ice hockey, student athletes compete at the nonscholarship, division III level.[3] While nearly one-third of students compete on an official intercollegiate team, the university regularly claims that nearly 96 percent of students participate in some athletic activity through dozens of club sports, intramural teams, or sponsored recreational activities during their undergraduate experience.[4] Without a physical education or sports studies related department, though, students interested in the academic study of sports generally take courses leading to a coaching certification or a minor in sports studies and exercise science. With an average of seventy-five students graduating each year with a sports studies minor, it is one of the most popular interdisciplinary minors at SLU.

With this institutional background in mind, it is not surprising that more than half of my seminar students were on a varsity team, and all the students competed in some sort of organized sport at the secondary school level. However, when I began to explore the students' personal experiences with athletics and their primary reasons for enrolling in the class, I noticed a common trend exhibited by many first- and second-year university students: students were drawn to the study of African history and sports by their own intellectual curiosity and experiences. When I asked about history/African studies as a potential major for this class of undeclared sophomores, however, many felt pressured by peers and family to focus on business or another degree perceived to be more marketable after graduation. As at many institutions across the United States facing a contested "crisis in the humanities" after the 2008 global recession, the number of history majors at SLU has declined, while majors such as the university's new business in the liberal arts have grown significantly.[5]

Getting to know these students in a small seminar setting as both an instructor and informal adviser, I could also tell right away that preprofessional academic pressures skewed the way students viewed the study of sports more broadly. For them, sports was not primarily a vehicle to examine social history but was represented by the lucrative professionalization of American sports, the science of sports psychology/physiology, and perhaps a vague interest in the global politics of mega-events such as the FIFA World Cup or the Olympic Games. Even though they had all had direct personal experiences with organized sports, few had thought about the broader social purpose and history of amateur sports or leisure.

More important, I found out during the first few weeks of the class that many students were going through an important transition in their personal relationships to sports. Several students confided in me how difficult the transition from high school to collegiate athletics was and how their particular sport was no longer "fun" and more like a job.[6] As sports psychologists have noted, those students who self-identified primarily as athletes in high school were more likely to experience athletic "burnout" in college.[7] Sharing my own struggles with burnout in collegiate wrestling opened the door to important theoretical discussions on the boundaries between sports and leisure and encouraged students to question the broader social function of sports in society. Students often reflected on their athletic careers in ways retired professionals do and were searching for a new sense of identity at the same time that they were choosing a major and potential career path. As an instructor, I saw this as an important moment of self-reflection, one in which students were more open to analyzing the role sports had played in their own development.

This connection between personal experience and academic insight was both an important entry point and an ongoing pedagogical challenge. Unlike other courses in African studies, in which few students have any direct connection to the continent or its diverse history, this course was different. Through the lens of sports, I was starting for once on somewhat familiar terrain, where each student had a personal history to draw from. Therefore, one of my biggest challenges throughout the course was how to engage their primarily American experience in the study of Africa's past without reinforcing a Eurocentric approach to studying African history in constant, comparative judgment to Western "development."

Course Introductions: Seeing Beyond the Pitch

Is New York marathon champion Meb Keflezighi truly American? Is South African Olympic gold medalist Caster Semenya too "manly" for women's track and field? During the first week of the seminar, my students grappled with the historic racial and gendered baggage of these questions coming from the world of sports journalism. When teaching African history in the United States, instructors often need to explicitly unpack misrepresentations in popular media so students can begin to question how contemporary discourse is rooted in the past.[8] A course on sports history is no different, and using contemporary examples from the world of elite professional sports challenges stereotypes; develops important analytical skills; and pushes students to move beyond essentializing wins, losses, and financial success as the default analysis for sports history.

The 2009 debates about Meb Keflezighi and Caster Semenya's dominant performances in athletics offered a contemporary window into histories of scientific racism and colonialism, which are often first obscured for students.[9] Caster Semenya's well-documented struggle with gender "testing" and discrimination provides an important opening conversation. While most had not heard of Semenya or the "controversy" specifically, her targeted and personal struggle was shocking to students and provided an extreme example to confront debates about gender and race in sports.[10] Starting first with coverage of Semenya's battle to compete on the world stage, I then moved to an example closer to home for my American students.

When Meb Keflezighi became the first American to win the New York marathon since 1982, his achievement was quickly branded as "foreign" and determined by his East African genetics. Keflezighi immigrated to the United States from Eritrea when he was twelve years old and won National Collegiate Athletic Association (NCAA) titles at the University of California at LA and a 2004 Olympic Silver Medal for the United States. Even with this elite American pedigree, a critic commented to the *New York Times*, "Keflezighi is really another elite African runner by birth, upbringing, and training. Americans are kidding themselves if they say he represents a resurgence of American distance prowess! On the other hand, he is an excellent representative of how we import everything we need!"[11]

Initially, students had a harder time identifying the stereotype because in some ways it was positive, referencing that East African nations (though not Eritrea) have long dominated long-distance running. However, when we dug a bit further, students began to draw comparisons between descriptions of Keflezighi and other professional athletes of African descent. Soon the discussion of the reasons for a professional marathon win became secondary to debates about race and how Black athletic achievement is often represented through dismissive arguments about genetics and "raw" talent, while White athletes are praised for their intellect and work ethic.[12]

To push the debate further, I showed students the infamous image of NBA superstar Lebron James and supermodel Giselle Bündchen from the cover of *Vogue* magazine in 2008.[13] On this controversial cover, shot by famous photographer Annie Leibovitz, James is framed in an aggressive stance. His mouth agape and bouncing a basketball with his left hand, he is embracing a delicately posed Bündchen on his right side. Though students are quick to point out the gendered contrast, the racial element of James's aggressive masculinity versus Bündchen's delicate femininity was not obvious to many of my White students until I introduced a historical comparison.[14] I placed the *Vogue* cover next to a racist World War I enlistment poster depicting a Black "King Kong" ape with a German military helmet carrying away a scantily clad White woman. Students gasped, as the comparisons with the James/Bündchen cover were now quite obvious. James's posture and Bündchen's dress, down to the color, are near mirror images of the 1918 lithograph.[15]

Throughout these early class sessions, our discussions about sports, gender, and race in a global and US context encouraged students to be critical of broader representations of Africa and Africans and how this prejudice is rooted in historical experience. Critiquing images and text from popular media allowed students to practice important analytical skills they would employ later in the semester. However, the introductory portion of the course was not complete until we had established the connections between sports and imperialism and equipped students with the ethnographic tools to analyze the significance of sports in a social and cultural context.

Keeping with the initial theme of contemporary representations and historical connections, I then had students analyze coverage of Eric Moussambani's 100-meter swimming race in the 2000 Olympic Games.[16] Hailing from Equatorial Guinea, Moussambani did not meet the Olympic qualifying time but was given a wildcard bid by the International Olympic Committee as part of an effort to encourage participation from developing countries. After only a few months' training, Moussambani's time of 1:52.72 in his qualifying heat was both mocked and pitied in the coverage of the Olympic Games. He came in a full minute slower than the gold medalist. My students watched coverage of the event via YouTube and debated whether commentators displayed empathy for Moussambani's humble origins or reinforced a patronizing view of Africans as victims of historical circumstance. While scholars clearly see the blatant colonial paternalism of the media discourse in Moussambani's case, for many students it was their first encounter with how African athletes can be portrayed using the familiar tropes of aid advertisements bathed in the twenty-first-century version of the "civilizing mission."

After considering the racial, gendered, and colonial context of these examples, my students had internalized the need for historical reflection and began to shift away from viewing sports from merely a performance or business aspect. However, before turning our attention to African sports history directly, I wanted students to first test their new analytical skills within their own community. This point of the semester conveniently coincided with the annual homecoming football game and a weekend packed with other matches and celebrations associated with sports across campus. I asked students to attend an event that weekend and practice their skills in participant observation. The assignment asked them to take ethnographic field notes on the various customs, rituals, and cultural aspects that are found both on and off the field and construct an argument about the cultural significance of sports and leisure at SLU. The day before homecoming weekend, we had a detailed discussion in class about research skills, in an attempt to draw a firm line between cultural analysis and sports reporting.

The class session following homecoming weekend culminated in a lengthy discussion of the culture of sports at SLU, based on this assignment. Despite our preparation, I first expected detailed discussions of the wins and losses of various SLU teams that weekend. However, I was pleasantly surprised when students first brought up the crowd, highlighting the gendered and generational makeup of football fandom at SLU. Students focused very little on what had happened on the field and turned their attention to the various rituals and etiquette of different constituencies (alumni, faculty, students, parents, etc.). Given their roles as cultural "insiders," students felt empowered to critique the connections between sports and alcohol, dress, music, and a whole host of other issues. While I left class that day impressed with their development as sports researchers, I realized later that this somewhat self-reflective assignment was essential in giving students the confidence to analyze sports history in a cultural context very different from their own.

Course Design: From Historical Survey to Research

Over the course of a fifteen-week semester, I had to move students from sports enthusiasts with no background in African studies to student researchers completing individual projects related to contemporary African sports history. The first three weeks of class were consumed by course introductions and lessons challenging students to critique representations of Africa and analyze sports through a social and cultural lens. From previous experience mentoring student research, I knew I needed to devote significant class time to research skills and individual mentorship. Consequently, I only had about six weeks, or twelve class sessions, to equip students with enough background knowledge for them to conduct their research projects.

In choosing readings and topics designed to broadly cover African sports history, my students and I grappled with the historiographical limits of the field. The limited coverage of pre-twentieth-century sports, and the dominance of colonial and soccer-inspired sports histories, at first limited our options.[17] I worried that despite scholarly attempts to show African agency, students would see African sports history as an inevitable cultural diffusion of colonial/European sports across the continent. Therefore, I had to balance a broad introduction to sports history with African history.

The two texts that anchored this section of the course were John Parker and Richard Rathbone's *African History: A Very Short Introduction*, and Peter Alegi's *African Soccerscapes*.[18] Parker and Rathbone's text is a staple in my thematic-based African history courses, as it provides a concise and thought-provoking introduction to Africa's past, without overwhelming students with dense encyclopedic knowledge or breaking the bank at the college bookstore. Alegi's superb examination of the history of soccer works as an ideal companion to the short history text, with accessible chapters broken down to provide important chronological and thematic examples. Within this overview, I provided additional examples for students to analyze primary sources related to sports and colonialism, neotraditionalism, the 2010 FIFA World Cup, and sports migration.[19] I also devoted a week to viewing the film *Otelo Burning*, which introduced students to South African surfing history, as a deliberate alternative to the dominance of soccer in the literature on African sports.[20] By providing a range of examples and themes related to different sports geography and chronology, I hoped students would be able to identify diverse research topics sparked by individual interests.

In mentoring undergraduate research for many years, I have learned to remove what I earlier thought was essential material to strike a more effective balance between content and process in the classroom. In courses where there is a significant research component, students need a multitiered approach to break down their projects into stages of feedback. In my seminar, several course periods were reserved to work on research methods, and students received formal feedback at the proposal, outline, and draft phases before the final project was due.[21]

The culmination of these semester-long projects was not a traditional research paper but a digital essay. Based on the practices of digital long-form journalism, we examined examples of digital histories and discussed how to translate a traditional paper for a digital audience.[22] Using a WordPress platform and the free plugin AESOP story engine, I worked with SLU's director of digital initiatives to create a public site for students to eventually publish their work.[23] With the ability to embed images and video, construct visual breaks, and pull quotes, the semester-long assignment challenged students to think critically about both research and the aesthetics of digital presentation. This took time to set up, and I devoted two ninety-minute sessions solely to practicing their skills with the WordPress platform.

Students embraced the project, given its public nature, and saw it as a chance to hone skills they would likely need for postgraduate careers in a world where digital communication is now the default. Research on sports history also opened up a wealth of digital primary sources for students, as they were required to incorporate at least two or three primary sources into their ten- to twelve-page papers/digital essays. Digital media archives such as allafrica.com and apimages.com gave students access to African media sources and historical images they could use to critique the representation of sports. Some students incorporated images and text from the growing Readex collection of African historical newspapers or from digital colonial era archives.[24] Access to primary sources and linguistic limitations curbed some students' research topics but also provided opportunities for discussions on the current scope and limits of digital sports histories in Africa.[25]

Student projects eventually fit into the mainstream historiography, as some were frustrated by the lack of material available on a number of topics in the relatively nascent field of African sports studies. Mapping topics onto student interests and backgrounds, six of the class's seven soccer players ended up studying soccer through topics related to the 2010 World Cup, sports migration, and development studies. Three other students chose biographical accounts of professional athletes Caster Semenya, Didier Drogba, and Mo Farrah. Other topics included long-distance running in Kenya, surfing and rugby in South Africa, and the gendered analysis of the sporting landscape through specific country studies. Students took ownership of their projects, with the public digital presentation allowing them to share the work easily with friends and family. Two students even logged in after the completion of the semester to continue to edit their papers, something that in my fifteen years of university teaching has never happened with a traditional research paper.

Mentoring fifteen individual research projects also taught me to reflect more on my own positionality as a researcher. For most of my students, their own personal sporting background influenced the research topics they chose. Given that topics tended to link to a sport they "knew best," I found myself consistently reminding students not to assume that the infrastructure or culture of sports was the same in various African historical contexts. These discussions reminded me of my own research on the social history of wrestling in East Africa, where my prior athletic experience had created opportunities but also challenges during field research.[26] My students inadvertently challenged me to reflect more openly on the ways my athletic preconceptions about the style and structure of wrestling had been colored by my personal background in American folkstyle and Olympic freestyle and Greco-Roman traditions.

By asking students to openly confront their own positionality as American athletes doing African historical research, I also began to see some of the more subtle bias I needed to confront in my own work. Sharing these reflections with my students helped them see research methods as a constantly evolving set of skills that even professional scholars have to continually revise and reevaluate.

African Sports in the Liberal Arts

Within a traditional liberal arts curriculum, breadth of knowledge is prioritized over specialized preprofessional education. Thus, the scope of a class's content is often secondary to the important skills students develop within course pedagogy. Critical analysis of popular media and primary sources, debate and communication skills, and writing for a digital audience were as important outcomes for my seminar as was detailed knowledge of African sports history. Curriculum committees at SLU responded well to this attention on skill development as well as the attention to personal reflection and personal development through sports.

A course designed for first- and second-year students also provides an important opportunity to recruit potential majors and tackle what scholars of higher education are increasingly calling the "sophomore slump."[27] Through the lens of sports, sophomores at SLU were able to reflect on their own development as student athletes during a time when students are at an increased risk for academic dropout and athletic burnout. Funded by grants through the Teagle and Mellon Foundations, my course was part of a wider effort at SLU and many other universities to focus on the sophomore year to increase retention and student academic success.

As scholars of African sports studies work to integrate the field into higher education curricula, courses on sports provide an important means to address this "slump" and can be "specifically designed to help second-year students answer vexing questions about their place and purpose on the campus and beyond."[28] As this volume demonstrates, though, more detailed examples and scholarship addressing the pedagogy of African sports studies and sports history more broadly need to be written.[29] Including the scholarship on sports studies pedagogy within broader liberal arts debates will provide important support for efforts to integrate these fields more widely across the undergraduate curriculum. Occurring during an important moment of academic and often personal transition in undergraduate education, my seminar made it clear to me that the familiar topic of sports and unfamiliar terrain of African history provided American students a significant moment of self-reflection and opportunity to develop important skills through doing social history.

Notes

1. Paul Robinson and Howard Brown, "Developing an Approach to Integrated Study in a Non-Western Context: The St. Lawrence University Kenya Semester Program," in *African Studies and the Undergraduate Curriculum*, ed. Patricia Alden, David Lloyd, and Ahmed Samatar (Boulder, CO: Lynne Rienner, 1994), 231–43; and David T. Lloyd, "African Studies and Study Abroad," *Frontiers: The Interdisciplinary Journal of Study Abroad* 6 (2000): 99–116.

2. St. Lawrence University Institutional Research, www.stlawu.edu/ir /masterstats.

3. Men's and women's ice hockey teams compete at the NCAA division I level and are the only two sports allowed to offer athletic scholarships at SLU.

4. SLU Fast Facts, https://www.stlawu.edu/about-st-lawrence.

5. Julia Brookins, "New Data Show Large Drop in History Bachelor's Degrees," *Perspectives on History* (2016): 10–11. At SLU, in 2008 only 10.2 percent of the graduating class was history majors; this portion had dropped to 3.7 percent by 2018. The university added an interdisciplinary business in the liberal arts degree in 2014, and by 2018 this major represented 20 percent of the graduating class. For more see St. Lawrence Institutional Research at www.stlawu.edu/ir.

6. Bill Pennigton, "It's Not an Adventure, It's a Job," *New York Times*, March 12, 2008, https://www.nytimes.com/2008/03/12/sports/12lifestyles.html.

7. Chang Wen Hsin, Chia-Huei Wu, Che-Chun Kuo, and Lung Hung Chen, "The Role of Athletic Identity in the Development of Athlete Burnout: The Moderating Role of Psychological Flexibility," *Psychology of Sport and Exercise* 39 (2018): 45–51; and Lisa Anne Martin, Gerard J. Fogarty, and Majella J. Albion, "Changes in Athletic Identity and Life Satisfaction of Elite Athletes as a Function of Retirement Status," *Journal of Applied Sport Psychology* 26, no. 1 (2014): 96–110.

8. For a broader introduction to African studies pedagogy, see Trevor R. Getz, *A Primer for Teaching African History: Ten Design Principles* (Durham, NC: Duke University Press, 2018); and Brandon D. Lundy and Solomon Negash, eds., *Teaching Africa: A Guide for the 21st Century Classroom* (Bloomington: Indiana University Press, 2013).

9. Gina Kolata, "To Some, Winner Is Not American Enough," *New York Times*, November 2, 2009; and Jere Longman, "Understanding the Controversy Over Caster Semenya," *New York Times*, August 11, 2016.

10. See, for example, Neville Hoad, "'Run, Caster Semenya, Run!' Nativism and the Translations of Gender Variance," *Safundi* 11, no. 4 (2010): 397–405; and Zine Magubane, "Spectacles and Scholarship: Caster Semenya, Intersex Studies, and the Problem of Race in Feminist Theory," *Signs: Journal of Women in Culture and Society* 39, no. 2 (2014): 761–85. For teaching purposes, the 2011 film by Maxx Ginnane, *Too Fast to Be a Woman: The Story of Caster Semenya*, is a valuable teaching tool available online at https://www.youtube.com/watch?v=f-UX0LE_tCg.

11. Kolata, "To Some, Winner Is Not American Enough."

12. See, for example, Luke Winslow, "Brawn, Brains, and the Death of Black NFL Quarterbacks," in *Sports and Identity: New Agendas in Communication*, ed. Barry Brummett and Andrew Ishak (New York: Routledge, 2014), 19–43; Laura Azzarito and Louis Harrison Jr., "'White Men Can't Jump': Race, Gender, and Natural Athleticism," *International Review for the Sociology of Sport* 43, no. 4 (2008): 347–64.

13. *Vogue*, April 2008, cover.

14. Clayton Zuba, "Monstrosity and the Majority: Defamiliarizing Race in the University Classroom," *Pedagogy: Critical Approaches to Teaching Literature, Language, Composition, and Culture* 16, no. 2 (2016): 356–67; and Karen Ritzenhoff and Cindy White, "Sports and Sexuality: Vogue's Photo Essays about Male Athletes and Supermodels Preceding the Olympic Games 2008," in *Sex and Sexuality in a Feminist World*, ed. Karen Ritzenhoff and Katherine Hermes (Newcastle, UK: Cambridge Scholars, 2009), 169–89.

15. Matthew Poth, "Analyzing Propaganda's Role in World War I," *Teaching with the Library of Congress* (blog), May 10, 2018, https://blogs.loc.gov/teachers/2018/05/analyzing-propagandas-role-in-world-war-i/.

16. John Nauright and Tara Magdalinski, "'A Hapless Attempt at Swimming': Representations of Eric Moussambani," *Critical Arts* 17, nos. 1–2 (2003): 106–22.

17. Marc Fletcher and Lizelle Bisschoff, "African Sport in the Global Arena: Contemporary Approaches and Analyses," *Critical African Studies* 6, nos. 2–3 (2014): 123–33.

18. John Parker and Richard Rathbone, *African History: A Very Short Introduction* (Oxford: Oxford University Press, 2007); and Peter Alegi, *Soccerscapes: How a Continent Changed the World's Game* (Athens: Ohio University Press, 2010).

19. A sample of the readings assigned to students to set up these different case studies/approaches includes Emmanuel Akyeampong, "Bukom and the Social History of Boxing in Accra: Warfare and Citizenship in Precolonial Ga society," *International Journal of African Historical Studies* 35, no. 1 (2002): 39–60; John Bale, "Capturing 'The African' Body? Visual Images and 'Imaginative Sports,'" *Journal of Sport History* 25, no. 2 (1998): 234–51; Matthew Carotenuto "Grappling with the Past: Wrestling and Performative Identity in Kenya," *International Journal of the History of Sport* 30, no. 16 (2013): 1889–1902; Ashwin Desai and Goolam Vahed, "World Cup 2010: Africa's Turn or the Turn on Africa?," *Soccer and Society* 11, no. 1 (2010): 154–67; and Jarvie Grant and Michelle Sikes, "Running as a Resource of Hope? Voices from Eldoret," *Review of African Political Economy* 39, no. 134 (2012): 629–44.

20. Sara Blecher, *Otelo Burning* (Johannesburg: Sara Blecher & Cinga Productions, 2011), DVD. For a useful set of readings for students, see the seven articles in the "Contemporary Conversation: Otelo Burning" section of the *Journal of African Cultural Studies* 26, no. 3 (2014).

21. Elizabeth Belanger, "Bridging the Understanding Gap: An Approach to Teaching First-Year Students How to 'Do' History," *History Teacher* 49, no. 1 (2015): 35–62.

22. Kasia Kovacs, "How to Engage Readers with Digital Long Form Journalism," American Press Institute, December 1, 2016, https://www .americanpressinstitute.org/publications/reports/strategy-studies/engaging -longform-journalism/.

23. For an example of the features of this free WordPress plugin, see http://aesopstoryengine.com/.

24. The subscription-based Readex African newspaper collection contains digitized copies of more than one hundred publications from 1800 to 1925. The collection has also recently acquired the South African *Rand and Daily Mail* from 1902 to 1985. For a methodological example of using sports reporting for African sports history, see Michelle Sikes, "Print Media and the History of Women's Sport in Africa: The Kenyan Case of Barriers to International Achievement," *History in Africa* 43 (2016): 323–45. Other archival sources consulted include newsreel clips from http://britishpathe.com/, film and images from http://colonialfilm.org.uk, the online Basel Mission archives (http:// www.bmarchives.org), and the UK National Archives project "Africa Through a Lens," http://www.nationalarchives.gov.uk/africa/.

25. There is a growing body of literature on digital sports history, but currently there is a need for more scholarly attention to resources and methods for African history. See, for example, Gary Osmond and Murray Phillips, eds., *Sport History in the Digital Era* (Urbana: University of Illinois Press, 2015); and "*Doing Sport History in the Digital Present*," special issue, *Journal of Sport History* 44, no. 2 (2017).

26. Matthew Carotenuto, "Crafting Sport History behind Bars: Wrestling with State Patronage and Colonial Confinement in Kenya," *History in Africa* 43 (2016): 289–321.

27. O. J. Webb and D. R. E. Cotton, "Deciphering the Sophomore Slump: Changes to Student Perceptions during the Undergraduate Journey," *Higher Education: The International Journal of Higher Education Research* 77, no. 1 (2019): 173–90.

28. See Sarah Barber and Robert Thacker, "We Can No Longer Ignore the Slump," *Inside Higher Ed*, September 29, 2017, https://www.insidehighered.com/views/2017/09/29/how-improve-retention-sophomore-students-essay.

29. Ryan Swanson, "The Wild West of Pedagogy: Thoughts on Teaching American Sport History," in *The Routledge History of American Sport*, ed. Linda Borish, David Wiggins, and Gerald Gems (New York: Routledge, 2016), 48–60.

FOUR

On Teaching South African Sports History at a US University

PETER ALEGI

Sports can deepen our understanding of the richness and complexities of African experiences, past and present. For more than two decades, this fundamental conviction has shaped my academic work as an Africanist specializing in the social and political history of modern South Africa. At Michigan State University (MSU), where I began teaching in 2005, I have incorporated sports into undergraduate African history and interdisciplinary African studies courses and placed Africans center stage in my global football surveys and seminars.[1] In this chapter I reflect more narrowly on pedagogical ideas and learning experiences drawn from "Sports, Race, and Power in South African History," an upper-level seminar for history majors I have taught three times in the past four academic years. The chapter makes two related arguments. First, African sports offers a personally engaging and intellectually stimulating opportunity for young men and women to *do* "serious" history: work that is methodologically rigorous, theoretically informed, and analytically incisive. Second, effective teaching about African sports requires thinking strategically and creatively about audience, goal setting, syllabus construction, format, assessments, and learning opportunities.[2]

"Sports, Race, and Power in South African History" (History 484) is a topical writing seminar, one of two capstone courses that MSU history majors are required to take. I offer it in the spring semester in alternate years. It represents a viable response to increasing student demand for innovative courses in history. It also makes a tangible contribution to a broader departmental effort aimed at addressing, if not reversing, the precipitous decline in the number of history majors in recent years, a trend currently affecting most colleges and universities across the United States. "The drop in the last decade," the American Historical Association noted recently, "has put us below the discipline's previous low point in the 1980s."[3] A tight geographical focus on South Africa draws on my research expertise while allowing for in-depth coverage of an important African nation whose history, while exceptional in some ways, also has much in common with that of the continent as a whole.[4] Per departmental requirements, the key learning outcome is the production of an original research paper approximately six thousand words in length. From my perspective, the main intellectual goals of this capstone seminar are to (a) develop specialized knowledge about South African history and (b) explore the inextricably linked and evolving relationship between sports and society.

The class meets twice a week for eighty minutes, and enrollment has grown from six to fourteen students, a typical size for an advanced history seminar at our public university. Approximately three-quarters of students who take the class are in their final year of a history BA degree. The remaining contingent is drawn from other social science and humanities programs. The class demographic is reasonably diverse, though the gender ratio skews slightly more male than in my other African history classes. Significantly, the undergraduates who take the seminar generally share a deep and abiding personal interest in sports, regardless of gender, race, socioeconomic status, and national origin. During introductions at the first meeting, male and female students alike often reveal to the group that they have played youth, club, and high school sports. It is quite common for students to volunteer descriptions of their casual or obsessive support for specific professional sports teams. Such declarations of emotional connections to the topic are relatively rare in the austere confines of a university classroom. While such affective ties are welcome, this advantage is partly offset by the discomfiting reality that MSU undergraduates, like most US students, arrive in my classroom with extremely limited knowledge about African affairs and not a few misconceptions about the continent and its people.

One way around this conundrum is to present the course's "big questions" in the syllabus and highlight them in the opening meeting: Have sports historically functioned as a tool for empowerment or disempowerment? Are sports a force for inclusion or exclusion? Do sports heighten or diminish racial consciousness and identities? What does it mean for athletes and leagues to be "political"? How has the sports business changed? Asking these kinds of questions underscores the universality of sports. It also prompts students to think about the connections between sports, race, and power in contexts closer to home, which frequently leads to US students mentioning more familiar stories, past and present, such as those of Jesse Owens, Joe Louis, Jackie Robinson, Muhammad Ali, Tommie Smith and John Carlos, Colin Kaepernick, and Megan Rapinoe. The conversation is under way.

Given the students' generally limited prior knowledge about South Africa and Africa as a whole, I open the course with a two-week mini-survey of South African political and economic history. This exercise serves two purposes. First, it gives everyone time to settle into the class during the drop/add period and to familiarize themselves with one another and with me. Second, it introduces students to South African history's periodization; key people, events, and themes; and distinctive racial terminology. Understanding this basic history enables seminar participants to properly situate later on the multifaceted agency of athletes, fans, organizers, and activists against a backdrop of powerful structural constraints. Mindful of the basic objectives of this unit and the intense work lying ahead, I assign readings from the Overcoming Apartheid, Building Democracy in South Africa website, a multimedia curriculum created at MSU before the social media revolution.[5] This digital resource is similar to an introductory textbook, a mix of synthesis and coverage. Unlike a textbook, however, Overcoming Apartheid is free of charge to internet users worldwide. Its essays, maps, documents, and audiovisual interviews help bring the past to life, while the embedded hyperlinks to external sources invite further user-driven exploration. This digital content is complemented by my concise lectures delivered in informal style, with plenty of time for questions and dialogue. This opening unit closes with an in-class assessment testing historical knowledge of indigenous societies, European colonialism and the mineral revolution, segregation and apartheid, and the liberation struggle.

With this foundational work completed, the course then adopts a complementary chronological and thematic structure, with case studies on specific sporting codes, biographies, and selected themes. A single historiography session maps the evolution of the field as well as some of the latest trends in South African sports history (broadly defined), followed by an engagement with precolonial sports.[6] This move is important because it establishes early on that the ship of history in (South) Africa did not arrive with European settlers. Historical ethnographies of Zulu stick fighting trigger a fulsome examination of agrarian athletic competitions, martial masculinities, youth socialization, and the existence in southern Africa of a *sportgeist*, a spirit of sport.[7] The seed is planted for our consideration of the nineteenth-century growth of modern sports under the British in the colonies of the Cape and Natal. The main focus is on rugby and cricket and their powerful role in the making of White identities, with an emphasis on men in the preapartheid era. In separate sessions, readings encourage discussion of cricket as a space for the production and reproduction of an English-speaking, White imperial masculinity and of rugby as a vehicle for articulating a manliness keenly in synch with crystallizing Afrikaner nationalist values and ideals.[8] As the class grapples with sports' relationship to racial segregation and colonial capitalism, openings appear through which to connect South Africa to similar shifts under way elsewhere in colonial Africa and world history as a whole.

At this point we turn our attention to the social and political history of Black soccer. By this time, most students tend to have a solid grasp of the country's sporting landscape and political context and can manage the weekly required reading load of about eighty to a hundred pages (with additional suggested journal articles or book chapters for the exceptionally curious). I assign the second edition of my book, *Laduma! Soccer, Politics, and Society in South Africa, from Its Colonial Origins to 2010*. The historical agency of football players, clubs, associations, and fans is placed in the context of segregated Black townships and mining compounds, harsh poverty and inequality, and Black-led liberation movements' struggle against the apartheid police state. This approach encourages students to analyze how soccer shaped power struggles and everyday lives in different cities around the country, including Johannesburg, Durban, and Cape Town. Some of the most productive discussions pivot around the stiff challenges of conducting archival research and oral interviewing in an African context. Many undergraduates come away from this unit with a firm appreciation of the porous boundaries between sports and society.

Having covered soccer, rugby, and cricket, the most popular sports in the country, the time is right for a deep dive into the South African sports boycott, "the most prominent extended antiracist campaign in the history of world sports."[9] The class goes backward in time. Fortunately, this does not seem to unsettle students. We begin with a lecture and the screening of *Fair Play*, part 4 of *Have You Heard from Johannesburg?*, Connie Field's eight-and-one-half-hour documentary film series.[10] This evocatively conveys a sense of the boycott's evolution over time, its main actors, protest actions, and ties to the Olympics and the Cold War. Moving from the general to the specific, and from the institutional to the individual, students then examine two dramatic episodes at the heart of this complicated history. The first is the D'Oliveira affair of 1968. This diplomatic incident was triggered by Prime Minister B. J. Vorster's refusal to allow Basil D'Oliveira, an exiled Capetonian cricketer, to return to South Africa as part of the England national team.[11] D'Oliveira's life story humanizes the fight for equality and freedom and illustrates how and why apartheid South Africa became a pariah of international sports by the 1970s. It also opens a window on the history of "coloured" identity and its interstitial place in South Africa's racial hierarchy. The second case study on the sports boycott movement centers on African American tennis star Arthur Ashe and his contentious decision to participate in the 1973 South African Open.[12] Here we consider African American connections with

South Africa as well as the social and political impact of Vorster's "multi-national sport" reforms (introduced in 1971) on the liberation movement at home and abroad.[13] The final episode in the unit looks at the rise and fall of the South African Council on Sport (SACOS). Its famous slogan, "No Normal Sport in an Abnormal Society," captured SACOS's function as, essentially, the domestic wing of the sports boycott movement until its rapid demise during the political transition of the early 1990s.[14] Such high-level work leads to a well-deserved spring break.

When we return to campus, there is a shift in the intellectual thrust and overall pace of the course. Team sports give way to individual sports, such as golf and athletics (track). The reading load lightens noticeably to allow students to commit more time and effort to their research projects. In a welcome break from the academic literature, we spend one week discussing Christopher Nicholson's essayistic biography of golfer Papwa Sewgolum. A caddie at the Whites-only Durban Country Club (where he was only allowed to play on Monday mornings), Sewgolum won the 1963 Natal Open against White competitors on that same course but had to suffer the indignity of being handed the trophy in the rain while the other golfers received their awards in the Whites-only clubhouse. The book also serves as an opportunity to grapple with aspects of the history of South Africa's Indian community and to extend previous discussions about biography as a genre of history.[15] Students seem to find the "prize giving that shook the world" a riveting read, despite its sad ending with Papwa's descent into alcoholism and death at the age of forty-eight. Moving swiftly from apartheid golf courses to the rubberized tracks of democratic South Africa, the next weeklong unit focuses on women and sexuality in sports through the story of Olympic and world champion middle-distance runner Caster Semenya.[16] The legal and institutional discrimination suffered by the intersex athlete, as well the history of gender testing (and the controversy over testosterone levels) in women's sports, often surprises and shocks students. Moreover, Semenya's self-identification as a woman and a lesbian elicits vigorous discussions about heteronormativity, patriarchy, and homophobia in sports.[17]

The course closes with a five-session sequence devoted to sports and nation building in the postapartheid era. The euphoria of rainbow nationalism in the mid-1990s comes into sharp relief with the Springboks' victory in the 1995 Rugby World Cup. Special attention is paid to how this history is represented (and glorified) in Clint Eastwood's film *Invictus*.[18] It is a reminder that sports feature films can certainly spark robust debates about the relationship between history and film.[19] The country's successful staging in 2010 of the most popular sporting event on the planet, the FIFA World Cup, adds another layer to our examination of sports as nation building in contemporary South Africa. Students evaluate the benefits of generating patriotic pride and of marketing "Brand South Africa" to the world, as well as the costs of massive public subsidies for stadium construction and guaranteeing tax-free profits for FIFA.[20] Last but not least, we scrutinize the status quo of South African sports, from the more racially representative composition of national teams and the administrative ranks to the gaping material inequality separating grassroots sports from elite sports.[21]

Generating and sustaining student engagement is the key to the success of this course. To this end, my main strategy is to run the class as both a reading-and-discussion seminar *and* a research seminar. Attendance and participation are required. Students are expected to read the assigned material *before* class and come ready to make informed comments, raise questions, and constructively challenge each other. While each student has his or her own personality and learning style, I make it clear at the outset that silence and passivity are not an option. Participation accounts for one-fifth of the final grade, and points are earned in two ways. The first is through qualitative contributions that advance peers' understanding of the material. The second is by leading class discussions. Each student does so once during the semester (sometimes twice depending on enrollment). On Wednesdays, discussion leaders upload a Word document to our learning management system site so that every member of the seminar can read it before coming to class the following day. This document presents a one-page summary of the assigned reading and then poses at least five questions to spark and sustain class discussion. This seems to be an effective way to put students in charge of their own learning and to increase meaningful engagement with the content.

While reading and discussion are vital ingredients, the most important assignment is the capstone research project: a journal-quality paper at least six thousand words in length that uses primary and secondary sources and accounts for 40 percent of the final grade. The intimate class size allows me to closely supervise the projects. During the first four weeks of the term, each student is required to meet with me in person at least once during office hours to discuss potential topics and available sources. The research process is carefully scaffolded, with evenly spaced due dates for topic approval, preliminary bibliography, research question(s), thesis and annotated outline, and draft (this last one is voluntary).

As members of the MSU community, students are fortunate and privileged to have access to one of the largest Africana library collections in the United States. A section of our course website lists the MSU Library Special Collections division's extraordinary African Activist Archive, which houses records of US activism to support the struggles of African peoples against colonialism, apartheid, and social injustice.[22] This vast collection includes the papers of the American Coordinating Committee for Equality in Sport and Society (ACCESS), founded in 1976 by Richard Lapchick, which advocated for the sports boycott of South Africa. Unsurprisingly, my students routinely mine ACCESS correspondence files, press releases, reports, and other documents covering mainly tennis, golf, and rugby. Our two African studies librarians also help students use databases such as the World Newspaper Archive and JSTOR's Struggles for Freedom Southern Africa, as well as interlibrary loan services and the rich collection of newspapers and political materials on southern Africa held by the Cooperative Africana Materials Project (CAMP).

For instructors at colleges and universities without the privilege of local access to extensive archival and library collections on African sports, there are alternatives to assigning a major research paper. In an earlier version of my seminar, for example, I decided to emphasize digital scholarship. Students created and maintained individual blogs on the WordPress platform for weekly assignments and completed a variety of digital capstone projects, including curated web galleries, data visualizations, podcasts, and e-books. This approach provides students more freedom to experiment with computer-based research and to present historical thinking in digital formats. My experience suggests that this approach can work well, as long as some of the units and assigned readings are replaced by hands-on sessions on basic digital humanities tools and methods. Like most instructors in advanced seminars (irrespective of pedagogy), I spend considerable time and effort tracking student progress, diagnosing challenges (e.g., availability of sources, feasible research questions, appropriate chronology), and providing constructive feedback.

This labor-intensive approach pays off in the final third of my course, as the focus turns decisively away from class discussions and toward the research paper. The reading load is reduced to about forty pages a week, with no readings at all assigned in the final two weeks. Instead, during the penultimate week students either workshop their papers with their peers during our regularly scheduled class period or voluntarily submit a draft for my review. The final class meetings are dedicated to students' formal ten-minute oral presentations of their research papers. As if attending a professional conference, I slide into my seat and diligently take notes while students present their findings with the assistance of slides, audio, video, and other technology. Then they field questions from the audience, including me. In the most recent iteration of the course, students wrote good quality papers on baseball in South Africa, golf and apartheid politics, boxing and Black identity, the economics of World Cup stadiums, and soccer in prison as a form of survival and resistance. The sports boycott was a popular topic, with some superb papers on Pan-Africanism in sports; a biographical study of activist Dennis Brutus; and a comparative analysis of the 1968 and 1972 Olympic boycotts against South Africa and Rhodesia, respectively.

Judging by learning outcomes and assessments, my course achieves its objectives and generally exceeds students' expectations. In terms of the latter, I share Trevor Getz's misgivings about student evaluations, which can "produce important insights, but often they merely become a data set of students' likes and dislikes."[23] Even so, "Sports, Race, and Power in South African History" has received high ratings in multiple categories, and the few negative comments tend to complain about the "heavy workload." Students appear to appreciate my enthusiasm, organization, and encouragement to express their different viewpoints and to generate new questions and ideas. Some actually enjoy the anecdotes about playing, coaching, watching, and researching soccer around South Africa. Finally, my willingness to connect South African sports to colonialism, racism, nationalism, and global capitalism seems to appeal to undergraduates who come to the course with different interests and limited preparation in South African history and African studies in general.

Teaching this course has influenced my scholarship in a number of unexpected ways. First, it has helped to generate new research presentations and publications on a range of new topics, such as women's leisure, youth development, and the impact of digital technology on South African history writing.[24] Second, while digging through analog and digital archives, I now collect written documents (and photographs) not simply because of relevance to my research project, but also for potential didactic value. Third, I like to believe that my academic writing has become more accessible to nonspecialist readers. This stems partly from having to synthesize complicated South African history into digestible mini-lectures. But it is also partly the result of teaching with (and writing) biographies, an alluring genre that humanizes history and brings out the contradictions and complications in people's lives. After all, "history is an anthology of stories, told by people with differing convictions and commitments, many of whom cannot even agree on the story line."[25]

African sports can be a valuable tool in social scientists' teaching arsenal. It can increase undergraduate enrollments in African history and African studies and also enhance students' skills in critical thinking, historical research, information management, oral communication, and writing. But it is important to recognize that "successful" teaching of African sports history is dependent on the quality and depth of instructors' strategic thinking about course design as well as their willingness to create engaging and intellectually lively, student-centered learning experiences. I hope this brief reflection can be useful to colleagues who are considering teaching similar courses or thinking of ways to incorporate more sports content into African history, global history, and African studies courses.

Notes

1. Peter Alegi, Amy Bass, Adrian Burgos Jr., Brenda Elsey, and Martha Saavedra, "Teaching Forum on Sport and Politics," *Radical History Review* 125 (2016): 187–98.

2. Trevor Getz, *A Primer for Teaching African History: Ten Design Principles* (Durham, NC: Duke University Press, 2018).

3. Benjamin M. Schmidt, "The History BA since the Great Recession: The 2018 AHA Majors Report," *AHA Perspectives*, November 26, 2018, https://www.historians.org/publications-and-directories/perspectives-on-history/december-2018/the-history-ba-since-the-great-recession-the-2018-aha-majors-report.

4. Mahmood Mamdani, *Citizen and Subject: Contemporary Africa and the Legacy of Late Colonialism* (Princeton, NJ: Princeton University Press, 1996).

5. Overcoming Apartheid, Building Democracy in South Africa, n.d., http://overcomingapartheid.msu.edu/.

6. André Odendaal, "Sport and Liberation: The Unfinished Business of the Past," in *Sport and Liberation in South Africa*, ed. C. Thomas (Alice, South Africa: University of Fort Hare Press, 2006), 11–38; John Nauright, "African Women and Sport: The State of Play," *Sport in Society* 17, no. 4 (2014): 563–74; and Ashwin Desai, "Sports Journalism and the Padding of History," in *Reverse Sweep: A Story of South African Cricket since Apartheid* (Auckland Park, South Africa: Fanele, 2016), 44–59.

7. Stephen Hardy, "Entrepreneurs, Structures, and the Sportgeist: Old Tensions in a Modern Industry," in *Essays on Sport History and Sport Mythology*, ed. D. G. Kyle and G. D. Stark (College Station: Texas A&M Press, 1990), 45–82.

8. David Black and John Nauright, "Making Imperial Men," in *Rugby and the South African Nation* (Manchester, UK: Manchester University Press, 1998), 22–37; and Albert Grundlingh, "Playing for Power: Rugby, Afrikaner Nationalism and Masculinity in South Africa," in A. Grundlingh, André Odendaal, and Burridge Spies, *Beyond the Tryline* (Johannesburg: Ravan, 1995), 106–35.

9. Rob Nixon, "Apartheid on the Run: The South African Sports Boycott," *Transition* 58 (1992): 70.

10. *Fair Play*, part 4 of *Have You Heard from Johannesburg? Seven Stories of the Global Anti-apartheid Movement*, directed by Connie Field (Franklin Lakes, NJ: Clarity Educational Productions, 2014).

11. Bruce Murray, "Politics and Cricket: The D'Oliveira Affair of 1968," *Journal of Southern African Studies* 27, no. 4 (2001): 667–84. See also Peter Oborne, *Basil D'Oliveira: Cricket and Conspiracy; The Untold Story* (London: Little, Brown, 2004).

12. Eric Allen Hall, *Arthur Ashe: Tennis and Justice in the Civil Rights Era* (Baltimore, MD: Johns Hopkins University Press, 2014), 143–78.

13. According to apartheid ideology, racial groups represented separate and distinct "nations." *Multinationalism* allowed racially defined teams to compete against each other in South Africa and against visiting foreign teams that included "non-Whites." In 1976 multinationalism was extended to club sports. For further analysis, see Christopher Merrett, "'In Nothing Else Are the Deprivers So Deprived': South African Sport, Apartheid and Foreign Relations, 1945–71," *International Journal of the History of Sport* 13, no. 2 (1996): 146–65; and Richard E. Lapchick, *The Politics of Race and International Sport: The Case of South Africa* (Westport, CT: Greenwood, 1975).

14. Douglas Booth, "The South African Council on Sport and the Political Antinomies of the Sports Boycott," *Journal of Southern African Studies* 23, no. 1 (1997): 51–66.

15. Christopher Nicholson, *Papwa Sewgolum: From Pariah to Legend* (Johannesburg: Wits Press, 2005).

16. Denise E. M. Jones, "Women and Sport in South Africa: Shaped by History and Shaping Sporting History," in *Sport and Women: Social Issues in International Perspective*, ed. Ilse Hartman-Tews and Gertrud Pfister (New York: Routledge, 2003), 130–32; Christopher Merrett, "Perpetual Outsiders: Women in Athletics and Road Running in South Africa," in *Routledge Handbook of Sport, Gender and Sexuality*, ed. Jennifer Hargreaves and Eric Anderson (London: Routledge, 2014), 93–97; and Ariel Levy, "Either/Or: Sports, Sex, and the Case of Caster Semenya," *New Yorker*, November 30, 2009, 47–59.

17. Alex Hutchinson, "An Imperfect Dividing Line," *New Yorker*, March 27, 2015, https://www.newyorker.com/sports/sporting-scene/dutee-chand-gender-testing-imperfect-line; and Claire F. Sullivan, "Gender Verification and Gender Policies in Elite Sport: Eligibility and 'Fair Play,'" *Journal of Sport and Social Issues* 35, no. 4 (2011): 400–419.

18. Albert Grundlingh and John Nauright, "The 1995 Rugby World Cup and the 2010 FIFA World Cup," in *Africa's World Cup: Critical Reflections on Play, Patriotism, Spectatorship, and Space*, ed. Peter Alegi and Chris Bolsmann (Ann Arbor: University of Michigan Press, 2013), 189–99.

19. See Vivian Bickford-Smith and Richard Mendelsohn, eds., *Black and White in Colour: African History on Screen* (Oxford: James Currey; Athens: Ohio University Press; Cape Town: Double Storey, 2007); and Robert A. Rosenstone, *Visions of the Past: The Challenge of Film to our Idea of History* (Cambridge, MA: Harvard University Press, 1995).

20. Alegi and Bolsmann, eds., *Africa's World Cup: Critical Reflections on Play, Patriotism, Spectatorship, and Space* (Ann Arbor: University of Michigan Press, 2013), 1–17; and Sifiso Mxolisi Ndlovu, "Sports as Cultural Diplomacy:

The 2010 FIFA World Cup in South Africa's Foreign Policy," *Soccer & Society* 11, nos. 1–2 (2010): 144–53.

21. See, for example, Ashwin Desai, ed., *Race to Transform: Sport in Post-Apartheid South Africa* (Pretoria: HSRC, 2010).

22. A selection of about ten thousand digitized items from the African Activist Archive is freely available at http://africanactivist.msu.edu/.

23. Getz, *Primer for Teaching African History*, 148.

24. See, for example, "The Izichwe Football Club: Sports, Youth, and Masculinity in Pietermaritzburg, South Africa," *Journal of Southern African Studies* 45, no. 5 (2019): 963–80; "Podcasting the Past: Africa Past and Present and (South) African History in the Digital Age," *South African Historical Journal* 64, no. 2 (2012): 206–20; and "Rewriting Patriarchal Scripts: Women, Labor, and Popular Culture in South African Clothing Industry Beauty Contests, 1970s–2005," *Journal of Social History* 42, no. 1 (2008): 31–56.

25. Sam Wineburg, *Historical Thinking and Other Unnatural Acts: Charting the Future of Teaching the Past* (Philadelphia, PA: Temple University Press, 2001), 168.

THREE

Resisting Discrimination and
Forging Identity through Sports

FIVE

"The Gist of the [Game] Is Played Out on the Edges of the Cricket Boundary"

The History of an Indian Cricket Team in Africa, 1934–95

TRISHULA PATEL

In 1987 Bharat Patel, a civil servant in Zimbabwe's Ministry of Justice, as well as a cricket player for the Sunrise Sports Club team of Harare, wrote an editorial about the state of Zimbabwean cricket. Sunrise, located in the city's Indian neighborhood, was made up primarily of members drawn from the country's Indian community. Patel's words were not exactly laudatory: "In almost every country where the game is played, cricket has come to acquire a certain mass appeal. Zimbabwe, however, appears to boast the exception to this rule: cricket continues to be the exclusive preserve of a privileged few. Admittedly, one cannot expect a broader popular base for the game to be built up overnight. But unless a concerned and thorough-going effort is made to 'Zimbabwean-ize' the game, cricket as a serious venture will flourish fleetingly and in isolation and will eventually die out in this country."[1]

"The privileged few" here referred to the fact that in Zimbabwe, cricket was played along racially exclusive lines, mainly by the country's White and Indian minority populations, not by the Black majority, who remained relegated to the lower economic working class, a hangover of colonialism, which had formally ended just seven years before. The players of the Sunrise Sports Club cricket team were certainly part of that advantaged elite. Yet in 1988, Sunrise's minutes from its annual general meeting revealed that the team was recruiting "African youngsters" in an effort to become more active in regional cricket to promote the national side's position on the international cricketing scene.[2] What had led to this seemingly sudden desire to participate in a wider sporting culture?

This chapter examines the history of the Sunrise Sports Club and its cricket players, exploring the issues of identity faced by the Indian community in Salisbury. The Sunrise Sports Club cricket team was formed in 1934, when the country was called Southern Rhodesia, during the colonial period of racial segregation, which meant that the sport was largely played along racially divided lines. The first generation of players participated in colonial society as subjects of the British Empire, reflecting a desire to participate in Rhodesian society. But as racial discrimination by the colonial government against the "Asian" population intensified in the 1950s and 1960s, and Rhodesia itself broke from the confines of empire, the next generation began to retreat to their Indian identity and tradition of playing the sport for a sense of security. After 1980, when the country gained its independence, the second and third generations of men of Indian origin born in Zimbabwe used cricket as a way to participate in the new state's national culture in an attempt to reconfigure themselves as African citizens.

These states of being—Indian and African—were not mutually exclusive, and the community's multilayered sense of identity played out, quite literally and sometimes simultaneously, on the cricket pitch. This chapter explores the moment of change that occurred in the years leading up to and just after the country's independence, focusing on the shift that took place, from Indians situating themselves within the colonial framework of empire to within that of an independent African nation. In a limited way, Sunrise had evolved from being an insular team that imbibed the notions of imperial racial segregation to embracing its status within a more national space. The game thus became a space for insertion into a national culture that typically excludes racial minorities from nationalist consciousness. The country's history is dominated by discourses of indigeneity and autochthony and the relationship between Black and White, with no shades of grey in between, both in academic and political spaces. It is in the space between Black and White that this exploration of identity and belonging locates itself.

As the British Empire consolidated its hold over Africa in the late nineteenth and early twentieth centuries, it created connections between its new African colonies and an older imperial holding: India. Requiring cheap labor for railways in East Africa and plantations in South Africa, Britain recruited Indian workers from the states of Punjab and Gujarat to migrate across the Indian Ocean in the late nineteenth century. By the twentieth century, Africa had become a "New World" for struggling Indian peasants seeking a new future in an old land.[3] Young Indian men began to voluntarily cross the ocean in the years leading up to World War I, landing on the coast of Mozambique. Finding that immigration restrictions made it difficult for them to join older generations of men who had ended up in South Africa, they began the long trek walking across Mozambique, ending up in what was then Northern and Southern Rhodesia. These migrants never made up more than 2 percent of Southern Rhodesia's population. Nevertheless, they were a significant presence in Rhodesia's economic landscape. Barred from purchasing farmland by the Land Apportionment Act of 1930, they turned instead to commerce, opening up businesses in Salisbury, Bulawayo, Umtali, and smaller towns.[4]

As these men put down roots in a new home, they looked for forms of recreation as a way to create a sense of civic spirit and space for socialization in a slowly burgeoning community. Seeking to locate themselves in Rhodesia's White settler–dominated society, they found cricket. Brought over to Rhodesia in the nineteenth century by the country's first White settlers, the English bat-and-ball game had come to represent the legacy of colonialism and empire for the men who played it. The sport was initially confined to the White minority community, an elite game played on a local league level and, after the formation of the Rhodesian Cricket Union in 1898, in international competitions.

In 1934, nine Indian men formed the Young Merchants Cricket Club in Salisbury, which in 1941 expanded and was renamed the Oriental

Cricket Club. The team, which would later become the Sunrise Sports Club cricket team, was one of the first non-White teams to form in the country. As the team transformed from being a ragtag group of men who played the sport merely for the sake of entertainment into a formally structured organization, it fell under the auspices of the Salisbury Indian Cricket Union, which was created to oversee the community's cricketing events in the city in 1947 and then in 1952 connected with the Southern Rhodesia Indian Cricket Board to become a national entity.[5] The Orientals were one of eight Indian teams located across the country, and they played not only against each other but also against the country's White teams, participating in the local league that served as the training space for selection into Southern Rhodesia's national side.[6] The most active Indian cricket unions were located in the larger cities of Salisbury and Bulawayo, with intertown fixtures a regular feature.[7]

These young Indian men aspired to become ideal colonial subjects, fulfilling their role as subjects of the British Empire in all its glory. They were, in a way, agents of colonialism, migrating to the land as British subjects and then participating in the construction of colonial society. Their identity as colonial subjects was thus grounded in the construction of frameworks through which they could affiliate as a settler population, rather than through identification with the Black majority population. They may have been subject to discriminatory segregation that governed racial hierarchies, but they were still given more rights than "Africans." For "their extraordinary services to the British Empire," including contributions to the British army in World War II, former residents of India in the colonies demanded rights as citizens of empire.[8] For the men of the Oriental Cricket Club, the game of empire provided a means of inclusion in colonial society.

White cricket players and officials, in turn, encouraged this behavior, reflecting what Arjun Appadurai describes as the "ideal way to socialize natives into new modes of intergroup conduct" in India.[9] But in Southern Rhodesia, these standards were applied by Indians *themselves,* suggesting a sense of self-socialization into colonial society. Indians voluntarily took on the standards of White settler cricket in order to fit in, highlighting a two-way process of negotiation between ruling and ruled. This desire to be part of broader colonial society is visible in the earliest examples of cricketing literature, which included minutes of meetings, programs created for circulation at tournaments, and tour books.[10] Meeting minutes articulated internal discourse regarding the importance of the game for imperial citizenship. At a meeting of the Rhodesia Indian Cricket Union, the board members noted that the most important goal of the board would be to foster cooperation between Indian teams as well as with White players, so that the "future generation will learn this and become good citizens."[11] In the following years, tour books and programs would reproduce imperial rhetoric that highlighted friendship and cooperation between different races from both Indians and Whites, who praised the playing of the game "in that spirit which had made cricket so popular all over the Empire."[12] N. V. Desai, president of the Rhodesian Cricket Union, exalted the game as one "of the Commonwealth of Nations. Second only to the Crown, it has been one of the greatest links of friendship between different members of the Commonwealth and Empire."[13] These publications were meant not only for the audience of Indian players and spectators but also for the leadership of the country's White cricketing boards, indicating a desire on the part of these Indian teams to conform to colonial standards for the game.

Indian men in Rhodesia thus used cricket and its associated literature to ingratiate themselves with the colonial state, and in this way advocated for their rights as "civilized" colonial subjects (figure 5.1). In so doing, they reproduced imperial notions that cricket should create harmony, unity, and cooperation between Whites and Indians in the colonial era. The Oriental Cricket Club team was the quintessential example of a group of men who complicated the relationship between metropole and colony, as both those who had been colonized on another continent and those who were now emulating the colonizers on another. Colonialism in Southern Rhodesia thus involved a negotiation not only between Black and White, but also with a third element of imperial society that erased the Black majority from its consciousness, in an attempt to create an identity as the ideal colonial citizen.

However, for the Indians of Rhodesia, a sense of imperial identity and belonging could not last long. Despite attempts to connect with

Figure 5.1. Oriental Cricket Club, 1941–42 season, representing themselves in this photo as the ideal imperial subjects. *Credit: Sunrise Sports Club*

colonial society, it was becoming clear by the 1950s and 1960s that Indians were to remain designated as colonized subjects, subject to colonial racial hierarchies that firmly placed them below White Rhodesians. Behind the scenes of the print literature that projected a colonial identity, discrimination against Indians was increasing, culminating in the creation of the physical space of Sunrise Sports Club as a way for the Indian community to consolidate itself against hostile, discriminatory policies. In many ways the rhetoric that projected Indian men as the ideal colonial subjects was part of an attempt to battle growing discriminatory policies against them as non-Whites. But lurking behind these laudatory words was the country's increasing imposition of formal segregation, which would cause Indians to question their status as colonial subjects of empire. Ironically, this led to the Indian cricket players of Rhodesia taking on an Indian nationalist identity as colonized subjects in the years after Indian independence in 1947.

As the Indian community in Rhodesia grew during the 1940s, both through continued migration and with new generations being born in the country, European resentment augmented as Indians began to demand equal treatment. Fearing competition from Indian businesses, the colonial government in Southern Rhodesia followed South Africa's lead and began restricting immigration in the 1940s, granting preference to migrants of European descent. Indians were very clearly "subject-citizens" rather than "citizen-subjects."[14] This distinction meant that while *de jure* Indians were not restricted from purchasing land or property, not being defined as "African" in legislation, *de facto* they were discriminated against by discretionary powers that prevented them from moving into European residential and commercial areas.[15] Their subimperialist claims gradually evolved into a critique of the colonial state for the discrimination they faced, as they became insular in many ways, retreating to the confines of community. In the 1950s, when Indians were blocked whenever they attempted to purchase properties in European neighborhoods, Suman Mehta pressured the City Council into allocating land specifically meant for settlement by Indians, a clear indication of self-segregation, while across the border in South Africa segregation was being imposed by the apartheid state. They were given the suburb of Ridgeview, land previously used by the Salisbury aerodrome.[16] Here, they put down roots.

In Ridgeview the Oriental Cricket Club members began thinking about creating a space of their own. The discrimination they faced as a community had permeated the boundaries of the cricket pitch, despite attempts to use the sport as an entry into elite colonial society. When invited to play games at White sports clubs before 1980, "Asian players were never invited into the host's club house either to shower and change or for refreshments. The Asian players consequently had to get changed in their cars."[17] "Lack of coaching, ground facilities and racial discrimination have been retarding factors" in the development of the game among Indians, wrote one of the members of the Orientals team in 1954, a hint amid the rhetoric propagating colonial friendship that all was not as rosy as it appeared.[18]

They needed a place that was their own, one that would serve as a space where they could play the sport on their own terms and create a sense of community that protected them from hostile, discriminatory policies. In July 1965 a group of cricket and tennis players came up with the idea to create Sunrise Sports Club in Ridgeview. The club would incorporate the Oriental Cricket Club team, which was later renamed the Sunrise Sports Club Cricket team.[19] Four months later, Ian Smith's Rhodesian Front government unilaterally declared independence from Britain, declaring itself an independent, sovereign state and refusing to give in to the terms laid out by the metropole for a transition toward Black-majority rule. As Southern Rhodesia became Rhodesia, it seemed that the Indians of the country too were breaking the constraints of empire, creating their own space, which in many ways would operate separately from the White settler society that had permitted Indians to become part of its sporting world, but with limits.

On October 25, 1969, the Sunrise clubhouse was officially opened for business. The guest of honor was N. J. Patel, a noted activist for Indian rights through the Southern Rhodesia Asian Organization, which aimed to protect "Asian" interests in the country as a whole.[20] The occasion was also marked by a reference to the fact that the club was being opened in 1969, the centenary year of Mahatma Gandhi's birth.[21] The magazine commemorating the official opening of the clubhouse demonstrated a distinct shift in tone in the community's sporting literature. Earlier productions had highlighted connections to empire, whereas the selection of a noted Indian rights activist as the guest of honor showed that the community was celebrating its *independent* Indian heritage, separate from its colonial one, as well as its right to break ground on a space all its own (figure 5.2). Although India had previously been imagined as part of the British Empire, it was now being reworked as a leader of the Global South and all that the newly decolonizing world was coming to symbolize. India, in particular, was emerging as a strong contender in international cricket postindependence, triumphing over its former colonizer. For the later generations of men who left India postindependence to settle in Rhodesia, the game would hold more meaning as an Indian one, rather than as an imperial form as it had for the men who had created the Young Merchants Club just over a decade earlier.

Facing rejection from colonial society despite efforts at integrating, Indians in Rhodesia thus turned to other Indian communities across the

Figure 5.2. President M. C. Desai performing a religious ceremony marking the opening of the Sunrise Club House, July 21, 1968, reflecting the Indian sporting community's reversion to its Indian roots and an Indian identity. *Credit: Sunrise Sports Club*

region, nurturing an Indian identity of cricket with links not only to the heritage of a homeland but to other diasporic groups on the continent. Games between the three Federation countries of Northern Rhodesia, Southern Rhodesia, and Nyasaland led to the formal organization of the Ramabhai Trophy in honor of one of Sunrise's first cricket players, and the first interregional tournament was organized in April 1958 in Livingstone, Northern Rhodesia. The success of the tournament persisted into the postcolonial era, and in 1985 the Ramabhai Tournament was renamed the Inter Club Cricket Tournament to include a team from Tanzania. Sunrise hosted the tournament in 1987, the first time it had accommodated "an ambitious four Nation cricket tournament."[22] "The aim of such a tournament would be, on the one hand, to establish bonds of friendship where none exist, while on the other hand, to consolidate old links, in the spirit of sportsmanship, competition and cooperation," wrote Rajendra Patel, chairman of the cricket section, on the occasion.[23] The same rhetoric that had been used to highlight connections with colonial society was now used to underline links with Indians in other countries, but continued to ignore the existence of the Black majority population.[24]

As the 1970s progressed, it became clear that the tides of change that had swept over the rest of the continent were permeating Rhodesia's tightly controlled and monitored borders. As the nationalist war of liberation gained momentum and Rhodesia began to face increasing international pressure through sanctions, it was obvious that White minority rule, and the segregation of society into neat lines that came with it, could no longer survive. By 1979 change was in the air. Talks were under way at Lancaster House in London, and the country's nationalists were pledging to work with the White farmers in the country, rather than against them. Fearing retaliation for the years of subjugation and discrimination if a Black-majority government came to power, white Rhodesians were unsure of their status in the new country. Upon his election in 1980, however, Zimbabwe's new leader, Robert Mugabe, called for reconciliation between Black and White, words that were to define the spirit of the country's first decade of independence.[25]

This spirit of racial reconciliation was pervasive, even breaching Sunrise's insularity in the years leading up to 1980. In 1979 the Sunrise constitution added a clause to the membership section of its constitution stating that members of all races would be able to join the club.[26] "The policy makers of the Club are to be complimented for their broadmindedness, especially in view of the positive changes taking place in our emerging nation in which the cementing of good relations obviously will help to pave the way for harmonious co-existence," wrote J. B. Patel, founding president of Sunrise, in an editorial. A year later the country was reborn as Zimbabwe. The decade that followed was one of hope and change, in which the Black-majority government led by Robert Mugabe promised free education, health care, and land reform. Before South Africa's "Rainbow Nation" came into being, Zimbabwe promised a peaceful multiracial society, one that would lead the continent into the sunset.

The 1980s were also a period of tumultuous change in general. Cricket, that quintessential colonial sport, had been turned on its head to become the sport of the formerly colonized. It was the decade in which the sport entered a new world, one in which England had lost its dominance of the globe. In 1987 future High Court judge and Sunrise member David Bartlett wrote in an editorial that "test cricket is not the same game that our grandfathers praised in its Golden era." It was no longer one of gentlemanly banter, delicate bowling, and graceful batting, but one of "venomous" fast bowling, aggressive "Blitzkrieg" tactics, and the triumph of the colonized over the colonizer, with the West Indies and India dominating the international cricketing scene.[27] It was a period when cricket players were refusing to conform to the colonial standards that had dominated the game for so long.

Less than a decade later, the management committee was actively recruiting "African youngsters" to play for the cricket team. They were a new generation of men, willing to embrace the new country's cricketing culture.[28] The team's standards at league level had dropped in the 1980s, and management felt that the best way to promote their players was to take part in the game at regional and national levels as part of Zimbabwe's efforts to attain test status with the International Cricket Council.[29] Rajendra Patel, chairman of the cricket section, argued in a 1988 section report that Sunrise had to make sure that the club was part of "current and future efforts to promote the game" in order to help the country as a whole reach the coveted test status.[30] "This is a step we, the present Committee" wrote Patel, "feel is necessary to further the attempts to involve ourselves in cricket in this country."[31] The game that had once been played as a colonial inheritance, and then as a legacy of an Indian identity, had become a way for the players of the team to find inclusion in a nationalist, Zimbabwean sporting culture (figure 5.3).

Indian players were also finally being recruited into the national side in the 1980s. Sunrise players, such as "skipper" Kish Gokal, made it to the Mashonaland provincial side in 1979.[32] In 1980 Sunrise player Ali Shah made the national side. The year that the team finally allowed a non-White player to represent the country, it played in the International Cricket Council World Cup for the very first time. Other Indian players who would make the national team in future years were Mac Doodhia and Mohammed Memmon. This transformation of the national side meant that international cricket games could become a space for Indian cricketing fans, including those who were members of Sunrise,

Figure 5.3. Sunrise cricket team on tour in the 1980s. The team now included Black players, reflecting its opening up to a more national space after independence. *Credit: Sunrise Sports Club*

to express either national or transnational identities in the teams that they chose to support, with the transnational frame of diasporic identity providing a model for reimagining the limits of a national identity.[33] For the first generation of Indian migrants, India and Pakistan held the Indian community's allegiance on the cricket pitch. For their sons and grandsons, who could now support one of their own playing for the Zimbabwean national side, those allegiances were transferred to their new country, even in games in which Zimbabwe faced India, as it did in 2001 at Sunrise Sports Club, "the heart of the Indian community in Harare," where India played a warm-up match against the Zimbabwe "A" team during their tour.[34] This generational shift reflected the desire of Sunrise players and fans to be included within national culture, in a country that in the postcolonial era erased Indians from its nationalist consciousness. Yet they were very much there: not just in the stands, but on the pitch, too.

The period of hope and change did not last long. Eventually it became clear that the era of multiracial intermingling that had allowed

Indians to enter the national space was an ephemeral one and perhaps was covering up deeper racial tensions that not even the hope of independent Zimbabwe could fully erase. In 1995 Henry Olonga was selected as the first Black player for the national side. His selection caused waves in Zimbabwean cricket, as Black members of the Zimbabwe Cricket Union leadership pushed for the selection of more Black players, and the remaining White members dug in their heels and insisted on keeping mostly White players on the team. Ali Shah retired in 1996. In 2003 several White players left the country in protest against the government's land reform scheme, which took land away from White farmers for redistribution without adequate compensation.[35] By this stage, professional league cricket in Zimbabwe had ended. The conflict over the racial composition of the national side translated to the local league level, which, once dominated by White cricket teams, has now been reduced to a few clubs who still participate in social tournaments. Zimbabwean cricket is currently in a state of disarray and chaos, wracked by financial scandals, the ongoing debate over the racial composition of the team, and pitiful performances in international matches and tournaments. Without the league cricket that teams such as Sunrise once participated in, players are recruited directly from schools without going through the training, both physical and emotional, that league games provided to growing players.

C. L. R. James argued in the mid-twentieth century that when cricket no longer "carries within its performative codes, norms and internal organization such as an edifying *esprit de corps*," this would lead to a "period of decline in the game and major changes in the society in question." His words would certainly ring true for Zimbabwean cricket half a century later.[36] Rajendra Patel's ominous words in 1988 had also been realized: "There is a possibility that cricket at Sunrise will continue for a few more years, but thereafter, at a very much lower keynote than it can and should be. Yes, we will have the ICCT and the Bulawayo links to concentrate on, but is this all we want?"[37] After that brief moment in which the players could aspire to the national side, the demise of league cricket was a disappointment. With nowhere to go beyond club cricket, interest in the sport died. It became more and more difficult over the years to recruit younger members for the team, and its standards dropped well below the requirements of first league cricket. Today, Sunrise only plays socially, reverting to an insularity that had been breached to a limited extent just after 1980. Just as Indians entered the country's national consciousness as citizens of the postcolonial state, the brief moment that had allowed them space in a multiracial civic society was cut off. In the conflict between Black and White, Indians were rendered invisible.

In many ways, this has been a story about Zimbabwean cricket, rather than one simply about the Sunrise Sports Club cricket team. The history of cricket in Zimbabwe was exemplified by the very existence of Sunrise Sports Club, a racially segregated team that not only imbibed colonial traditions of the sport in the country but used cricket to link itself to an Indian identity that came to dominate that sport the world over in the second half of the twentieth century. Sports, and specifically cricket, provided a way for Indians to make themselves visible and navigate the racial hierarchies and structures of colonial and postcolonial society in Zimbabwe. Although cricket has been seen as both a British and an Indian sport, the case of the Sunrise team suggests that they drew from both these inheritances in the 1980s to aspire toward an *African* citizenship. Cricket provides a lens not only into the cosmopolitanism and dynamism of Zimbabwe's sporting culture, but also into its larger colonial and postcolonial history. Cricket shows that the country had a dynamic connection with cultural forces and traditions that extended beyond the confines of the relationship between the metropole and the colony, and that in spite of being landlocked, it is part of a broader methodological framework of an Indian Ocean history of migration, cultural transference, and hybridity.[38] When we focus on cricket, and on an Indian cricket team in particular, it becomes clear that these pluralistic influences were a significant part of the country's transition from Rhodesia to Zimbabwe, as well as of negotiations of postcolonial citizenship, aspects that are often lost in the translation of the conflict between the White minority and the Black majority. By including the men of Sunrise Sports Club within this reimagining of a Zimbabwean national culture, it becomes clear how the country's history played out, quite literally, on the cricket turf.

Notes

The quote in the chapter title is from program of the 6th ICC Tournament, Lusaka, Zambia, April 1991, p. 9, file SP0037, Hindoo Society Archives, Harare. I would like to thank the Taylor and Francis Group and the *Journal of Southern African Studies* for permission to reproduce parts of my already published work in "Played Out on the Edges of the Cricket Boundary: The History of an Indian Cricket Team in Rhodesia/Zimbabwe, 1934–1995," *Journal of Southern African Studies* 45, no. 3 (2019): 465–83.

1. B. Patel, "Editorial," program of the Inter Club Cricket Tournament, Harare, 1987, p. 11, file SP0017, Hindoo Society Archives, Harare.

2. Cricket sectional report, presented at the section AGM, July 28, 1988, p. 1, file SP0049-03, Hindoo Society Archives, Harare.

3. D. M. Desai, "The Indian Community in Southern Rhodesia," September 1948, p. 9, file HIS0001, Hindoo Society Archives, Harare.

4. After independence, Salisbury was renamed Harare, and Umtali became Mutare.

5. Desai, "Indian Community in Southern Rhodesia," p. 5.

6. Souvenir program, South Africa versus Rhodesia (non-Europeans) cricket tournament organized by the Rhodesian Indian Cricket Union, September 1958, p. 11, file SP0052, Hindoo Society Archives, Harare.

7. G. D. Govender, "410 'Not Out,'" 1952, p. 59, file SP0059, Hindoo Society Archives, Harare.

8. Desai, "Indian Community in Southern Rhodesia," pp. 3 and 18.

9. Arjun Appadurai, "Playing with Modernity: The Decolonization of Indian Cricket," in *Consuming Modernity: Public Culture in a South Asian World*, ed. Carol A. Breckenridge (Minneapolis: University of Minnesota Press, 1995), 27.

10. Anthony Bateman has explored the ways in which cricket literature "produced and reproduced ideas of the national and imperial cultures," in this way emulating a "construction of Englishness through cricket." Print culture, according to Bateman, was critical in the construction of national and imperial identities within "the culture of colonialism," both in the metropole and in the colonies, with this discourse suggesting that the colonized "could be refashioned into English gentlemen." What he does not account for, however, is the ways in which non-White populations appropriated these quintessentially English values into their own discourse. See Anthony Bateman, *Cricket, Literature and Culture: Symbolizing the Nation, Destabilizing Empire* (Surrey, UK: Ashgate, 2009), 2, 122, and 129.

11. Minutes of meeting of the Rhodesia Indian Cricket Union at the Coronation School in Livingstone, Northern Rhodesia, April 6, 1958, p. 19, file SP0051, Hindoo Society Archives, Harare.

12. J. C. Graylin, Federal Member of Parliament, in souvenir program, cricket tournament between Northern Rhodesia and Southern Rhodesia, Bharat Sports Club Ground, Livingstone, Northern Rhodesia, April 1958, p. 7, file SP0056, Hindoo Society Archives, Harare.

13. Tour book of the Rhodesia Indian Cricket Union's Ramabhai Trophy Cricket tournament between Southern Rhodesia and Northern Rhodesia, Dayalji Sports Ground, Bulawayo, April 20–21, 1957, p. 2, , file SP0002, Hindoo Society Archives, Harare.

14. Desai, "Indian Community in Southern Rhodesia," p. 4.

15. Desai, "Indian Community in Southern Rhodesia," p. 12.

16. Deepak Mehta, "History of the Indian Community," 2015, p. 2, file HIS0004, Hindoo Society Archives, Harare.

17. Mehta, "History of the Indian Community," p. 3. This segregation continued until independence in 1980, when racially divisive policies in residential areas formally ended.

18. Program, Salisbury Indian Cricket Union's first inter-town tournament for the Nagrani Shield, April 1953, p. 2, file SP0015, Hindoo Society Archives, Harare.

19. Constitution of the Sunrise Sports Club, incorporating the Oriental Cricket Club, Salisbury [n.d., draft], file SP0036. Hindoo Society Archives, Harare.

20. Souvenir magazine marking the opening of the new Sunrise Sports Club house by N. J. Patel, October 25, 1969, p. 3, file SP0038, Hindoo Society Archives, Harare.

21. Souvenir magazine, p. 7.

22. Program, Inter Club Cricket Tournament between Sunrise Sports Club (Zimbabwe), Dar Brotherhood-Upanga Club (Tanzania), Indian Sports Club (Malawi), and Lotus Sports Club (Zambia), Harare, 1987, p. 6, file SP0017, Hindoo Society Archives, Harare.

23. Program, Inter Club Cricket Tournament, p. 8.

24. Bateman's arguments about the colonial nature of cricketing literature cannot, then, account for this change over time in the cricketing print literature of the colonies. See Bateman, *Cricket, Literature and Culture*.

25. Robert Mugabe, "Address to the Nation by the Prime Minister Elect, 4th March, 1980" (Harare: Ministry of Information, Immigration and Tourism, 1980).

26. Constitution of Sunrise Sports Club (incorporating Oriental Cricket Club), October/November 1987, pt. XV, sec. 59, file SP0044. Hindoo Society Archives, Harare.

27. David Bartlett, "Test Cricket Today," in program of the Inter Club Cricket Tournament held in Harare in 1987, pp. 29–30, file SP0017, Hindoo Society Archives, Harare.

28. Winch refers to the inclusion of "African" players in recruitment efforts by cricketing boards, a move he believed would "further enhance the already vibrant and progressive atmosphere pervading Zimbabwean cricket." See Jonty Winch, *Cricket's Rich Heritage: A History of Rhodesian and Zimbabwean Cricket 1890–1982* (Bulawayo: Books of Zimbabwe, 1983).

29. Minutes of annual general meetings at Sunrise Sports Club, presented at the section AGM, July 28, 1988, file SP0049-03, Hindoo Society Archives, Harare. Test games, considered to be the highest standard of the sport, are usually played for four innings, or five days, and only the world's top-ten-ranking teams play each other at this level. Zimbabwe was granted test status in 1992 and played its first game against India at Harare Sports Club in October of that year.

30. Minutes of annual general meetings, p. 2. MCA refers to the Mashonaland Cricket Association, ZCU to the Zimbabwe Cricket Union.

31. Minutes of annual general meetings, p. 1.

32. "Gokal, Hunt Sink O.H.," *The Herald*, October 22, 1979, file SP0029-02, Hindoo Society Archives, Harare.

33. This idea, articulated by Susan Koshy and R. Radakrishnan, permeates studies of South Asian diaspora and their cricketing affiliations. See Susan Koshy and R. Radakrishnan, eds., *Transnational South Asians: The Making of a Neo-diaspora* (Oxford: Oxford University Press, 2008). Manu Madan discusses the different rankings that international cricket teams hold for members of the Indian diaspora: "For the Australian diasporic Indian collective, support for India comes first; then, other non-White national teams and, more problematically, non-White players in White national teams; and finally, former colonies (such as Australia, New Zealand, and Zimbabwe) have priority over the colonizer." See Manu Madan, "'It's Not Just Cricket!' World Series Cricket: Race, Nation, and Diasporic Indian Identity," *Journal of Sport and Social Issues* 24, no. 1 (2000): 33. Keith Sandiford has similarly explored how ethnic tensions in the Caribbean mean that Indians will cheer for the Indian or Pakistani touring sides when they play against the West Indies, arguing that "a strong sense of nationalism cannot be nurtured on cricket alone." Keith Sandiford, "Cricket and a Crisis of Identity in the Anglophone Caribbean," in *Sport and*

National Identity in the Post-War World, ed. Adrian Smith and Dilwyn Porter (London: Routledge, 2004). Fahad Mustafa suggests that "immigrants' continued support for the teams of the nations of their origin is a reflection of their exclusion from national culture." Like Madan, he does not, however, account for how this sense of exclusion can change over time from generation to generation. See Fahad Mustafa, "Cricket and Globalization: Global Processes and the Imperial Game," *Journal of Global History* 8, no. 2 (2013): 335.

34. John Ward, "Indians Not Stretched by Zimbabwe A," *ESPN News*, June 22, 2001, http://www.espncricinfo.com/zimbabwe/content/story/103511.html.

35. Ironically, their departure to England, where they were recruited for the English team or were hired as coaches, led to England's resurgence on the international cricketing scene. The scheme, also known as the fast-track land reform program, continues to be debated by scholars. Some scholars who have contributed to the discussion of the results of land reform are Walter Chambati, "Restructuring of Agrarian Labour Relations after Fast Track Land Reform in Zimbabwe," *Journal of Peasant Studies* 38, no. 5 (2011): 1047–68; Godfrey Magaramombe, "'Displaced in Place': Agrarian Displacements, Replacements and Resettlement among Farm Workers in Mazowe District," *Journal of Southern African Studies* 36, no. 2 (2010): 361–75; Nelson Marongwe, "Farm Occupations and Occupiers in the New Politics of Land in Zimbabwe," in *Zimbabwe's Unfinished Business: Rethinking Land, State and Nation in the Context of Crisis*, ed. Amanda Hammar, Brian Raftopoulos, and Sting Jensen (Harare: Weaver Press, 2003), 155–90; Prosper Matondi, *Zimbabwe's Fast Track Land Reform* (London: Zed Books, 2012); and Blair Rutherford, "Commercial Farm Workers and the Politics of (Dis)placement in Zimbabwe: Colonialism, Liberation and Democracy," *Journal of Agrarian Change* 1, no. 4 (2001): 626–51.

36. See C. L. R. James, *Beyond a Boundary* (London: Stanley Paul, 1963), xiii.

37. Minutes of annual general meetings, p. 1.

38. This draws from Isabel Hofmeyr's use of the Indian Ocean as a methodological framework for comparative histories between Africa and South Asia. See Isabel Hofmeyr, "The Complicating Sea: The Indian Ocean as Method," *Comparative Studies of South Asia, Africa and the Middle East* 32, no. 3 (2012): 584–90.

SIX

Nigeria, Women's Football, and Resisting the Second Fiddle

CHUKA ONWUMECHILI AND JASMIN M. GOODMAN

The struggle of African women footballers against marginalization is similar across the continent, particularly regarding remuneration, media coverage, homophobia, unequal treatment, and undervaluation of the women's game.[1] Unfortunately, essays on women footballers in Africa rarely focus on resistance to oppression and inequality. Although Nigerian women footballers face marginalization, they have found ways to confront those challenges by developing an array of strategies. We argue that their employment of those strategies belies their subordinate status and demonstrates their willingness to challenge existing patriarchy. These strategies include sit-ins/standoffs, denying renegotiation, training boycotts, and co-opting media publicity. However, it is notable that ongoing female resistance has not effectively countered all forms of oppression, particularly homophobia. The focus of this chapter is a narration of critical moments of resistance in Nigerian female football. Analyses of these moments help unpack strategies of resistance and evaluate their effectiveness.

Historical Background to Women's Resistance in Nigeria

We argue that understanding women's resistance to marginalization in Nigeria's football requires understanding the cultural history of the environment. Scholars such as Oyeronke Oyewumi, Bibi Bakare-Yussuf, and Ifi Amadiume have argued that precolonial history among Yorubas and Igbos in what today is Southern Nigeria provides evidence of gender-lessness, or at least gender fluidity.[2] While some of that scholarship have been criticized, by and large there is agreement that the arrival of evange-lists and colonialists introduced a high sense of gender roles whether pre-colonial Nigeria was genderless, gender fluid, or patriarchal.[3] The clash between precolonial life and coloniality was a major upheaval, which nov-elist Chinua Achebe described with the phrase "things fall apart."[4]

That things were, indeed, falling apart was demonstrated in the early twentieth century by women's resistance to colonial rule in southeastern and southwestern Nigeria. Early European scholars describe this resis-tance as riots and framed them from the perspective of colonialists, with a focus on the women's refusal to accept taxation designed to develop their own communities.[5] However, recent scholarship has challenged and reframed the 1929 events as *Or-gu Umu nwaanyi* (women's wars) in southeastern Nigeria and women's revolt against marginalization in southwestern Nigeria. The demonstrations were not just about taxation but also about protesting increasing colonial infringement on cultural institutions.[6] One such publication is by Marc Matera, Misty Bastian, and Susan Kent, who link local culture to successful women resistance to colonial rule in Southern Nigerian communities.[7] They note, for in-stance, that the events of 1929 began when women in Bende (southeast Nigeria) employed a local means of resistance that involved sitting in at a place of protest until a grievance was acknowledged and restitution was promised. The colonial gendered decision of hiring only men[8] and then extending taxation to women was bound to attract resistance to a system that further affected the way of life in their society. Judith van Allen's work helps to explicate this larger context for the events.[9]

Marginalization of women in the colonial Nigerian social sphere, which gave rise to the events in 1929 and the late 1940s, helps explain, or at least understand, the resistance of Nigerian women footballers to the marginalization in which they find themselves today. Strategies for resistance, which included "sitting on" (making war on) an oppressor and demonstrations, among others, were used by women in the late 1920s and 1940s[10] and are used today by women footballers.

UNWANTED FEMALE INTRUSION?

The conflict between local cultural values and the new colonial values created opportunities for women to resist by participating in football alongside men, against the dictates of authority and power. The evangelists, who controlled schools and their playgrounds, refused and/or restricted women's participation. In addition, media coverage was virtually absent. It is noteworthy that the first mention in the media of women playing football in the country was not a report of an actual game. Instead, it was a letter to a newspaper editor inquiring if playing football was good for women. This letter, which appeared in the *West African Pilot* in 1939, is significant because it suggests that Nigerian women had already participated in football before the late 1930s. Second, it points to the ambivalence of the population about women's participation in football under colonial rule. That such ambivalence continues to exist today is a testament to the effectiveness of and hegemonic effects of colonial rule.

Although it is difficult to pinpoint the beginning of women's football in the country, the decision by colonial authorities to stop it is well documented. Weibe Boer and Chuka Onwumechili point to a June 1950 Football Association edict broadcast by the national media, which specified the date of proscription of the women's game.[11] In other words, while the media found no space to report on women's football, they found space to report its proscription. Otherwise, the media ignored women footballers during that period.

The proscription by colonial authorities in Nigeria had deep effects. Not only did it last through the last day of official colonial rule in the country, but it persisted long afterward, with no known competitive women's football in the country until the early 1970s. One of Nigeria's football magazines, *Soccer International*, reported in 1974 that women were forming their own football clubs, such as Adesukhumu Ladies

FC of Benin and Ubiaja Women FC.[12] Later, in 1984, the Youth Sports Federation of Nigeria (YSFON) introduced the Alhaja Simbiat Abiola Cup, a national competition for women. Pauline Walley reported in 1987: "As football fans and other curious personalities trooped to the stadium (Ilorin) the next morning ... they wanted to be doubly sure that women play competitive soccer."[13]

What persists today is the struggle by women's football to be considered a competitive sport, for media to focus on the performance of the participants, and for equal treatment. These issues are understood through the lenses of valuation of women's football labor, sexual stigmatization, homophobia, underreporting of female football, and gender marking.

Adaobi Nwaubani highlights the undervaluation of female football in Nigeria: "The Falcons (Female national team) were handed a paltry 10,000 naira each ($50, £35) after they successfully booked a ticket to the 2016 Africa Women's Cup of Nations," which stood in stark contrast to the male players, who were "paid $4,000 each for a draw and $5,000 for a win."[14] In 2016, even the youth male national teams were paid more than the Falcons. The irony in this disparity is that the female national team often wins more trophies than its male counterpart. The undervaluation of the female national team can also be inferred from other means beyond pay disparity. For instance, the women are housed in substandard accommodations, and they train and play exhibition games on the practice fields of the National Stadium, while male players stay in five-star hotels and train in the main bowl of the National Stadium.[15]

In Nigerian football, women suffer the most from sexual stigmatization. Sexual stigmatization is described as "labeling of a biological sex group with extreme disapproval. A person who performs outside the expectation of his or her biological sex group is seen as being on the fringe and not part of the norm. This stigmatization promotes hegemonic masculinity in sport."[16] This type of stigmatization occurs globally. Some scholars believe that this stigmatization of female football as being weaker stems from Victorian ideals of frail women and muscular men.[17] Successful female footballers are regarded as nonfemale, and some have been directly labeled as men. This stems from the fact that they do not fit the frame of play expected of female footballers and therefore must not be female.

Sexual stigmatization creates an environment for widespread homophobia, according to Marie Engh.[18] She argues that women have to "prove" themselves by becoming *feminine apologetic*, which refers to women working to prove their femininity through makeovers in order to be sexually appealing and attractive and, above all, to escape being labeled as lesbian. Although feminine apologetics exist among Nigerian female footballers, there remains widespread labeling of female footballers as lesbians.

Furthermore, Asakitikpi demonstrates that media consistently underreport sporting activities of women's football in Nigeria while negatively framing their performance.[19] Although such underreporting is a global phenomenon, it underlines how women are treated differently in the media. This is evinced by the amount of space provided for such reports and the number of media outlets reporting the activities compared to reports of male football. For the women's game, coverage includes a few paragraphs of text, infrequent television broadcasts, and far less mention on other media platforms.

Media reports also include gender marking, which Onwumechili describes as an athlete's performance or activity being marked, denoted, or restricted to a certain gender scope.[20] For instance, reporting a competition as the "Women's Federation Cup" restricts it to women, whereas the men's competition is known simply as the "Federation Cup." In essence, it means that the women's cup exists as the *other* cup.

Nigerian Women's Resistance

The undervaluation, stigmatization, homophobia, underreporting, and gender marking have not gone unnoticed. Angela King notes: "Foucault claimed that resistance exists wherever there is normalization and domination. Power is never total, uniform or smooth but shifting and unstable."[21] That is precisely the case for women footballers in Nigeria. Historically, they have resisted playing second fiddle and the attempt to erase or belittle their activities and imprint on Nigerian football, but such resistance, while notable, has not always been successful.

In the following discussion we argue that traces of Nigerian women footballers' resistance can be found in various strategies, including sit-ins/standoffs, denying renegotiation, training boycotts, and co-opting media publicity. Each strategy has been used successfully and is described in detail.

Sit-ins/standoffs. A critical sit-in in South Africa in 2004 demonstrates a successful resistance strategy used by Nigerian women footballers.[22] The women were protesting nonpayment of financial benefits. They had just won the African championship in South Africa but refused to fly home to Nigeria for further celebrations. Instead, they demanded their benefits; refused to board their scheduled flight; and stayed in the hotel with the championship trophy, refusing to hand it over to officials. In spite of promises made by officials, including their coaches, the footballers refused to budge. One of the players stated: "We will . . . hang on and it does not matter how hungry we get. It [the sit-in] is something we have decided to do and we will do it together."[23] The sit-in at the hotel differs slightly from the sit-on strategy used by women protesters in the late 1920s, but both strategies were ultimately used to resist marginalization. Whereas the sit-on strategy was employed within the home or place of the oppressor, the sit-in strategy used by women footballers involved occupying a space valued by the oppressor. The value was that with the women occupying the space, administrators were required to pay for the continued stay. The sit-in was not an easy decision for the footballers, disobeying male officials and managers in a patriarchal society. In response, their managers denied the team's agency in order to avoid cultural and patriarchal disruption. The managers attributed the women's actions to the influence of agitators for a regional secession from Nigeria, the Movement for the Actualization of Sovereign State of Biafra (MASSOB). Since most of the team were members of the Igbo ethnic group (the region represented by MASSOB), it was easy to link MASSOB to their actions. This interpretation psychologically restored the postcolonial social order of males dictating female action and women not having agency of their own. There was never compelling evidence provided to support the involvement of MASSOB. Nevertheless, the players' sit-in was successful. It embarrassed the Nigerian government and forced it "to send funds for [their] payment and [fly] players back home to a reception hosted by the country's President."[24]

The footballers learned that resistance could help their cause and that they could use it when necessary in the future, which they did again in 2016.[25] This time, the sit-in was in a hotel in Abuja, Nigeria, where the team stayed after winning the championship game in Cameroon. The players refused to leave the hotel, stating: "They can't treat the Super Eagles [the men's national team] like this. The only thing we understand right now is for them to pay and stop making promises."[26] Those statements speak volumes regarding the angst and the perennial struggle to resist being treated as second fiddle.

But while these sit-ins have been successful, there are repercussions for this type of resistance in a patriarchal society. For instance, the football authorities took a hard line following the 2016 protests. There were reports that one player, Francisca Ordega, was uninvited from future play after she told the media that she regretted playing for the country.[27] In addition, some journalists attribute the decision not to renew Florence Omagbemi's coaching contract to her role in the Abuja sit-in.[28] Omagbemi is not wanted by the Nigerian Football Federation (NFF) because of her role in the players' protests over unpaid allowances and wages after the 2016 AWCON in Cameroon.[29]

Denying renegotiation. A subplot to the 2004 sit-in was the players' steadfast refusal to renegotiate previously agreed payments. In the past, football authorities have taken unilateral decisions on player remunerations pertaining to women and youth teams. The players, viewed as subordinates, are expected to obey. Arnold Pannenborg describes this as the Big Man syndrome in African football.[30] He attributes the phenomenon to colonialism, in which the relationship between colonial officials and Africans was "that of a master tutoring his children who were to show respect and obedience in return.... [T]his pattern of role expectation between the powerful and the powerless was copied by the African elites."[31] In this social order, a young woman maintains a position slightly higher than that of children. Thus, total obedience is expected of Nigerian women footballers when faced with unilateral and adverse financial decisions by federation officials. However, Nigerian women footballers resist such actions. "On several occasions, promised allowances and bonuses were delayed, unilaterally reduced, or went unpaid. As the competition [2004 African championship] progressed, team officials attempted to unilaterally slash the amount due to the team. Players reacted by threatening to boycott training until officials agreed to make no change to the amount owed to players."[32] This unified action of resistance successfully rebuffed attempts to deny players the promised remuneration.

Boycotting training. Another strategy is to boycott training in order to call attention to various problems.[33] An example occurred when, while "the team was practicing . . . the football federation ordered their [the women's] team bus commandeered for the use of the male national team. The women completed practice in heavy rain, without the bus, they had to hitch rides in private cars, taxis, and motorbikes as they scurried back to their hotel rooms."[34] Although on many occasions boycotting training is ineffective, it is a strategy that women footballers continue to utilize because it attracts media attention, which forces officials to respond.

Co-opting media publicity. The strategies previously identified require public awareness to hasten the possibility of achieving the goal. Nigerian women footballers are keenly aware of this, and they aim for maximum public awareness in their struggle against oppressive situations. They use media interviews and leaks to achieve publicity. In several media reports, only the best players are directly quoted. For instance, team captain Nkiru Okosieme used a media interview to publicize the federation's poor preparation of the team for the 1995 Women's World Cup in Sweden.[35] However, sources for media stories are also disguised in various ways, including unnamed sources, or a "player wishing to be anonymous." Disguising the informant often protects footballers from retaliation by top federation officials.

Lingering Homophobia

The aforementioned strategies have not always helped to avoid oppression. In fact, many areas of oppression persist in women's football in Nigeria. One that remains troubling is the issue of homophobia. In Nigeria, this is both significant and dangerous because of the country's laws. In 2014, Nigeria made homosexuality illegal, punishable by imprisonment of up to fourteen years.[36] Adam Nossiter writes that Nigeria is not unique in Africa, as "[h]omosexuality is illegal in 38 of 54 African countries."[37] The danger for Nigerian women footballers is that it is too easy for the media, coaches, and fans to label them lesbians when they do not act sufficiently feminine. Such situations can put them in danger of prosecution and, possibly, imprisonment.

Unfortunately the Nigerian media focus attention on sexuality within their meager reporting of women's football. This type of coverage both silences and endangers women. Its effects include discouraging young women from playing football. Kari Fasting notes the possibility of such an effect in Norway: "Then we get more 'mothers' who will not permit their children to play soccer. . . . [T]he whole junior team left the club, because parents were afraid their daughters would become lesbians. . . . [P]arents think that one can be infected by it [lesbianism] as if it were a virus."[38] It is conceivable that this is occurring in Nigeria, where lesbianism is illegal. Moreover, religious restrictions in northern Nigeria prevent many women from participating in football.[39]

Why have women footballers not resisted this label as they have resisted other instruments of oppression? The answer is simple. There are two major factors, each institutionally strong, that make it difficult to voice or resist homophobia easily or successfully. The first is the law, which criminalizes homosexuality and puts anyone who publicly resists the law in harm's way. The law also punishes people who advocate for homosexuals. "Advocates have been forced to go underground."[40] In essence, there is significant risk for anyone who dares to resist the law. Second, homosexuality is considered a religious violation and therefore both un-Christian and un-Islamic.[41] This belief places homosexual discourse within the realm of religion and makes questioning it untenable.

A person who questions the law's value becomes guilty of heresy and unfaithfulness and has committed a sinful act. In such circumstances, resistance is neither advisable nor possible.

Women's resistance to unequal treatment in football in Nigeria has a long history. As we have argued, women footballers have borrowed, modified, or developed strategies against oppression, leading us to examine implications for the resistance and the strategies that women use.

Women's use of sit-ins or standoffs, denying renegotiation, and boycotting training or games may not always be effective. Although they make team officials uncomfortable and affirm the women's use of resistance strategies, officials who are determined to have their way can overcome these tactics. What appears to be the trump card for women is the co-opting of media publicity, a key strategy moving forward. This is particularly crucial when resisting homophobia, especially when resistance appears to oppose national laws and widely held religious beliefs. Perhaps this explains why women don't openly resist the label as lesbians. To resist is to highlight the issue, and they risk adverse consequences given extant law. Therefore, it is conceivable that the women choose silence over a pushback strategy, particularly when the accusations are not directed at a publicly identified player. To date, there is no known strategy to resist the homophobia labeling. The dangers are clear. However, if such resistance is to arise, using media will be critical to widely publicize the issue to a more sympathetic global audience, including the powerful International Federation of Association Football (FIFA).

With more Nigerian women moving outside the country to play professionally, the probability of more confrontation with Nigerian football officials increases. Players like Asisat Oshoala and Francisca Ordega may face inequality in foreign leagues, but such inequalities may be less about pay disparity and oppression; thus, the women are more likely to move toward resistance while playing for Nigeria.

Ultimately, with continued inequality in how women footballers are treated compared to their male counterparts, women footballers will continue to resist. As shown in this chapter, they have developed effective strategies for such resistance and are not hesitant about using them.

Notes

1. Martha Saavedra, "Football Feminine, Development of the African Game: Senegal, Nigeria, and South Africa," *Soccer and Society* 4, nos. 2/3 (2006): 225–53; Aretha Asakitikpi, "Media, Sport, and Male Dominance: Analysis of Sport Presentations in a Nigerian Newspaper," in *Gender, Sport and Development in Africa*, ed. Jimoh Shehu (Dakar, Senegal: Codesria Books, 2010), 47–62; and Chuka Onwumechili, "Urbanization and Female Football in Nigeria: History and Struggle in a 'Man's Game,'" *International Journal of the History of Sport* 28, no. 15 (2011): 2206–19.

2. Oyeronke Oyewumi, *The Invention of Women: Making an African Sense of Western Gender Discourses* (Minneapolis: University of Minnesota Press, 1997); Bibi Bakare-Yusuf, "'Yorubas Don't Do Gender': A Critical Review of Oyeronke Oyewumi's *The Invention of Women: Making an African Sense of Western Gender Discourses*," in *African Gender Scholarship: Concepts, Methodologies and Paradigms*, ed. Signe Arnfred, Bibi Bakare-Yusuf, Edward Kisiang'ani, Desiree Lewis, Oyeronke Oyewumi, and Filomena Steady (Dakar, Senegal: CODESRIA, 2004), 61–81; and Ifi Amadiume, *Male Daughters, Female Husbands: Gender and Sex in an African Society* (London: Zed Books, 2015).

3. Carole Boyce Davies, "Pan-Africanism, Transnational Black Feminism and the Limits of Cultural Analyses in African Gender Discourses," *Feminist Africa* 19 (2014): 78–93.

4. Chinua Achebe, *Things Fall Apart* (London: William Heinemann Ltd., 1958).

5. Harry Gailey, *The Road to Aba: A Study of British Administrative Policy in Eastern Nigeria* (New York: New York University Press, 1970); and Margery Perham, *Native Administration in Nigeria* (London: Oxford University Press, 1937).

6. Judith van Allen, "Aba Riots or the Igbo Women's War? Ideology, Stratification and the Invisibility of Women," *Ufahamu: A Journal of African Studies*, 6, no. 1 (1975): 11–39; Gloria Chuku, *Igbo Women and Economic Transformation in Southeastern Nigeria, 1900–1960* (New York: Routledge, 2004), and Judith Byfield, "Taxation, Women, and the Colonial State: Egba Women's Revolt," *Meridians: Feminism, Race, Transnationalism*, 3, no. 2 (2003): 250–77.

7. Marc Matera, Misty Bastian, and Susan Kent, *The Women's War of 1929: Gender and Violence in Colonial Nigeria* (New York: Palgrave Macmillan, 2012).

8. Lisa Lindsay, "Working with Gender: The Emergence of the 'Male Breadwinner' in Colonial Southwestern Nigeria," in *Africa after Gender?*, ed. Catherine Cole, Takyiwaa Manuh, and Stephen Miescher (Bloomington: Indiana University Press, 2007), 241–52.

9. Allen, "Aba Riots or the Igbo Women's War?"

10. Allen, "Aba Riots or the Igbo Women's War?"

11. Weibe Boer A Story of Heroes": *The Story of Football in Nigeria* (Ibadan, Nigeria: Bookcraft Publishing, 2018); Onwumechili, "Urbanization and Female Football"; and Chuka Onwumechili, *Chukastats, 2: Youth and Female Football in Nigeria* (Bowie, MD: Mechil Publishing, 2010).

12. Onwumechili, *Chukastats, 2.*

13. Pauline Walley, "Simbiat Abiola's Cup for Women: An Overview," *National Concord*, April 26, 1987, 22.

14. Adaobi Nwabuani, "Letter from Africa: Why Nigeria's Women Outkick the Men," April 20, 2016, http://www.bbc.com/news/.

15. Nwabuani, "Letter from Africa."

16. Chuka Onwumechili, *Sport Communication: An International Approach* (London: Routledge, 2018), 148.

17. Ben Carrington, *Race, Sport, and Politics: The Sporting Black Diaspora* (London: Sage, 2010); and J. Mangan and Roberta Park, *From Fair Sex to Feminism: Sport and the Socialization of Women in the Industrial and Post-Industrial Eras* (New York: Routledge, 2013).

18. Marie Engh, "The Battle for Center Stage: Women's Football in South Africa," *Agenda* 24, no. 85 (2010): 11–20.

19. Asakitikpi, "Media, Sport, and Male Dominance."

20. Onwumechili, *Sport Communication.*

21. Angela King, "The Prisoner of Gender: Foucault and the Disciplining of the Female Body," *Journal of International Women's Studies* 5, no. 2 (2004): 37.

22. Onwumechili, "Urbanization and Female Football."

23. Onwumechili, "Urbanization and Female Football," 2215.

24. Onwumechili, "Urbanization and Female Football," 2215.

25. Lucy Clarke-Billings, "Nigeria: Women's National Football Team Stage Sit-In Hotel Protest," *Newsweek* (US ed.), December 7, 2016, http://www.newsweek.com/; and Oluwashina Okeleji, "African Women's Champions Nigeria in Fight for 'Welfare,'" BBC News, December 9, 2016, http://www.bbc.com/sport/football/38230355.

26. Clarke-Billings, "Nigeria."

27. Ifreke Inyang, "I Regret Playing for Nigeria: Super Falcons' Francisca Ordega," *Daily Post*, December 6, 2016, http://dailypost.ng/2016/12/06/regret-playing-nigeria-super-falcons-francisca-ordega/.

28. Steve Dede, "Florence Omagbemi: She Has Just Been Nominated for FIFA Women's Coach of the Year Award, but NFF Don't Want Her Anymore," Pulse, August 18, 2017, http://www.pulse.ng/sports/football/florence -omagbemi-she-has-just-been-nominated-for-fifa-womens-coach-of-the-year -award/695q8c6.

29. Dede, "Florence Omagbemi."

30. Arnold Pannenborg, *Big Men Playing Football: Money, Politics and Foul Play in the African Game* (Leiden, Germany: African Studies Centre, 2012).

31. Pannenborg, *Big Men*, 177.

32. Onwumechili, "Urbanization and Female Football," 2215.

33. Okeleji, "African Women's Champions"; Onwumechili, "Urbanization and Female Football"; and Onwumechili, *Chukastats*, 2.

34. Onwumechili, *Chukastats 2*, 159.

35. Janine Anthony, "China '91, 25 Years On: Nigeria Women Journey to the World Cup," Unusual Efforts, April 20, 2016, http://www.unusualefforts .com/nigeria-women-world-cup/.

36. Adam Nossiter, "Nigeria Tries to 'Sanitize' Itself of Gays," *New York Times*, February 8, 2014.

37. Nossiter, "Nigeria Tries to 'Sanitize' Itself of Gays."

38. Kari Fasting, "Sexual Stereotypes in Sport: Experiences of Female Soccer Players," Play the Game, June 18, 1997, http://www.playthegame.org/news /news-articles/1997/sexual-stereotypes-in-sport-experiences-of-female -soccer-players/.

39. Onwumechili, *Chukastats*, 2, 136.

40. Nossiter, "Nigeria Tries to 'Sanitize' Itself of Gays."

41. Onwumechili, *Chukastats*, 2, 154.

FOUR

Crossing Racial Boundaries

Sports and Apartheid

SEVEN

Beyond South Africa's Draconian Racial Segregation

Transkeian Surfing Narratives, 1966–94

DAVID DRENGK

As a young researcher, my image of South African apartheid historiography was always influenced by narratives of structural segregation directly connected to the argument for noncontact between races. In public urban spaces like beaches, this separation was visible in the form of designated areas for "Whites only." There, the different racial groups were not permitted to intermingle. But as a traveling historian who also happens to be an enthusiastic surfer, I moved away from the urban centers into one of the former *bantustan*, the Transkei, in search of waves. In these rural settings along South Africa's Wild Coast, I came across a social phenomenon under apartheid rule that challenges the stereotypical narratives of racial confrontation. During the early decades of South African surfing, from the late 1960s onward, a period in which surfing became increasingly prominent globally, young White South African surfers traveled to these remote coastal areas. During their journeys, they needed somewhere to stay; they had to eat, drink, and fetch firewood, and many also sought to procure marijuana. But above all, their hunger for waves had to be satisfied, and this quest for waves led to interracial contact between these young travelers and the local population of coastal Transkeian communities.

This chapter examines the encounters between visiting White surfers and the Black Xhosa-speaking residents of the Lwandhle community between 1966 and 1994.[1] This period is marked by the release of the surf movie *Endless Summer* in 1966, which had a tremendous influence on the growing young generation of traveling surfers around the globe and in South Africa. The year 1994 marks the official end of the apartheid regime; from that point onward, the borders of the Transkeian territory no longer existed. Consequently, journeys by White surfers to the Wild Coast became a much more common trend within South African surfing.

Surfing offers a unique point of entry into the history of apartheid South Africa, featuring local community members' memories of past encounters. Via their oral testimony, we are treated to the formation of new local labor relations, the local trade in dagga (marijuana), spontaneous campsites, and campfire sessions. In turn, these revelations challenge reconstructions of apartheid-era South Africa in which racial groups remained strictly segregated, and when they did interact, these exchanges were uniformly hostile and often violent. Instead, interactions between local residents and visiting surfers on the beaches of the Transkei were marked by cooperation and mutuality, rather than racial animus, suspicion, and distrust. The transgression of racial and social practices by both White surfers and Black locals suggests that scholars should also reconsider notions of apartheid as governing the full array of interracial interactions, as in these instances, the racist system was patently disregarded by these relatively marginalized historical actors.

The first section of this chapter provides historical context for the Transkei within South African history and offers background information on the main research site in Lwandhle. The ensuing part is divided into two sections, the first dealing with local villagers' perceptions and classification of visitors, as well as local demography, and the second with temporary labor relations and food exchanges between the visiting surfers and local communities. In the last section I consider the narratives of young local Black residents who actively crossed social boundaries in a variety of ways when interacting with visiting surfers.

The Bantustan, *Mining Recruitment,*
and a Marginalized Community

I conducted the main part of my research in Lwandhle, which can be seen in figure 7.1. The community is located at South Africa's Wild Coast, whose name derives from the numerous shipwrecks that can be found along this strip of coastline. Due to rough and fast-changing weather patterns, the sea along this coast often becomes unpredictable.[2]

Nowadays, as well as during the days of apartheid, there is a preponderance of children in the area. Since the Transkeian coastal areas used to be important areas for mining recruitment, the men who were fit for work went to the various mines across the country to provide for their families back home. The recruitment process primarily began either in Coffee Bay or in Umtata, where men had to register with the respective mining recruiters.[3] People's detailed memories of these processes reveal that mining was an omnipresent issue in coastal Transkei.[4]

Figure 7.1. View of parts of Lwandhle in the former Transkei, 2015. *Photograph by the author.*

Consequently, at the time of the encounters described to me, most local men were away, and the remaining population in the area consisted of the elderly, children, and women. Since girls and women typically stayed in the homesteads to take care of younger children and the household, it was teenage boys who could escape to the beach and spend time with the visiting surfers.[5] This scenario illustrates a major aspect of racial inequity in both the rural Transkei and the rest of the country: traveling to other destinations outside the *bantustan* was usually not possible for Black residents of the Transkei due to apartheid policies and financial challenges. As mentioned previously, most travel was by men, who went to cities as well as mining and plantation areas to secure employment. So, while traveling was already a rare event, traveling for leisure activities somewhere away from home was almost nonexistent. This reality speaks for itself and illustrates the tremendous racial, as well as class, differences between White and Black South Africans.

The labor market in the area continues to be marked by high unemployment. However, there is a vibrant so-called informal sector. In Lwandhle, informal labor included fishing and the selling of fish and marine resources, such as lobster or mussels.

Lwandhle was a marginalized community within South Africa owing to the structural marginalization of the entire area by the apartheid government. The complex political history of pre-independent Transkei and the Republic of the Transkei was marked by confusing power relations and contesting political and economic interests. Following the nominal independence of the Transkei in 1976, the political sphere was dominated by problematic representation, structural weaknesses, and political power struggles.[6] Moreover, the elected Transkeian government of Chief Kaizer Matanzima did not bring any positive change to the coastal communities along the Wild Coast.[7] In fact, the opposite was true. Matanzima's government was always backed and supported by the government in Pretoria.[8] Internal political rivalries and constant power struggles led to the further deterioration of local infrastructure and the educational and health-care sectors. I can therefore argue that the past and present degree of underdevelopment is attributable to durable political shortcomings. These issues, and the isolation of the area, generated an increasing degree of inequality between the Wild Coast and the rest of the country. And in apartheid South Africa, race differences between Whites and Black residents also meant class differences. Financial wealth was unequally distributed.

This situation was also favorable for White traveling surfers, because the White government was essentially still controlling the area. Therefore, young surfers enjoyed the same privileges at the remote Wild Coast as they did in the urban White core of South Africa. Despite their "lifestyle consumption" and their "ideals and values that pushed against apartheid's political regulation of social life and the moral authoritarianism of the apartheid state," their status as "a privileged social class in apartheid deprived competitive surfing of the possibility of unshackling itself from this history."[9]

Encounters on a Transkeian Beach

My local informants recalled that young White surfers used to travel to the area roughly from the late 1960s onward for recreational purposes. The late 1970s and 1980s appear to have been the peak period for young White South Africans' surfing explorations along the Wild Coast, a time of incoming "waves of combis."[10]

In other globally emerging surfing centers like Hawaii, California, and Australia, surfing has a much older history, and foreign surf travelers were already touring the world in search of waves before surfing became a widespread activity in South Africa. In the early 1960s, for instance, South African waves were still unknown to most young Western surf travelers. This changed tremendously in 1966, after Bruce Brown's movie *Endless Summer* was released. The country's wave potential became widely known, and surf explorations along the coast started to flourish.[11] In Lwandhle, community members recalled that the surfing visitors used to come from all over the country, but particularly from the main urban centers along the coast, such as Cape Town, Port Elizabeth, East London, and Durban, and even from the United States and Australia.[12]

As an unoccupied open and public space, the beach served as a location for a range of interracial encounters between these visitors and local residents. Unlike in urban areas in South Africa, there were no legal regulations that structured or racially segregated this open space at the Wild Coast. After the apartheid regime had passed the Reservation of Separate Amenities Act No. 49 in 1953, beaches were categorized into separated spaces in accordance to the different racial groups. These public beaches were organized to adhere to the policy of noncontact between the races. At the Wild Coast, however, this was not the case, and the surfers described these coastal areas as places "where you could suspend all that [racism] crap" and "basically strip naked and party and carry on."[13] It was the freedom that people could experience on the beach that attracted them to this locale.

In some cases, interviewees even referred to bonds of friendship that developed.[14] Sometimes people stayed in touch for many years, even after they had left the area for good.[15] For example, a White Capetonian surfer who used to live in the Transkei with his family after 1976 recalled: "Obviously, we made friends with some guys and people worked for our parents and we got to know their kids and we got to know them very well and we had a close relationship with them, spoke a bit of Xhosa with them and shared some of their lives."[16] This proves that some South Africans' lived realities under apartheid were anything but uniformly informed by racial confrontation and contempt.

Perception, Classification of Visitors, and Local Demography

The villagers I interviewed generally made a distinction between English- and Afrikaans-speaking White South Africans who visited the beaches. The distinction was often manifested in the respective endeavors of the visitors.[17] Afrikaans-speaking visitors were widely remembered as older fishermen, who were regarded as being rough and often impolite.[18] They used to bring their big motorboats for high sea fishing along with them, on which they often used local community members as guides and ship's boys.[19] To a person, my informants mentioned that fishing was, and still is, very important in the area for both local and (predominantly White) visiting fishermen.[20] Afrikaaners were often regarded as the embodiment of discrimination and racial classification of society. Usually it was the older interviewees who shared such negative experiences and impressions. In fact, it was predominantly older male villagers, who were also former miners, who differentiated among the White visitors. I suggest that these and other negative experiences, from the mining areas, continued to shape people's impressions even when they were far removed from these infamous worksites.

In contrast, boys from the ages of eight to eighteen years old used to spend time with the surfers on the beach. They were born in the 1960s and 1970s and were sometimes younger than ten when they met the surfers. Eric, for instance, stressed that they did not even know what apartheid meant. They had no clue about the systematic racial oppression that was going on elsewhere in the country and usually had no problems with any of the visitors who came to the area.[21] This outlook derives from their positive perceptions of the visitors and the fact that they did not subdivide White South African visitors into Afrikaans- and English-speaking groups, as older fellow community members did. The visiting White surfers were mostly remembered as English-speaking students who were perceived as being interested in the area and its people.[22] They were generally referred to as being friendly Whites who did not have much to do with the racial segregation between Black and White in the wider country.[23] They were usually not interested in politics and were therefore seen as apolitical.[24]

Nevertheless, these travelers' journeys were embedded in daily apartheid realities and their Whiteness. Some surfers might have morally rejected apartheid policies, including by avoiding conscription and smoking dagga. However, socially they capitalized on their Whiteness and the privileges afforded them by apartheid. It was their privileged position as young White middle-class men, their financial capability, and their freedom of movement within South Africa and the Transkei that enabled them to travel to and surf along the Wild Coast. As Glen Thompson accordingly argues, "[t]he consumption of pleasure and fashioning of surfing identities should rather be seen as impetus for maintaining, and not challenging, the status quo in South Africa".[25]

Temporary Labor Relations and Food Exchanges

The surfing and little surf camps piqued the boys' curiosity. Surfing was a relatively new activity in the area, and surf tourism as it is known today was only just beginning in the 1970s and 1980s. Fascination and curiosity may partly explain why the young boys longed to spend time with the surfers on the beach. Perhaps just as important, both surfers and local community members all remember that their presence on the beach meant an opportunity for temporary employment for a few in the community.[26] One of the oldest women in the community, who is now in her eighties, remembered early labor relations between Whites and local community members dating back to the late 1930s and early 1940s,[27] when a White family from Umtata traveled for the first time by bicycle and ox wagon to the coastal community, where they employed local community members to collect sand, probably for the first construction of a road around 1945.[28] Henceforth, labor relations developed between the White owners of local cottages and entire families from the community. Two of the families have worked for cottage owners for several generations, and these labor relations are still in place today.[29] For those families, these engagements constitute an important source of income, which is generally scarce in the community.

In the visitors' camps the youngsters used to complete a number of small jobs for the surfers, such as fetching firewood, preparing bonfires, washing the dishes, cooking, and guarding the camp and cars while the surfers were in the water.[30] Ordinarily, if the surfers ran out of food and needed new supplies, they sent local youngsters to buy them for them at one of the old trading stores, "dusty dark old musty buildings with a lot of cheap Chinese stuff and then sacks of millet meal and sometimes some clothing."[31] There, visitors could usually get basic food supplies like sugar, bread, and tinned food.[32] In such cases, the surfers and local community members generated a trusting relationship.[33] The temporary work was important for the youngsters because they could contribute to their families' households and, in some ways, assume the role of head of the household, if only figuratively, as many men were away in the mines. The income from such temporary work and the work in the cottages augmented the money that the men sent home from their work in the mines, which "created an economy in the Transkei . . . and that kept the trading stores in business."[34]

The White employer–Black employee relations on the beach were definitely characterized by race and class inequities. And local community members' position within apartheid did not improve owing to their interactions with the surfers. But the labor relations were less rigid in this case than they would have been otherwise. Many interviewees, such as David, enthusiastically told stories about joint dinner gatherings with the surfers and several community members on the beach.[35] After the "boys" had cooked the dinner, they were often invited to eat and hang out a little longer with the surfers.[36] So in a sense, the jobs often served as door openers for further interaction between people, while further testimony revealed tales of cheerful evenings with spontaneous guitar jams around campfires on the beach in a rollicking atmosphere.

The surfers' presence also often generated further material benefits for local residents. The visitors usually brought most of their supplies, such as water, luxury foodstuffs, coffee, tobacco, and alcoholic beverages, and would often leave behind what they had not consumed; at times they even left some of their clothing behind: "If you had fishing gear, you would often end up giving . . . fishing line to your guide. You give him some cash and you give him stuff he needed."[37] These things could be given as gifts or payment for the boys' help and work. Given that foodstuffs like bread and meat, for example, used to be scarce and expensive in the area, such food gifts caused people to refer to the surfers as generous and generally "good" people.[38]

Both the opportunity of temporary employment and gifts of food and clothing fueled the youngsters' degree of excitement. One anecdote from Lwandhle impressively illustrates how excited the young boys were about the opportunities that the surfers generated. When telling the story in their green clay rondavel on one of the many hills in the community, Marie and Andrew, a couple in their mid-fifties, laughed out loud. Andrew was close to tears when he recalled how he and his friends used to follow the surfers as they moved along the coast. He explained that infrastructure was in a poor condition and even gravel roads, which mark the area today, hardly existed. Since he and his friends sometimes wanted to follow the surfers to their next beach destination, they had to come up with an idea to keep track of the surfers' routes. Subsequently, once Andrew found out about the visitors' departure plans, he quickly gathered his friends from the village, and they started to collect all the fresh cow dung they could find. With great effort, as he described enthusiastically, they placed the dung at different points where they expected the cars to turn left or right. Hiding at a safe distance, they observed the turns of the cars; the marks they left in the fresh cow dung served Andrew and his friends as road signs to the surfers' next stop along the coast. This anecdote illustrates to what creative lengths children would go just to meet the surfers again and possibly be employed once more.

Crossing Social Boundaries

The mothers of these children remembered their concerns regarding the youngsters' schooling because they often ran away from school in order to spend time on the beach and in the surf.[39] Once the children spotted the surfboards on the tops of the cars and combis passing their schools, they abandoned their classrooms to chase them.[40] One villager in his late forties laughed when he recalled that he and his friends sometimes stayed away from school for days or even weeks, depending on how long the surfers stayed.

This absence had implications for family relations in the community and schooling in the area. Often, parents disapproved of their children spending time with the surfers, which can be explained in various ways.[41] First, the parents feared the dangers that their children could encounter on the beach. One such danger was, in fact, contact with White South Africans. After all, some parents had had negative experiences in the cities or in the mines, where racial confrontation and systematic oppression were experienced daily. On one occasion, William mentioned that his parents always stressed that if he saw a man with long hair like a horse, he should run away as fast as he could.[42] Other times, parents disapproved of these interactions because it meant that the children were not attending school. At the time, most children did not have access to education because it was very costly.[43] In addition, livestock was and still is an important and integral part of local society. Cattle herding is a task that all men, at some stage, must perform. In coastal rural Transkei, where most men were recruited to work in the country's mines, often only their sons were left to herd and watch the families' cattle. If cattle were left unattended, they could easily be seized by others or run away. Such a loss could be devastating for families because cattle equated to social wealth. Therefore, parents often meted out corporal punishment for leaving the cattle unattended to run off to the beach.[44] Thus, cattle herding, school attendance, and the elders' disapproval of interracial contact with White surfers constituted social boundaries in Lwandhle. Such social structures marked the young boys' possibilities and limits in their daily lives. But although there were more important social expectations and duties at hand, the majority of these children crossed those social boundaries anyway, chasing after the newly arriving cars and intermingling with the visiting surfers.

This chapter has demonstrated that studies of sports and sporting activity can provide important insights into human interaction and dynamics. Studying sports can also mean looking beyond the sport itself to consider social structures and historically generated societal phenomena. In the case of South African surfing along the Wild Coast, this approach entails shifting the narrative away from political and economic history to engage with the peripheries and rural areas. This chapter has attempted to illustrate that racial segregation and the impacts of the racist apartheid system on social dynamics and interaction, as South African historiography often and rightly reflects, were not uniform. We must also be cautious not to romanticize these narratives of beach encounters. Different positions of power and racial privileges were still crucial, even on the Transkeian beaches. The visitors' privileged position, which derived from their Whiteness and their financial capability, needs to be considered when examining these encounters. Class and race hierarchies were still always subliminally present, although not explicitly remembered and recalled as such by most of the surfers and community members. As elsewhere in apartheid South Africa, the provision of Black labor, which existed not only in the urban centers but also in the seemingly detached peripheries of the rural Wild Coast, typically reinforced the White capitalist policies of apartheid South Africa.

Nevertheless, as a remote rural setting along the Wild Coast, the local beach of Lwandhle served people of different races and classes as a meeting point where they could encounter each other in a respectful manner, far removed from the more racially hostile urban settings and social control of the South African state. Although also racially informed during times of employment, these interactions offer a more nuanced understanding of the impact of apartheid on people's daily lives, suggesting that in certain times and places, South Africans could situationally disregard apartheid's most draconian features, transgressing boundaries intended to keep people apart, to reach across durable socioracial divides and appropriate these interactions to serve their own ends.

Notes

As can probably be said of most academic work, this chapter could not have been written without the support and devotion of many other people. I would like to express my gratitude to all my interviewees from Lwandhle, my research assistant, and for their trust. I am thankful for all those who agreed to meet me, answer my questions, and talk about my academic interest in the history of surfing and their own village communities.

1. I have changed the name of the community and anonymized my interviewees because I realized that I have dealt with issues in the research that are sensitive in nature in a South African context and can cause reactions and evoke emotions among certain people that I do not have the ability to predict. Such reactions could again induce certain social and political dynamics that can easily get out of hand. Names in this chapter are therefore changed. Interviews are identified using numbers rather than names. In total, I conducted forty-one semistructured, face-to-face interviews in a variety of locations along the Coast between Cape Town and Lwandhle at the Wild Coast between September 2014 and February 2015. Seventy-five percent of these interviews were conducted in the community at the Wild Coast and in the near vicinity.

2. Hazel Crampton wrote a magnificent book on the history of the Wild Coast, which illustrates among many other issues the lives of such shipwreck

survivors in local communities. See Hazel Crampton, *The Sunburnt Queen* (London: Saqi Books, 2006).

3. Interview 35.

4. Ten out of twenty-three male interviewees from the community stated that they went to several different mines across South Africa, particularly the gold mines in Rustenburg and Johannesburg.

5. For example, interview 39.

6. An extensive examination of the internal power struggles and structural administrative weaknesses can be found in: J. B. Peires, "The Implosion of Transkei and Ciskei," *African Affairs* 91, no. 364 (1992): 365–87.

7. For a detailed analysis of the life of Matanzima and his politics, see Barry Streek and Richard Wicksteed, *Render unto Kaiser: A Transkei Dossier* (Johannesburg: Verso, 1981).

8. For further information on the supposed independence of the Transkei see Roger Southall, *South Africa's Transkei: The Political Economy of an "Independent" Bantustan* (New York: Monthly Review Press, 1983); and Roger Southall, "The Beneficiaries of Transkeian 'Independence,'" *Journal of Modern African Studies* 15, no. 1 (1977): 1–23.

9. Glen Thompson, "Pushing under the Whitewash: Revisiting the Making of South Africa's Surfing Sixties," in *Radical Politics, Global Culture: The Critical Surf Studies Reader*, ed. Dexter. Z. Hough-Snee and Alexander S. Eastman (Durham, NC: Duke University Press, 2017), 159; and Glen Thompson, "Certain Political Considerations: South African Competitive Surfing during the International Sports Boycott," *International Journal of the History of Sport* 28, no. 1 (2011): 44.

10. Interviews 14 and 30. The only specific reference to the legendary VW combi was in interview 28.

11. For more information on South African surfing history and the influence of *Endless Summer* (dir. Bruce Brown; New York: Bruce Brown Films, 1966), see Spike (Steve Pike), *Surfing South Africa* (Cape Town: Double Storey, 2007), as well as the numerous publications by South Africa's leading surf historian, Glen Thompson.

12. Interview 17.

13. Interviews 2 and 8.

14. Interview 18.

15. Interviews 2 and 17.

16. Interview 2.

17. The described perception was anything but ruled by fixed poles. These two categories of White South African visitors could often also be in a rather fluid state.

18. For example, interview 15.

19. Interviews 15 and 27. Young men from the community can still be spotted near the launching area waiting for the fishing boats to be launched or return from their daily fishing trips. So this relation between visiting White fishermen and local young men continues to exist.

20. Interviews 19 and 15.

21. Interview 36.

22. Interviews 14, 18, and 17.

23. Interviews 14, 18, and 17.

24. Interview 25.

25. Thompson, "Pushing under the Whitewash," 159.

26. Interview 18.

27. Interview 29.

28. Interview s29 and 30.

29. Interview 19. Further information derives from informal talks with a few cottage owners who visited the area during my research stay and talks with members of the respective families from the community.

30. Interviews 20 and 24.

31. Interview 2.

32. Interviews 30 and 40.

33. Interview 30.

34. Interview 2.

35. For example, interview 30.

36. Interview 18.

37. Interview 2.

38. This can be found in basically every interview in which people mentioned the food gifts from the visitors; for example, interviews 18 and 41.

39. Interviews 24 and 36.

40. Interview 26.

41. In only one account does an interviewee mention that his parents liked it that he spent time on the beach and worked for the visitors. It could be that he brought home some money, food, and clothing. However, he does acknowledge that the teachers were anything but happy about the boys' absence. Interview 41.

42. Interview 13.

43. Interview 31.

44. Interview 29.

EIGHT

Racing out of the Shadows

Black Competitive Cycling in Johannesburg and Cape Town, ca. 1900–1964

TODD H. LEEDY

The history of sports in South Africa, like that of many countries and regions, remains understudied. Although the "big three"—football (soccer), rugby, and cricket—which dominate today's market, have all received attention from multiple scholars, very few publications examine the varied historical landscape of sports that included athletics, boxing, cycling, golf, swimming, tennis, and others. Given the highly racialized nature of South African society, particularly prior to the democratic transition of 1994, it should come as no surprise that even less scholarship exists on sports in the various communities collectively termed "Black" or "non-White."[1] Yet sports have long shaped individual identities and have occupied a vital space in the fabric of marginalized communities. The nature of these roles of course changed across geographic location, social class, and personal or family interest. This chapter focuses on the bicycle racing scene in South Africa's major cities of Cape Town and Johannesburg from its earliest days until the suspension of South Africa from the Olympic movement in 1964.

Blackness and Racing in South Africa

The evolution of racial categories in South Africa occurred over many decades, and a full account of the process is beyond the scope of this chapter. A long history involving Dutch settlement, slavery, frontier encounters, White settler expansion, British colonial rule, industrialization, and migrant labor had produced a widely understood set of race-based social practices by the onset of the twentieth century. Yet as in all such attempts to make sense of a social environment, racial categories remained fluid at their edges and could even break down completely when seriously challenged. The language or terms used to refer to these groupings also changed over time. Following its rise to power in 1948, the Nationalist Party sought to harden the definitions of such categories and extend a formal legal framework that would govern all manner of socioeconomic relations according to racial codification. This became the system known as *apartheid*, under which separate groups each had different rights as citizens or subjects. Each of the commonly utilized categories of that period—White, Asian, "coloured," and Bantu—in fact contained numerous subgroupings. However, only Whites had access to full political rights prior to 1994. In this sense, all the other groups can be considered "Black," even though rights and resources might differ between them. Although competitive cycling structures existed in each of these communities, this chapter focuses on "Black" racing in Johannesburg (predominantly "Bantu" or indigenous African ethnicities) and Cape Town (predominantly "coloured" or mixed race identities).

Sources

For most of the era under examination, few government offices dealt with sports and almost none dealt with such matters among non-White communities. Therefore, official archives have yet to yield substantial evidence. Primary materials for reconstructing this history for the most part exist only in newspapers and periodicals. Since the major newspapers of the time rarely covered Black affairs, and almost never covered sports, historians must rely on the few publications that targeted a growing Black urban population. Although the earliest such papers emerged in South Africa prior to 1900, these contain little to no sports coverage until the late 1920s. But by the early 1930s, several new weekly papers had emerged, and they began to include regular sports pages. These include *Umteteli wa Bantu*, *The Bantu World*, *The Sun*, and *The Cape Standard*. Beginning in the 1950s, the groundbreaking *Drum* magazine provided sports features, as did its lesser known competitor *Zonk*. Only in the early 1960s did the major Johannesburg paper *Rand Daily Mail* begin to cover Black sports in its "township" supplement.[2]

Origins and Early Growth

The exact origins of Black bicycle racing in South Africa remain murky, but the first "bicycle boom" that swept Europe and North America beginning in the 1880s did not miss the Southern Hemisphere, as Australia and South Africa also saw the rapid rise of cycling for transport, leisure, and sports. Although the expanding popularity of cycling in South Africa is somewhat documented for the politically and socially dominant White minority population, competitive racing among the Black population has received almost no attention from scholars of sports. Yet racing by these groups in South Africa goes back at least to 1900, as available accounts from both Cape Town and Mafikeng demonstrate.[3]

The huge growth in all forms of cycling that began in the mid-1880s quickly led to the construction of purpose-built racing tracks in Cape Town, Johannesburg, Durban, and Kimberley. Depending on the level of financial commitment, these could be flat or banked with dirt or concrete surfaces. Some tracks arose within the grounds of private clubs (Wanderers in Johannesburg) or in ostensibly public spaces (Green Point Common in Cape Town).[4] While there is no specific data on how Black cyclists first began racing, some reasonable deductions can be made within the socioeconomic context of those decades in South Africa. Regardless of track location, Black workers likely performed much of the manual labor involved in construction and maintenance. Black workers would also have staffed the earliest race events featuring White riders, even in otherwise all-White venues. Racing on public roads also grew in popularity alongside competitions on the track, and since the cities of these years had yet to develop into the models of spatial segregation we know from the mid-twentieth century, virtually any urban resident, White or Black, could witness the spectacle of bicycle racing on a regular basis.

Clearly, exposure to this new sport could occur through a number of avenues. One should not discount, however, that a more organic route to racing may also have factored into this process. As urban Black populations expanded and more individuals participated in the cash economy, bicycles provided both labor-saving transport as well as a level of mobility otherwise unattainable. As objects, they also came to mark a level of prosperity, even modernity, as well as a certain form of sophistication or cosmopolitanism. With both practical and representational incentives to own a bicycle, Black ridership increased greatly even before 1900. A prominent example was Sol Plaatje, later one of the founding members of the South African Native National Congress, who worked as a bicycle messenger after moving to Kimberley in 1889. With such expansion, just as one only needed two people to make a phone call, cyclists really only needed two people to make a race. In larger groups, there's also a popular saying, "Every ride is a race." Given all these variables, it does not take much imagination to envision how irregular, informal competitions between friends or acquaintances could easily transform into publicized events sponsored by organized clubs, with common standards ensured through local or regional governing bodies.

In Cape Town, South Africa's oldest city, at least one Black cycling club had formed by 1898. Other clubs apparently emerged quickly, which led to the establishment, in 1901, of the Western Province (Coloured) Amateur Athletic and Cycling Association. Farther north, riders had formed clubs in Bloemfontein by 1918. The early evidence for Johannesburg is sparse, but a sufficient density of clubs existed to prompt the founding of the Witwatersrand Bantu Cycling Association, which organized a variety of races in 1932. By the early 1950s, clubs could even be found in small cities such as Kroonstad (halfway between Johannesburg and Bloemfontein). Some clubs elected officers, while others had managers to provide logistical support.

Organization and Structure

Clubs participated in a wide variety of races on both track and road. Most events welcomed all riders, but many clubs also held their own annual championship races for members only. While some riders certainly gained reputations for better results in particular events, almost none became specialists, and therefore they tended to race in whatever format organizers chose. On the track, most meets featured quarter-mile, one-mile, five-mile, ten-mile, and even twenty-five-mile races, with victory in the twenty-five-mile race generating the most prestige for a rider. Track races frequently occurred in tandem with athletics to produce full-day events, usually held on public holidays such as New Year's Day, Easter Monday, Empire Day, Wiener's Day, and Dingaan's Day. When clubs held larger meets, which could attract dozens of racers and hundreds or sometimes thousands of fans, race entry fees and proceeds from ticket sales would go into club coffers to support travel expenses for racers heading to inter-provincial or national meets. Such events could be lucrative enough that even other community organizations would hold occasional "sports days" to raise funds for a particular cause.

Although road races did not draw the same level of attendance as those on the track, in some ways they exposed even more people to racing, since these events occurred in fully public spaces. Aside from the occasional "novice" and "second-class" events, road races largely remained open category events. Individual time trials over distances from ten to one hundred miles, on both out-'n'-back and circuit courses, retained a consistent popularity during this period. Handicap starts, a form of racing largely forgotten by contemporary racers, also featured regularly in most racing programs. This format required race organizers to rate the form of each entrant and create a staggered starting grid. Slower/weaker riders went off first, with each faster ranking going off in a subsequent wave. The strongest rider(s) started last. This type of racing both gave slower racers a chance to win and pushed the strongest to ride consistently hard. It certainly did not favor the sprinter, who could sit in for many miles only to jump out of the bunch to win at the line. Finally, the currently more familiar mass-start races often tended to attract the fewest entrants, as the top end of the field would make quick work of anyone not on good form.

Regardless of race format, the regular use of certain courses inscribed them on the cycling heritage landscape of South Africa. In Cape Town, the Paarden Island circuit course hosted time trials, handicap races, and mass starts for several decades before and after World War II. Its location near the harbor, while essentially flat, frequently produced challenging wind conditions against which even top riders struggled. Another well-used course in these years, the "Round the Mountain" race, ran between Green Point and Mowbray, with the direction determined by local organizers. Either way, racers faced a tough route into or out of Hout Bay, having to climb both Constantia Nek and Suikerbossie. In the late 1950s and early 1960s, the Tour de Mountain routed entrants over Bainskloof and DuToitskoof passes, resulting in both significant attrition and thrilling racing. For Johannesburg racers, the road to Potchefstroom (today the N12) saw lots of action for various events departing from Soweto. Frequently, mass start races would finish inside the stadium at Moroka—à la the famous Paris-Roubaix road race—to cheering crowds. The "Race around the Houses" utilized a more spectator-friendly circuit on public roads entirely within Soweto to cover twenty-five miles over a series of laps.

Sponsorship and Publicity

Racing drew enough public attention that a variety of sponsors supported the sport though named trophies and shields. Prominent local individuals could sponsor a prize—usually named after themselves—such as the "Geyer" and "von Diggelen" trophies in Cape Town. Others might come from local businesses, such as Nimmo's (bike shop) "Success" trophy. Eventually, even larger corporate entities got involved; Bokomo (biscuit/cookie manufacturer), Dunlop (tire manufacturer), and Coca-Cola provided shields. Often these prizes would "float" between the winners of specific races, with a stipulation that after a certain number of wins (usually three) the prize could become a racer's permanent possession. Sometimes prizes could even "float" among different races at the discretion of the sponsor, as occurred with the Geyer Cup in the 1940s, when different event organizers sought to attract the prize to their races in hopes of gaining more high-level entries.

A select few riders gained enough public attention that businesses saw an opportunity for promoting consumer products. On a very local level, this might amount to displaying a winning rider's gear in a shop window, as one store did with the bicycle of Cape Town star Toby Dreyer. On a larger scale, as corporate entities in the 1950s and 1960s increasingly recognized that urban Blacks constituted growing consumer markets, some used sports figures in their targeted advertising campaigns. Although football (soccer) players and boxers dominated this sector, Johannesburg's most dominant racer of the 1950s, George Mazibuko, secured endorsements with Raleigh (bicycle manufacturer), 3-in-1 Oil (bicycle/general purpose lubricant), and Wilson's XXX Mints (candy). Mazibuko's young successor on the track, Thomas Tumo, found himself promoting Gold Star condensed milk. Cycling imagery (racing, leisure, and transport) also featured in a wide variety of consumer advertising, from pain relievers to tea, batteries to clothing.

Cycling and the Mining Industry

Consumer brands, however, were only following the lead of the mining industry, which had begun incorporating bicycle racing in their sponsored leisure activities in earnest after 1945. Mine managers viewed sports primarily through the utilitarian lenses of worker productivity, social control, and public relations.[5] Much of this perspective came out of earlier White liberal views on the value of sports for easing newly arrived Africans into the rhythms of the city. Certain forms of recreation and leisure were thought to promote healthy living, thereby buffering communities against the urban ills of drunkenness, prostitution, and violent crime. For the mines, whose officials put a premium on order and stability within their migrant labor forces, sports would become a regular part of life in worker compounds, whether one was a participant or spectator. Cycling featured prominently not, as some might believe, because the mines originated the sport for Blacks in South Africa, but rather because the sport's preexisting popularity made it an obvious choice for inclusion by mine management.

Mine cycling occurred in a number of formats, with racing as part of larger public holiday sports meets being the most common. In the 1940s and 1950s, much of the racing took place on flat running tracks within the mining facilities, but eventually some of the larger, more capitalized mines began to install banked velodromes as a supplement to their 400-meter athletic tracks. Bicycle racing thereby featured in a spectacle that the mines hoped would keep some workers active and the remainder away from "unhealthy" distractions. In larger operations, different mine sections or job divisions might compete against each other, with the best racers across all areas then selected to compete against squads from other mines. Anglo-American, the largest gold mining company in South Africa, held its own championship, with a team of athletes from its various operations then competing against other geographically based selections at the South African "Non-European" Championships. The best cyclists might even find themselves reassigned to different job duties in order to facilitate time and energy for proper training and travel to competitions.

Inclusions and Exclusions

Participation in racing fostered social networks within one's locality as well as on regional and national levels. Since cyclists trained in public spaces, most serious racers would quickly become known entities in the community. Racers often rode long distances to venues only to ride home again after finishing the day's event. Beyond such regular visibility, race results frequently appeared in the newspapers, allowing for at least some name recognition well beyond one's immediate friends and acquaintances or event spectators. Some racers participated in or organized local charity fund-raising events, which also bolstered their public profile. Cycling clubs held social events such as concerts and dances to raise funds that supported travel to interprovincial or national meets. Cyclists from wide geographic areas would show up at the biggest events, such that top riders developed their own "elite" networks.

Local cycling clubs often hosted visiting racers, thereby generating ties between sports organizations.

Well before the onset of formalized apartheid policies following the Nationalist Party election victory in 1948, accepted social practices meant that nearly all sports events remained completely segregated. This policy impacted racing cyclists on a number of fronts. At the local, provincial, and national levels, annual championships and "official" records remained the exclusive domain of White athletes belonging to clubs affiliated with the South African Cycling Federation (SACF). Black clubs affiliated with several different national organizations held their own championship events but could not compete head-to-head with White riders. Following the formalization of practice into policy by the apartheid government in 1957, even White racers who crossed the racial divide to compete against Black fellow cyclists could face sanction or suspension by their federation. In a sport where team tactics, road or track conditions, and weather on any particular day all factor prominently in race outcomes, this effectively meant that several generations of Black cyclists raced in the shadows of Whiteness, never knowing how they might have performed at a truly national level if given full opportunity.

Exclusionary practices, and eventually legislation, also limited access to training and racing facilities. Already in the late 1930s and early 1940s, racers in Cape Town could only access the Green Point track for training for a few hours on certain days. They faced infringement on even these limited times from White footballers and on occasion were also denied use of the locker/shower facilities. Organizers in Paarl sometimes struggled to access track facilities, which occasionally forced the cancellation of major annual events. In Johannesburg, track racing occurred for several decades on the flat oval at the Bantu Sports Grounds. Although this space did not feature the same usage issues as some of those around Cape Town, it did not constitute a proper cycling track (velodrome), such that racers faced considerable disadvantages whenever competing elsewhere on a banked hard surface. Only in the 1950s, as the city council accelerated the build-out of the various townships that became collectively known as Soweto, was a fully surfaced, banked track constructed as part of the new Elkah Stadium in Moroka.

As mentioned previously, cycling clubs, and sports teams more generally, comprised an important part of the social fabric in many urban communities. Despite struggles for access to facilities and resources, clubs and regional organizations managed to continue holding competitions on both road and track. However, as the new apartheid state sought to intervene more aggressively across a wide range of public policy sectors, the obstacles to regular participation only mounted. The Group Areas Act of 1950 (and its many subsequent revisions) forcefully disassembled long-standing neighborhoods and communities in the name of racially based residential uniformity.[6] The impact on clubs was immediate and sometimes permanent. As residents of Salt River, Woodstock, and Claremont underwent removals to the distant Cape Flats, a number of long-standing clubs folded, never to reemerge. Even the Springboks Cycling Club, captained by their star George Mazibuko and dominant on the 1950s Johannesburg scene, could not survive the destruction of Sophiatown, which included the removal of its residents to various sections of Soweto. Yet circumstances varied, and in other locales clubs did manage to withstand these impacts, such as in Paarl, where the Yorkshire Club celebrated its centenary in 2019.

Between 1896 and 1964, not a single Black cyclist made the SA Olympic team in any discipline (nor in any other sport, for that matter). Cyclists and athletes protested against this exclusion as early as 1936, following the multiple gold medals won by Jesse Owens at the Berlin Olympics. Even in the United States, with its own deeply racist sporting institutions of the day, Owens had risen to win on the international level through competition with White athletes, as had Marshall "Major" Taylor (world champion track cyclist) and Joe Louis (world champion boxer). None of these possibilities existed in South Africa. Some White cycling officials occasionally offered timekeeping services, and others eventually began to provide coaching, but Black racers simply did not receive consideration for or invitations to trials. When the idea of separate trials emerged in the late 1950s, many Black racers still struggled with inadequate facilities, equipment, and travel funding. Facing international pressure over these practices ahead of the 1960 Games in Rome, South African officials put forward a plan for proposed affiliation between the

SACF and various Black cycling bodies that would allow consideration for Olympic qualifying but still avoid mixed race competitions in South Africa while subsuming erstwhile independent associations under the authority of the SACF. Black associations widely rejected these proposals, and while South Africa was still allowed to compete as a Whites-only team in Rome, it subsequently found itself suspended in 1964 as global opinion moved heavily against racially exclusive sports.

Why Cycling? Why Sports?

This chapter is only an overview of key themes and topics for the history of Black bicycle racing in South Africa. In a fuller form, this history will present a valuable addition to the broader existing literature on sports in South Africa. For many decades in the twentieth century, cycling held an important place in the array of competitive pursuits in which urban residents participated, spectated, discussed, and consumed through media accounts. Cycling and other sports therefore offer a means to more fully examine the social fabric and daily rhythms of urban life. Cycling clubs and associations provided structures that for many years buttressed community resilience in a political landscape of segregation and apartheid. Racing comprised an important element in the formation of masculinities and social identities. South African labor history must also grapple more fully with sports and recreation as a part of, not something separate from, working life. All of these items point to a need for more work by historians.

Alongside academic inquiry, however, lies the restorative power of revealing a "hidden" history. Decades of competition produced many stars, even "heroes" or "legends," in South African Black cycling. Yet today they remain largely unknown. Official records seemingly do not exist, so families and their communities have only a few personal photos, some newspaper clippings, and their own recountings of a past era. A palpable, chronic pain runs through the nostalgia surrounding these racers. A focused historical examination can hopefully produce the recognition or acknowledgment, denied for so many years, in order to assuage past injustices. The current generation of competitive riders in South Africa (where cycling is undergoing a resurgence in popularity), who have no direct links to this bygone era, also need access to the struggles and achievements of these ancestors. Only with this knowledge can they situate their own cycling goals and efforts on the arc of history.

Notes

The chapter title is inspired by several online pieces by Geoff Waters (d. 2018), who also generously provided encouragement and contacts at the outset of this project. See "Competitive Cycling in Apartheid's Shadow: The Development of Cycle Sport in the Coloured Community of Natal Province, South Africa in the 1970s," http://www.classiclightweights.co.uk/cycling-apartheid-rem.html; and "Racing in the Shadows of Mine Dumps: Black African Cycle Sport on South Africa's Gold Mines in the Apartheid Era," http://www.classiclightweights.co.uk/extras/racing-in-shadows-waters-extras.html.

1. See for example, Robert Archer, "An Exceptional Case: Politics and Sport in South Africa's Townships," in *Sport in Africa: Essays in Social History*, ed. William J. Baker and J. A. Mangan (New York: Africana, 1987), 229–49; André Odendaal, "South Africa's Black Victorians: Sport and Society in South Africa in the Nineteenth Century," in *Pleasure, Profit, Proselytism: British Culture and Sport at Home and Abroad, 1700–1914*, ed. J. A. Mangan (London: Frank Cass, 1988), 193–214; John Nauright, *Sport, Cultures and Identities in South Africa* (Cape Town: David Philip, 1998); Peter Alegi, *Laduma! Soccer, Politics and Society in South Africa* (Pietermaritzburg, South Africa: University of KwaZulu-Natal Press, 2010); and Tyler Fleming, "Now the African Reigns Supreme: The Rise of African Boxing on the Witwatersrand, 1924–1959," *International Journal of the History of Sport* 28, no. 1 (2011): 47–62.

2. The sources for this chapter include only English-language periodicals. Coverage of sports in Afrikaans, isiZulu, SeSotho, and other local language newspapers does exist, but integrating other languages and other urban centers remains the project of an up-and-coming South African historian!

3. See D. Coghlan, "The Development of Athletics in South Africa: 1814–1914" (PhD diss., Rhodes University, 1986); and Francois Cleophas, "A Historical Social Overview of Athletics in 19th Century Cape Colony, South Africa," *African Journal for Physical, Health Education, Recreation and Dance* 20, no. 2 (2014): 585–92.

4. See Thelma Gutsche, *Old Gold: The History of the Wanderers Club* (Johannesburg: Howard Timmons, 1966).

5. For an extensive treatment of this topic see Cecile Badenhorst, "New Traditions, Old Struggles: Organized Sport for Johannesburg's Africans,

1920–50," in *Ethnicity, Sport, Identity: Struggles for Status,* ed. J. A. Mangan and Andrew Ritchie (New York: Routledge, 2004), 116–43.

6. For a useful overview of these issues see Paul Maylam, "Explaining the Apartheid City: 20 Years of South African Urban Historiography," *Journal of Southern African Studies* 21, no. 1 (1995): 19–38.

FIVE

On the Margins

Informal Engagements with Sports

NINE

English Premier League Football Kiosks and the Emergence of Communal Television Viewing as a Sporting Practice

The Case of Eldoret, Kenya

SOLOMON WALIAULA

This chapter is based on the football (soccer) kiosk as an emergent space for viewing live English football in Eldoret, Kenya. I emphasize the sociality that goes into the construction of this space, as well as the ludic activities that accompany the viewing process. I have argued that this "sportified viewing" reflects the real-life experiences of those who engage in the activity. In this chapter, I contend that the viewing of English football in Eldoret kiosks is a creative process that emerges from and also responds to the immediate socioeconomic conditions of life in this setting. This approach constitutes a novel way of considering the significance of global sports in parts of sub-Saharan Africa. The fact that the viewing experience is processed through a playful and locally meaningful context revises the relevant scholarship, especially studies by James Tsaaior, Godwin Siundu, Gerard Akindes, and Olomuyiwa Omobowale.[1]

As Tsaaior has observed, "the viewers are victims of the efflorescence of European football and 'the allure of its irresistible spectacle' through satellite television."[2] This observation links to work by Omobowale, who has argued that local audiences exposed to global soccer trends "are momentarily brought to the fore of western culture, which is apparently seen as superior."[3] In Akindes's study of the phenomenon in the West African Francophone world, this mediated spectacle creates "glocal stadiums" that have an underlying logic of neocolonialism; in the same manner, Siundu has observed that in western Kenya the fans' experiences in such glocal stadiums "camouflage their deep seated aspirations towards cosmopolitan citizenship within the wider dynamics of globalization."[4] This study does not dispute the aforementioned sociocultural force on local viewers of European football. Nevertheless, it argues that local viewing contexts and practices adapt the technology and cultural logic of European football to the immediate social experience. The kiosk is perceived as one of the spaces where European football is locally situated and consumed and its perceived standard technological and cultural identity is reconfigured. Most important, this experience grants the viewers a sense of agency. Significantly, a number of studies have also recognized viewing English football as sporting and playful activity, the most elaborate of which was published by Senayon Olaoluwa and Adewole Adejayan.[5] Their work explores viewing experiences in local video showrooms, where watching English football includes a playful grafting of Nollywood Video films' characters onto English footballers in a process that has been termed *christening*, but that could also be interpreted as a sport in and of itself.

Methodology and Conceptual Framework

In this study, I adopted a media ethnography approach and, in particular, employed participant observation and in-depth, semistructured interviews to collect data between November 2015 and May 2016. This approach echoes Eric Rothenbuhler and Mihai Coman's emphasis on "observation of and engagement with the everyday situations in which media are consumed."[6] The setting for the study is Eldoret municipality, with a closer focus on two low-income neighborhoods, Huruma and Kipkarren, selected because they have featured in my long-term ethnographic research on English football viewing in Eldoret. I used field notes, audio recordings, and photography to collect data, but I also reflected on my personal experiences watching English football.

The study is theoretically framed by the concept of media as practice. In this light, the football kiosk is understood as a (local) media practice, a concept I borrow from media anthropology that explains how media are incorporated into the everyday experiences of life. I seek to show how the football kiosk operates according to a distinct technological and cultural logic that is not necessarily determined by the perceived standard configuration of viewing sports. David Rowe refers to kiosk viewers as "mediated audiences," describing them as "electronically reconfigured versions of the stadium audience."[7] Tsaaior further contends that the logic of postmodern culture and the new media architecture through which "football is transmitted from one corner of the world to another remote corner consequently shrinks and erases spatial and temporal boundaries."[8] I utilize specific examples from Eldoret to demonstrate that the so-called electronic audience is not a homogenized and invisible community of local viewers of English football but locally constituted sets of communities that use various strategies to situate this football in their immediate circumstances.

In his study of this phenomenon in southwestern Uganda, Richard Vokes has posited a similar argument. He has contended that the rapid uptake of English Premier League football in western Uganda is not only a consequence of globalization, but is attributable to a preexisting culture of electronic media reception, the communal consumption of electronic media that goes back to the time when radio was introduced in the region. He observes: "Specifically, from the early 1940s onwards, in the period before the address of cheap, portable transistor radio, early experiments in radio broadcasting in Uganda by the colonial government through communal listening posts . . . resulted in radio broadcasts becoming coded as essentially public goods, and as especially powerful, and these aspects have continued to shape patterns of consumption ever since."[9] Vokes describes one case of English Premier League communal consumption in which a village entrepreneur purchased satellite television equipment and "also converted his homestead's entire compound into a large viewing hall."[10] This development redefined the viewing experience, locating it in an elaborate set of locally determined and contiguously meaningful practices.

From Mainstream Fandom to the Football Kiosk

The football kiosk located at the heart of Huruma shopping center is one of the oldest in Eldoret town. It is in such places that "middlemen" first introduced satellite television technology into low-income neighborhoods. Previously, satellite television and the live European football it mediated were mainly associated with local upmarket establishments in the town center and in private homes of the well to do. This was not a social reality limited to Eldoret; as has been observed by Marc Fletcher, Richard Vokes, and Leah Komakoma—in South Africa, Uganda and Zambia, respectively—it was part of local socioeconomic segmentation in most parts of sub-Saharan Africa.[11] Significantly, viewing live

Figure 9.1. Spectators watching a football match on a television screen in a restaurant in Eldoret town. *Photo by Solomon Waliaula.*

European football was part of the local performance of middle-class social identity and, in particular, was one dimension of the culture of consumption associated with the local middle class. I argue in this chapter that the kiosks served to translate European football into the "language" of local, low-income neighborhoods (figures 9.1 and 9.2).

By 2016, when the research was conducted that is reported in this chapter, this kiosk had been in operation for slightly over ten years, having been established in 2006. It is named "Jaguar," which also happens to be the owner and proprietor's pseudonym, which he acquired while hawking secondhand shoes from 1998 to 2000. He later engaged in video show entrepreneurship, a venture that was highly successful for him because of the strong social networks he had cultivated throughout the Huruma slums. His pseudonym stuck and was arguably at the heart of a playful and charming engagement with his clients. In turn, his small video shop, located at the far end of the shopping center, evolved into one of the largest football kiosks, right in the heart of the Huruma

Figure 9.2. Spectators watching a football match in a football kiosk in a low-income neighborhood. *Photo by Solomon Waliaula.*

Figure 9.3. A notice for an upcoming screening of a football match in a low-income neighborhood. *Photo by Solomon Waliaula.*

commercial district. Using this example, I contend that the evolution of the football kiosk in Huruma was also a metaphoric representation of the socioeconomic dynamics of local life. In this sense, the football kiosk became a form of "multimedia technology" that enabled locals to access European football but also, in its evolution and actual operation, was a medium through which we are afforded a nuanced picture of everyday life in neighborhoods such as Huruma (figure 9.3).

In my in-depth interview with Jaguar, he insisted that his success as a football entrepreneur was attributable to his "social intelligence." He incorporated live European football in his video show business in the year 2006, and within a year he had relegated the video-show component to the periphery because the live football business had picked up beyond his wildest imaginings. When I inquired how this had happened, he said: "Somebody gave me the idea of purchasing satellite television equipment and paying monthly subscriptions so that I could show live English Premier League football in my video show room. Remember, at that time a decoder was retailing at Kshs. 30,000, and a monthly subscription for the premium package was Kshs. 6,000. So, I asked him, 'What if I do not attract any customers?' He assured me that they would come, because people liked EPL football."[12]

People did, indeed, love European football, but for those in lower-income neighborhoods it was not yet part of their everyday experience of life. One could argue that they loved viewing football not just for the novelty of it, but also because it gave them a chance to enter the ludic mode. Yet it had not been adapted to their world and made to flow with the rhythms of their lives, with where they lived. Even though he was unaware of it at the time, Jaguar was ideal for this adaptation role. He had cultivated sufficient social capital to be guaranteed the goodwill of the community of European football enthusiasts in the neighborhood, even though he admitted that he was not a football fan and did not know much about European football. In practice, this disconnect exists in most entrepreneurship in the low-income neighborhoods of Eldoret, in which business enterprises not only need financial capital, but also "social connections" between the entrepreneur and the immediate neighborhood. The business has to be adapted to the situation on the ground. Indeed, Jaguar initially incorporated English Premier League football in his video-show business in a way that fit within existing physical and social landscapes. As the number of clients increased, he decided to construct a stand-alone kiosk out of loose iron sheets and waste lumber. Commenting on his experience at that point, he observed: "I had saved some money and bought this piece of land where the kiosk now sits. When I started the construction process people were curious and kept asking me, 'What are you building? Is it a church?' I told them it was a place where people could come to watch football, like a stadium. Most of them did not believe me, because this was a very new idea in these parts. I decided to use temporary material so that the structure could be expanded or contracted depending on the number of clients."[13] He kept the entrance fee at 20 Kenyan shillings, about a quarter of a dollar, but crammed many benches into a small space to accommodate as many viewers as possible. In practice, this is the logic of the kiosk. It aims to accommodate everyone, even when that means reducing the quality of services delivered. Jaguar also accommodated those who could not pay the entrance fee, on the understanding that they would pay later, although some never did. In this way, he managed to retain most of his clients and also to gradually attract more. At the same time, he cultivated good rapport with his clients; they felt like they, too, owned the space. Indeed, according to Jaguar, and in my own estimation, the "sacred status" of his football kiosk was manifested during the month of ethnic violence that shook Kenya between late December 2007 and late January 2008, when, following a disputed presidential poll, the situation in the country rapidly deteriorated. Eldoret was one of the regions significantly affected by this violence, with most houses and business premises being razed. This occurred during the middle of the European football season, between Christmas and New Year's, when there is a congested schedule of English Premier League matches. Yet Jaguar's football kiosk was among the structures that were not touched. He observed:

> We were disrupted by the post-election violence. People fled the
> town. Suddenly, I was the only one in the football kiosk business
> in the whole of the Huruma region, and the larger part of this
> side of town. I can say I was very lucky. The number of customers
> went up. I expanded the viewing space. Indeed, I had to expand
> this kiosk to three times its size, then. Now, as you can see, it is
> a fairly big space and I make a profit of between Kshs. 40,000
> to 50,000 per month. I have other smaller kiosks in other parts
> of Huruma, Road Block, and Mwanzo. So, now when you see
> people playing football in England, it is also a chance for me to
> make money.[14]

He may have imagined that his kiosk survived the destruction and thrived because of luck, but it's arguable that he had established informal, but very strong, social security around the structure, composed of his considerable number of loyal clients. These football kiosk patrons had been consuming their football in social conditions that engendered a ritual-like attachment to the space.

The Playful Viewing Experience in Football Kiosks

This section describes the experience of viewing football in a kiosk. I intend to make the point that the viewing experience of European football plays out in, and also helps to sustain, local patterns of social interaction whose main currency is play. In one sense, the beauty of the experience is not necessarily in the viewers' admiration of the glamorous moving-picture images of European footballers, but in the simple and more immediate sense of group identification that is facilitated by the sporting nature of the viewing experience. I use this specific example to argue that communal viewing experiences play an integrative function by providing a playful sense of shared and/or contested fandom that could also be useful as a template upon which to maintain social cohesion. This social element is prevalent in most football kiosks but will obviously play out differently in another kiosk, even just a few meters away.[15] This phenomenon is not limited to the Kenyan experience; James Omotosho he observes in his study that educated youths in the low-income urban spaces of Edo Ekiti, Nigeria, use communal viewing experiences to plug into what they consider the social substance of their everyday lives. He quotes one of them: "When we are waiting for a match to start, we gist [discuss] about our boys-to-boys talk . . . hope you understand what I meant . . . we talk about school, our lecturers, the way our leaders govern, and we talk about our female friends.'"[16]

This practice constitutes a specific kind of social interaction through which the youth link themselves to their social contexts. Nevertheless, I argue that the communal viewing experiences in these football kiosks gradually build a specific kind of group interaction. The Kipkarren kiosk, which I examine in the following section, hosts youths and young

Figure 9.4. Branded local football kiosk. *Photo by Solomon Waliaula.*

adults with low to average education who tend to hinge their social identification on close and fairly intimate local networks that revolve around
their immediate neighborhood. As a result, the group interaction that
accompanies the viewing experiences is characteristically carnivalesque.

The kiosk is run by a Kenyan Somali businessman and is part of a
chain of enterprises that also includes a retail store and an eating house.
The kiosk blends in with the landscape of the Kipkarren business center
(figures 9.4 and 9.5). Frequently, two matches will be shown simultaneously, and participants choose which to follow. But in practice, it is difficult to completely ignore one match in favor of the other; it is almost

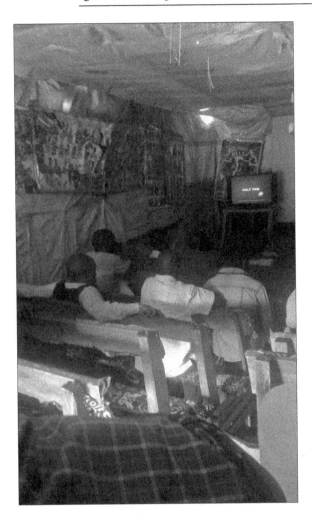

Figure 9.5. Interior design of a local football kiosk. *Photo by Solomon Waliaula.*

always a case of vacillating between them, while also momentarily disengaging to participate in the vibrant social interactions within the space. This is normally an engaging experience that is comparable to a performance, an experience that arguably redefines the practice of viewing live, televised football. I have been part of many such experiences, but here I reconstruct a particular one that I consider most illustrative.

On this day, only one match was on, in this case between Tottenham Hotspurs and Chelsea. The room was about half full. Everyone seemed to be glued to the TV set. The viewing experience turned out to be a well-choreographed verbal performance revolving around the entrepreneur himself. He was hailed by his pseudonym, "Oria," a form of address that the Somali frequently use, which translates to "comrade." He moved around, continuously engaging with the audience. He knew his clients by name and addressed his comments, curses, jibes, and threats directly to individuals, constantly engaging in playful, verbal duels. At the sixty-fifth minute of the match, however, there was a power blackout. This is a normal occurrence in Eldoret, but some viewers ferociously cursed and swore at Oria. He reciprocated, while also cursing Kenya Power. He left the room, announcing that he was going to call "the Kenya Power people," and that he would "viciously harangue them." A few minutes later, the power was restored and he rushed in, triumphantly shouting, "You see, you see. I don't joke with these people."

While the satellite television system was reconnecting, there was more lively banter. Someone shouted from the back: "Oria, beware. If Chelsea has conceded a goal during the blackout, I will castrate you." He responded, "In fact, I hope they have conceded twice. You, Mourinho [the Chelsea manager], and all his players are dirty adulterers." Someone in front then shouted, "Oria, we know you are a gifted wife snatcher, thank God you are too weak." It went on this way, with the audience engaged in a host of activities including verbal duels, curses, and swearing. Even when the comments and retorts were related to the ongoing match, the language used was characteristically ribald. For instance, dribbling and goal scoring were described in sexualized undertones. Most of the time, the audience seemed to be much more actively engaged in their own performance than they were with the ongoing football match. I understood this scenario not just as a viewing session, but as a playful and fun-filled experience in which the European football on display was not necessarily the dominant factor. Rather, it was only one of the elements that contributed to the carnival-like group interaction, which itself was a key part of the overall pleasure of viewing the match.

The football kiosks considered here are comparable to many other such spaces in sub-Saharan Africa in which local enthusiasts of European football watch the games live on television. Studies examining this phenomenon have tended to define local fandoms of European football as extensions of media/cultural colonialism; in this light, they don't critically engage with the physical and social processes that act as local filters through which this supposed global cultural form is translated into the local fans' contexts. Conversely, I have argued that the Eldoret football kiosk constitutes one example of how, as a media practice and cultural form, English Premier League football fandom is a social practice that feeds into the local realities of everyday life, in particular the infusion of a playful element into this broader process. In this sense, the space and experience of viewing European football in the kiosks is comparable to a multimedia complex in which the satellite television broadcasts the match, but in physical and social conditions that mediate aspects of the local experiences of life in low-income neighborhoods. I have traced the evolution of the football kiosk in Eldoret within the wider frame of the socioeconomic realities of this setting. Ultimately, the emergence of the football kiosk in sub-Saharan Africa was prompted by the pragmatic need to generate affordable access to enthusiasts who were not necessarily able to patronize standard football bars, the very same social segment that employs "play" to cushion itself from the harsh realities of daily life.

Notes

1. Gerard Akindes, "Transnational Television and Football in Francophone Africa: The Path to Electronic Colonization?" (PhD diss., Ohio University, 2010); Godwin Siundu, "European Football Worlds and Youth Identifications in Kenya," *African Identities* 9, no. 3 (2011): 337–48; James Tsaaior, "Football as Social Consciousness or the Cultural Logic of Late Imperialism in Post Colonial Nigeria," in *Popular Culture in Africa: The Episteme of the Everyday*, ed. Stephanie Newell and Onookome Okome (London: Routledge, 2014), 275–91; and Olomuyiwa Omobowale, "Sports and European Soccer Fans in Nigeria," *Journal of Asian and African Studies* 44, no. 6 (2009): 624–34.

2. Tsaaior, "Football as Social Consciousness," 285.

3. Omobowale, "Sports and European Soccer Fans in Nigeria," 624.

4. Akindes, "Transnational Television"; and Siundu, "European Football Worlds," 540.

5. Senayon Olaoluwa and Adewole Adejayan, "Thiery Henry as Igwe: Soccer Fandom, Christening and Cultural Passage in Nollywood," in *Gender, Sport, and Development in Africa: Cross Cultural Perspectives on Patterns of Representations and Marginalization*, ed. Jimoh Shehu (Dakar: Codesria, 2010), 79–94.

6. Eric Rothenbuhler and Mihai Coman, introduction to *Media Anthropology*, ed. Eric Rothenbuhler and Mihai Coman (London: Sage, 2005), 2.

7. David Rowe, "Sport and Its Audiences," in *The Global Handbook of Media Audiences*, ed. Virginia Nightingale (London: Wiley-Blackwell, 2011), 515.

8. Tsaaior, "Football as Social Consciousness," 282.

9. Richard Vokes, "Arsenal in Bugamba: The Rise of English Premier League Football in Uganda," *Anthropology Today* 26, no. 3 (2010): 13–14.

10. Vokes, "Arsenal in Bugamba," 11.

11. Marc Fletcher, "Reinforcing Divisions and Blurring Boundaries in Johannesburg Football Fandom," in *Identity and Nation in African Football*, ed. Onwumechili Chukwu and Gerard Akindes (New York: Palgrave Macmillan, 2014), 133–51; Vokes, "Arsenal in Bugamba"; and Leah Komakoma, "An Investigation into Fan Identity among Supporters of the English Soccer Premier League in Lusaka, Zambia" (MA thesis, Rhodes University, 2005).

12. Jaguar, conversation with author, Eldoret, Kenya, May 21, 2016.

13. Jaguar, conversation with author, May 21, 2016.

14. Jaguar, conversation with author, May 21, 2016.

15. Solomon Waliaula, "Electronic Football Fandom as Verbal Art Performance in Eldoret, Kenya," in *Sports Global Influence: A Survey of Society and Culture in the Context of Sport*, ed. Skye Arthur-Banning and Solomon Waliaula (Oxford: Inter-Disciplinary Press, 2015), 79–85.

16. James Omotosho, "Patronage of Local Cinema Halls among Urban Youths in Ado Ekiti, Southwest Nigeria," in *Negotiating the Livelihoods of Children and Youth in Africa's Urban Spaces*, ed. Michael Bourdillon (Dakar: Codesria, 2012), 176.

TEN

The Gambling Games

"Unorganized Structure" of South African Soccer

TARMINDER KAUR

If play is timeless across human geographies, it is gambling that fuses seriousness to seemingly trivial activities.[1] C. L. R. James brings to life such an interplay of sports and gambling at a historic cricket oval:[2]

> At their matches, cricketers ate and drank with the gusto
> of the time, sang songs, and played for large sums of money.
> Bookies sat before the pavilion at Lord's openly taking bets. The
> unscrupulous nobleman and the poor but dishonest commoner
> alike bought and sold matches. Both Sir Donald Bradman and
> Mr. Neville Cardus think that cricket is too complex a game to
> encourage betting. The history of the game is against them. There
> is nothing too complex for men to bet on.[3]

Thomas Reefe opens his essay on gambling in traditional Africa by equating gambling to play: "Like the other forms of play, gambling can be a most serious undertaking."[4] It is at the intersection between serious and not-so-serious forms of contest that I discuss soccer gambling games in this chapter. The links between sports and gambling are discussed in historical writings on popular leisure practices among the masses. Various modern sports, including cricket and soccer, trace their origins to nonstandardized forms, in which they were contested according to a variety of inconsistent rules, usually agreed upon at the start of the game, and yet the ultimate stakes of any contest were determined by the bets placed on it.[5] For example, Wray Vamplew argues that gambling influenced the development and standardization of rules and regulations to create "equality of opportunity to win" and "to eliminate cheating and sharp practice."[6] And it was standardization of rules that effected the "diffusion of a sport: without standardized rules a game cannot spread."[7] Soccer emerges as the most widely diffused of all standardized, rule-bound competitive activities.[8]

Although the standardized rules provide a recognizable form for soccer, the actual performances take on a life and flavor of their own. The soccer gambling games I discuss here are just one example. I draw on my ongoing research (since 2012) on sports among the working-class people in and around Rawsonville, a small, rural town surrounded by fruit farms and wineries, in the district of Cape Winelands, South Africa. Autonomously organized sports contested for stakes are neither unique nor novel to Rawsonville. Forms of everyday soccer have drawn and continue to draw ethnographers in their search for broader and deeper meanings that such popular practices may contain. For example, Eric Worby sketches different forms soccer takes in the public parks of Johannesburg to discuss spontaneity and temporalities within which racial, classed, gendered, and nationality-based identities and divides are suspended and reinforced on the urban fields of pickup soccer.[9] Similarly, Susann Baller attends to the transformation of "vacant plots" into soccer fields, where Senegalese youth reconstruct and renegotiate their "urban identities, conflicts and socialities."[10] Laura Fair also shows how the colonial sport of soccer in Zanzibar is transformed into popular practices imbued with locally significant meanings.[11] Beyond these localized ethnographies of soccer, Peter Alegi's *Soccerscapes* lucidly conveys the overarching point that soccer not only reflects regional peculiarities but also effects social change and is changed by the continent.[12]

The subject of my ethnographic enquiry is based on a structure that, as a research participant explains, is "unorganized." Although an oxymoron, *unorganized structure* retains a more accurate sense/feeling for these games than, say, referring to them as *informal* or *amateur*. The widespread practice of unofficial and less-than-organized soccer gambling games relies on the structure that these are attached to: stakes. This structure of soccer could be identified in the broader working-class appropriations of the sport and the ways in which it continues to be cherished by disenfranchised South Africans.[13] Despite the growing scholarly interest in uncovering the dynamics and potentialities of African soccer, this kind of gambling at soccer games has been given only a passing reference in literature.[14] Just as Stephen Louw notes about Fahfee (an unregulated numbers' gambling game), it may well be because of their ubiquitous presence that soccer gambling games have "escaped serious academic enquiry."[15] Scant academic attention is given to unregulated gambling in Africa, but the few studies on the topic do offer an insightful analysis of urban working-class cultures and how they negotiate their marginality, leisure, and morality.[16]

My analysis takes place at the intersection of soccer and gambling among the rural working classes of South Africa. The chapter is organized in four parts. After presenting a generic description of the games from my fieldwork, I discuss the particularities of these games in the lives of farmworkers of Rawsonville. While Rawsonville's location in the agrarian economy certainly influences who plays soccer and how it is played, the focus on soccer draws the agricultural workers into relationships with the urban working classes, presenting an opportunity to analyze urban working-class traditions in rural- and farm-based settings. It is in the socioeconomic relations, contradictory logics attached to identify *(un)organized* and *structure*, and layers of micropolitics that I search the for dynamics that create and sustain the soccer gambling games.

Defining the Soccer Gambling Games

More often than not, the soccer gambling games among the working class of Rawsonville are arranged between two soccer clubs or teams. If there are more than two teams competing for a single pot of money, it is referred to as a *tournament*. A tournament is usually organized in an elimination format and involves no more than eight teams at a time. The venue and time may remain uncertain until the players start gathering, the referees and stakes are all loosely agreed upon at the field, just before the start of the game. Almost all the games that I attended were played for money, but brandy or sheep as stakes also featured in the stories local soccer enthusiasts told. In a one-on-one contest, in which two soccer teams would put forward anything from R300 to R700 each, the winner takes the lot. In a tournament, however, there is no fixed rule as to how the prize money is to be divided among the winners and/or runners up, but the split is agreed upon at the venue. Tournaments are organized by a host, either a soccer club or an individual, who invites other (often only selected) teams, informing them about the money each is required to pay as entry fee. The word might go around a week in advance, but it is only on the day of the tournament that the host knows the exact number of participating teams, and it is not unusual to announce or adjust the distribution of the prize money while the games are already under way. Late arrivals are neither unusual nor unwelcome; they are accommodated into the tournament with neat swiftness. While hosting a big tournament (i.e., by inviting a large number of clubs) could certainly increase the stakes, the social dynamics of farm life are such that the stakes and numbers per tournament are kept quite small. This dynamic varies according to the location of the field, whether it is on private property or on municipal ground. Although the tournaments organized by booking Rawsonville's centrally located municipal field could be played out late into the evening, under the floodlights, and over both days of the weekend, sports fields on farms required no prior permissions or arrangements, so long as these games did not disturb the owners living on the property (but these farm-based fields also lacked floodlights for late evening games).

This description obviously applies to a particular time and place and reflects my subjective observations. Glimpses of similar practices can be found in historical references to South African soccer. For example, Tim Couzens describes "another kind of football. This was a much more informal activity played in the streets of suburbs like Doornfontein and locations such as Sophiatown, Eastern Native Township, Western Native

Township and Pimville. . . . Each team would collect a small amount of money (a pound or two) and hand this to the referee. The winning team would take the jackpot. Other forms of gambling no doubt sprang from this form."[17] That other kind of football is a close approximation, but the gambling games were never played on the streets of Rawsonville, nor would these games be considered "informal" by those invested in them. In the same essay, Couzens concludes that soccer in South Africa "moved through the stage of spontaneous organization, through organized amateurism, to small professionalism, to the present [1983] generation of large-scale sponsorship and near full-time professionalism."[18] Therefore, it is possible to argue that gambling games are a parallel offshoot of the stages through which soccer achieves "full-time professionalism." In the early 1980s, Robert Archer and Antoine Bouillon noted that soccer in the townships was social in nature, meaning that it did not form part of the official competitive sports structures through which individuals or teams might attain national or international recognition.[19] Peter Alegi's seminal monograph *Laduma!* details how soccer remains embedded in Black urban working-class traditions in postapartheid South Africa, despite the professionalization of the sport.[20] Alegi also describes the presence of gambling at and around the fiercely contested soccer games with high stakes and prestige attached to them in African townships, but his discussion does not touch on the kind of rural gambling games I strive to theorize. The gambling tournaments that "Angolan teams outfitted in full kit played" in Worby's ethnography are a closer and more contemporary depiction of the soccer gambling games under discussion.[21]

Many of my research participants who lived in Johannesburg before they moved to Rawsonville in the early 1990s suggested founding connections between the soccer gambling games and South Africa's top professional clubs, like the Orlando Pirates FC and Kaizer Chiefs FC. Their contentions find some corroboration in the anecdotes found in the popular soccer magazines. These include personal accounts of soccer players who remember being drawn into soccer through similar gambling games. For instance, *Soccer Laduma* covered a story on Motsau Joseph "Banks" Setlhodi, a goalkeeper for the Kaiser Chiefs FC during the early 1970s, depicting how he was drawn into the sport through a "pick up" soccer game. In this story, Banks (as he is popularly known) recounts: "I saw the guys coming to fetch me to play in one of the 'pick up' games. Eventually they convinced me to come and play and I even had to put five bob (that's the money we used in those days before Rands and cents) into the soccer money for the game. As you know, the pick-up games between street teams were played for 'winner takes all.'"[22]

On February 8, 2001, *IOL News* published a story on "gangster soccer leagues," which reported that these leagues operate "across the Cape Flats in Cape Town and are funded and run by drug lords and gang leaders . . . drawing in hordes of youngsters with the lure of big money."[23] The incident that prompted the report was the murder of two people "when a gang war erupted during the games." This report explained the professional manner in which these gangster leagues were run for prize money, as much as R30,000 to R50,000. Recounting the participation of some famous South African soccer players, the article vividly showed how fluid and interconnected the official and the unofficial are in South African soccer: "Household names like Bafana striker Benni McCarthy, his brother and Santos winger Jerome, Bafana striker Bradley August, Sundowns striker Alton Meiring and Ajax defender Jeremy Jansen are still well remembered for their exploits in these 'Sunday league' games which easily attract 5000 supporters."[24]

The presence of high-profile soccer players in such games is evidence of how the history of racial segregation and utter neglect of soccer as a Black sport in White South Africa influenced the development of soccer in the country.[25] The gambling games I describe are certainly not as professional as the gangster soccer leagues, but they are less spontaneous than pick up soccer, operating in autonomous realms without affiliation with any official sports governing bodies, much like the "street matches" described by Ian Jeffrey:

> In most street matches teams compete for a prize, usually
> monetary, which, in the 1950s ranged from a penny to three pence.
> The money was lodged with a trusted spectator and the match
> began. Usually the winner was the first team to score two goals
> before the other team scored or the first team to go two goals

ahead. So, as Thabe recalls, "If the teams were well-matched, the game could go on for a couple of weeks." There was no official referee for the matches: "Everyone was the referee. Everyone would be shouting at the same time. 'Handball! Handball!'"[26]

Rivalries did exist between more established soccer clubs in Rawsonville and were best contested at the sites of gambling games. The dynamics among and between the farm, rural, and urban soccer clubs, however, were not simply a product of their participation in the soccer gambling games, but were also influenced by the specific localities and histories of their domicile, their temporary residence, their livelihood options, and their aspirations and access to the official soccer leagues. In an ethnographic study of soccer in Kayamandi, a township on the outskirts of Stellenbosch, also surrounded by commercial agriculture farms and therefore closest to Rawsonville's socioeconomic context, Sylvain Cubizolles notes the presence of similar yet somewhat different performances of the gambling games.[27] In his more recent work he theorizes the limitations of seeing these games as "informal," arguing that these have a clear "form" and express aspirations for professionalism within the constraints of their rural and township boundaries.[28] My analysis concurs with his, and building on this discussion, I focus on the dynamics of the "unorganized structure" of soccer in Rawsonville. But first I present some more context for my research.

Farmworkers, Soccer, and the Cape Winelands

The peculiarities of Rawsonville's placement in the racialized agrarian economy and the history of paternalistic labor relations render novel the context of this study of soccer.[29] Cubizolles's article on soccer in a rugby town reflects on similar perceptions of and challenges facing organized soccer in the Cape Winelands, but his study does not extend to the vast and distant farmlands, where permanent farmworkers and seasonal migrant workers live (at least part of the year) and make lives. As he correctly argues, it is rugby, not soccer, that is known as the dominant sport of the region.[30] Examining the contestations over securing a venue at which to play soccer in Stellenbosch, he is able to show that soccer not only exists but is more popular among the majority of the region's residents. Likewise, soccer, despite its widespread practice across the farmlands of Rawsonville, hovers just below the radar of popular knowledge about sports in this locale. The inequality that separates all aspects of life of the wealthy farm owners and the poorly paid farmworkers is one reason that workers' leisure practices linger in the shadows of the centrally located and well-kept rugby fields and associated clubs. Development discourses, often in response to poor conditions of workers at the farms, portray the workers' circumstances as lacking in opportunities for sports and positive recreation.[31] Yet over the course of my fieldwork, I found seemingly abandoned, at times overgrown, sports-field-like spaces with soccer goal posts throughout the vast farmlands. Created with little concern for official parameters, most of these soccer fields were on private land, usually situated close to workers' on-farm housing, and sometimes shared with grazing animals. Only a few fields of these sorts were visible or accessible from the tarred roads, and thus locating them required knowledge of local geography and history. Unless these spaces were totally barren and unfit for farming, there was always a chance that they might end up being plowed for farming purposes.[32] On Saturday and/or Sunday afternoons, anywhere from two to eight soccer teams (often outfitted in uniform jerseys), a few cars or pickup trucks parked along the boundaries, young children in a kickabout at a corner, and from twenty to two hundred spectators (men and women) of all ages gathered in small groups, setting the scene for soccer gambling games.

On a weekend in May 2012, I had almost accidently stumbled upon a soccer gambling game, a fiercely competitive game played in somewhat informal conditions. This discovery was to change the scope of my research; from trying to figure out how sports could be structured into farmworkers' lives, I turned my attention to learning how they structured soccer in their everyday lives. Over the course of my yearlong fieldwork, I recorded interviews with players, coaches, and managers of about twenty-three soccer clubs at the farmlands in and around Rawsonville.[33] Only five of these were affiliated with the Local Football Association (LFA), part of the official governing body of soccer, the South African Football Association (SAFA), but all twenty-three had played in the gambling games.[34] Still, *gambling games* was not how I was first introduced to these activities. Earlier in my fieldwork, some soccer players had avoided using the term *gambling* by either calling them *friendly* games or dismissing them as not so serious. The intensity of play would suggest otherwise. For some time, I also referred to these as friendly games, until a fellow spectator at a game corrected me: "This is not a friendly game. They are playing for money!"[35] Not only were these games played for a sum of money, brandy, sheep, or other stakes, the reference—*gambling games*—was very much part of the vernacular. The reservation in referring to them that way on the part of some of my earlier interlocutors might be an attempt to purge them of the negative judgments gambling could attract. Of course this was not a concern for every soccer enthusiast, and once I became familiar with the colloquialism, it allowed me to ask more specific and frank questions. As I elaborate later in the chapter, treating the gambling games as a structure promises a dynamic understanding of soccer in the rural farming landscape within which farmworkers negotiate urban soccer gambling traditions.

Dynamic Life of the "Unorganized Structure" of Soccer

Explaining the broader structure of soccer in the rural Cape Winelands region, the executive of a better resourced soccer club explains:

> So, the [soccer] union have two different kinds of structures now: there's the organized structure and there's the *unorganized structure*. The organized structures are this: where the competitions are endorsed by SAFA, and the unorganized structure is this: where anyone can come and organize a competition for money and any team can come and play.[36]

Although the *organized structures* were considered more prestigious and desirable for most soccer clubs to compete and perform well at, they were, at least indirectly, sustained by the *unorganized structure* of gambling games, "where anyone can come and organize a competition for money." To elaborate on this dynamic, I (T) quote from my conversation with the same executive (E):

E: But SAFA say that they are not allowing clubs affiliated to the union [LFA] to play unorganized soccer, and vice versa. You have to belong to SAFA in order to benefit from SAFA. If you don't belong, you don't benefit.

T: That's a good point you raise. What's the benefit of being with SAFA?

E: That is something we all still want to see! (*He laughs.*) We don't know! We are being told that the benefits are being promoted to Castle [now SAB, regional] league, Vodacom [provincial] League, and the possibility of one day playing PSL [Professional Soccer League], getting sponsorships from SAFA. . . . But there is more money being invested in unorganized soccer than there is money being invested in organized soccer.

T: But that is private money, no?

E: Yes, that is not SAFA's money, that's private money! . . . According to the constitution, they [SAFA] are in charge of all soccer in South Africa, but they are not managing it. Why not? Because they don't make soccer inclusive for everybody. They only make it inclusive for a small part. And to be included you have to be affiliated. And you cannot always afford affiliation being paid, transport for games, and stuff like that. I would rather play for R500 this afternoon, than for R200 at the end of the season. You understand that? That is the mind-set that we have in our region for soccer.[37]

   Although SAFA, in principle, may not want soccer to be played in an unorganized (or rather unaffiliated) manner, policing such practices would be beyond any sports governing body. The real pull for the vast majority of the soccer clubs to SAFA's organized structures was the opportunity for "being promoted to Castle league, Vodacom League, and the possibility of one day playing PSL." However, the costs of affiliation, traveling to the weekly games, and maintaining professional standards were often much higher than what most rural soccer clubs could consistently afford. It is in this context that "more money [was] being invested in unorganized soccer than . . . in organized soccer." The "private money" I referred to did not mean involvement of the formal private or corporate sector, but rather the money individuals or groups contributed to their soccer clubs from their own means. I did learn about the involvement of minibus taxi owners, *shabeen* (tavern) owners, and other actors (with relative economic or political power) from the informal economy of the urban townships, who sponsored or managed their own soccer clubs, teams, and gambling games, but their influence in the farmlands was limited. From time to time, farmworkers were able to secure sponsorships from their employers, but these were limited to transport, team jerseys, boots, and soccer balls.[38]

Instant gratification may well be one of the reasons for the popularity of soccer gambling games, as E suggests: "I would rather play for R500 this afternoon, than for R200 at the end of the season." However, the chance of getting any real return on the R200 was, if not totally unreliable, at least contingent upon factors beyond the control of most rural/farm soccer clubs, who were unable to actively participate in the executive committee of the LFA. On the other hand, the structure of gambling games guaranteed at least a 50 percent chance to win money, without any real overhead. The gambling games also served as a training ground for the more ambitious soccer clubs to test their prowess, get practice matches, and build a strong foundation before venturing into the official soccer leagues. The money won from these games, as some coach-managers justified, could be used to manage the expenses of the soccer club. Some soccer clubs played in the gambling games with a clear goal of earning money for the affiliation fees. Even the less ambitious or those who considered their chances to be competitive in the official leagues unrealistic would regularly organize and participate in the gambling games. They argued that there was little else to do at the farms, so it was easy to get into recreational alcohol consumption. Soccer helped to "keep the guys busy" over the weekends.[39] It kept them healthy and fit, and they were ready for work on Monday morning, one farmworker-soccer manager argued. Soccer provided a flexible and affordable leisure pursuit, and gambling added to the excitement of and expectations from the games for the low-income soccer clubs. One could always organize a game when transport and money were available, without having to worry about the penalties that the LFA imposed for absentees.[40]

Nevertheless, in "gambling games, you lose some and win some," as the soccer coach of the Rawsonville Gunners FC, Tanduxolo "Kolly" Mkoboza, pointed out.[41] Although Kolly was no longer involved in the gambling games at the time of this comment, he had played, coached, and managed soccer in Rawsonville for many years (1998–2014). He went on: "In those days we did not look at it that way, it was just another way of trying to make money to sustain the club. The stronger you are, the more are chances of winning games. Then we can be able to buy soccer kits. But in the mean time we enjoyed playing soccer."[42] At one level, it might seem logical that the stronger the soccer club, the more money it could potentially win. In practice, however, being recognized as distinctively stronger came with another kind of burden. Kolly added:

> Yes, if your team is stronger others will refuse to play against that team. There were times that some other teams don't want to play against us, because we were stronger. They knew we were stronger than them. Then we will tell them, 'Okay, guys, go and sit down as a team, and decide for how much you can play against us.' And they will come back and say they can only bet R50. Then we'll say, 'Ok, it's fine, we can play for R50!' Just because we wanted to play soccer! (Then) most of Rawsonville teams were only betting R100 against Gunners.[43]

It could be argued that gambling games worked best when both teams felt that they had a fair chance at winning. A stronger soccer club that uses gambling games for training and to save up money may not be able to do so for too long. The much-needed sponsorship to manage a soccer club was unlikely to come from the SAFA, at least not to the small and marginal soccer clubs of Rawsonville. Given the dominance of urban soccer clubs in executive positions of the official league and the sheer number of soccer clubs looking for sponsors, the rural, let alone farm, soccer clubs were much further down in the long line of potential beneficiaries. While farm-based soccer clubs were, from time to time, able to access sponsorship from their employers, someone like Kolly, who worked for the local municipality, relied on his income and a network of soccer friends who were equally passionate about nurturing a strong soccer club to manage the expenses of the Gunners. Both the possibility and inconsistency of support for a soccer club, which is also devoid of any consideration of the club's actual performance on the field, played an important role in maintaining the significance of soccer gambling games.

Moral discomfort with gambling existed alongside the perceptions that soccer was a desirable, constructive, and healthy pursuit, especially for the youth. Sites of gambling games were often criticized for their "lawlessness" and for inviting brawls and disputes. The disputes were not limited to rival clubs and their supporters but extended to conflicts among the players, coaches, and managers of the same club. While disagreements over fouls, bad tackles, or cheating were obvious and fairly easy to resolve, the disputes over money and the moral weight of gambling were more complex and harder to work through. For example, a game I attended at a farm soccer field ended after fifteen minutes of play. The participating soccer coach explained that the other team was being violent and did not play fair, so they called the game off. Each club took its money back and left without further contestation. The disputes and brawls were also part of the official league games, and these were not always resolved so amicably. The presence of an official referee shifted the responsibility for finding resolutions onto the professional. The frustrations and misunderstandings between the players, coaches, and managers of the same club were at times even more challenging to reconcile. A season after the Gunners had won the LFA winter league in 2012, Kolly and his players found themselves in a disagreement. Despite winning the league, the Gunners never received their financial reward from the LFA. The gambling games also were not paying off much, as Kolly noted previously. Explaining the downfall of the club, Emmanuel Yolo Thoba shared the players' side of the story:

> Disputes over money just before the [official] games not only made us late to the field, but all the players started to feel demotivated. Normally, when we played a soccer match, we all would talk playing strategies, and laugh and joke around before our games. But now, we were just quiet, frustrated, and not in the same spirit. . . .We could not understand why he [the coach] was . . . (asking for money for transport and referees' fees) just before the game. If money was the problem, he knew that we could earn him money from the gambling games, but he would not let us play the gambling games.[44]

However, it was a sponsor from a local farming business that caused the Gunners to dissolve. Kolly questioned why a farming business would offer their club a sponsor, searching for ulterior motives. However, the players were less interested in the 'why' and went with the offer, parting ways with Kolly for good. Kolly decided to take a complete break from soccer; the newfound sponsorship, as Kolly had feared, did not last; and a smaller core group of players found another member from the community with a stable job to manage the Gunners. Despite the less than prestigious association with gambling games and limitations on the kind of soccer exposure these games could offer to more ambitious soccer players, the gambling games do offer a sense of empowerment, however unrealistic, to craft one's way to success on the official or professional soccer circuits. Still, the material realities, urban-rural-farm divides, and multidirectional forms of power relations and conceptions of prestige both sustain and disrupt how soccer is played and where aspirations attached to these may take those who invest in the sport.

Meanings and Structures of Soccer and Gambling

Gambling appeals to and gives expression to that age-old human desire to control our own fates. Soccer, similarly, has come to claim universality with its globally recognized rules and forms of play. Within these universally familiar outlines, the scenes of soccer gambling games at Rawsonville are painted in the particular social dynamics of a time and place but also express an escape from the realities into the fields of dreams and desires. This form of gambling and soccer generates its own informal economy, shapes particular psychological experiences, and plays into social and material relationships. These games provide "a fleeting sense of control and importance," as Albert Grundlingh argues in the case of betting in dog racing.[45] Particular to the context of farmworkers, Leslie London argues that the spaces of recreational alcohol consumption create "a social focus around which farm workers could construct their own cultural identity," away from the control of their bosses.[46] I argue that soccer gambling games play a similar function, allowing farmworkers to craft another, seemingly less stigmatized and more positive, identity as soccer players, coaches, and managers. To this end, Louw's reflection on Fahfee as "a medium through which individuals enter into relationships with each other, form communities, share hopes and dreams, have fun, and develop autonomous competing conceptions of the good life," rings true, however temporarily, as is evident in the Rawsonville Gunners FC's example I presented.[47]

The concept of unorganized structure works to the extent that it allows for a contrast to what these gambling games are or are not, to whom they belong, and who belongs to them. At its simplest, *unorganized* serves as a proxy to refer to soccer played without affiliation to the governing structures of the sport. The structure that gambling provides to soccer, on the other hand, expresses and embodies the working-class masculine aspirations and practicalities of organizing and controlling one's own leisure spaces. Soccer gambling games thus serve as a stepping-stone, a strategy, and a mimicked inferior of their organized counterparts.[48] Anthropologist of money Keith Hart argues: "For a large number of people without much money, in making bets, opens up the chance to participate actively in the money force, not just as a passive bystander."[49] The gambling games also offer those without access to or real chances at the organized structures of soccer an opportunity to create a world of soccer that they can participate in and control. Implicit in the concept is a lingering desire to be a part of the organized structure, but more than that, it is to benefit from becoming a part, to excel at it, to be seen, to be recognized, and to bring the art and theater of soccer to the world. The aspirations and striving to become a professional soccer player that so many young men display are no less a gamble—but a gamble that sustains the organized professional structures. By way of conclusion, it is the logic of gambling, big or small, that inadvertently sustains both the organized and unorganized structures of soccer.

Notes

Earlier versions of this chapter were presented at the New England Workshop on Southern Africa (NEWSA) in Burlington, Vermont, in October 2017; the Sports Africa Conference in Lusaka in March 2018; and the Emerging Scholars and New Research in Southern Africa workshop in Zomba, Malawi, in July 2018. In addition to the comments received at these academic platforms, the paper particularly benefited from the constructive feedback of Dr. Lyn Schumaker and Dr. Hikabwa Chipande.

1. Clifford Geertz, "Deep Play: Notes on the Balinese Cockfight," *Daedalus* (1972): 1–37; Niko Besnier, Susan Brownell, and Thomas F. Carter. *The Anthropology of Sport: Bodies, Borders, Biopolitics* (Berkeley: University of California Press, 2018).

2. C. L. R. James, *Beyond a Boundary* (London: Yellow Jersey Press, [1963] 2005).

3. James, *Beyond a Boundary*, 211.

4. Thomas Q. Reefe, "The Biggest Game of All: Gambling in Traditional Africa," in *Sport in Africa: Essays in Social History*, ed. William J. Baker and James A. Mangan (London: African Publishing Company, 1987), 47.

5. Wray Vamplew, "Playing with the Rules: Influences on the Development of Regulation in Sport," *International Journal of the History of Sport* 24 (2007): 843–71; Tim Couzens, "An Introduction to the History of Football in South Africa," in *Town and Countryside in the Transvaal: Capitalist Penetration and Popular Response*, ed. Belinda Bozzoli (Johannesburg: Ravan Press, 1983), 198–214; Lloyd Hill, "Football as Code: The Social Diffusion of 'Soccer' in South Africa," *Soccer & Society* 11, nos. 1–2 (2010): 12–28; David Goldblatt, *The Ball Is Round: A Global History of Soccer* (New York: Riverhead Books, 2008); and Baker and Mangan, *Sport in Africa*.

6. Vamplew, "Playing with the Rules," 857.

7. Vamplew, "Playing with the Rules," 844.

8. Goldblatt, *The Ball Is Round*.

9. Eric Worby, "The Play of Race in a Field of Urban Desire: Soccer and Spontaneity in Post-Apartheid Johannesburg," *Critique of Anthropology* 29, no. 1 (2009): 105–23.

10. Susann Baller, "Transforming Urban Landscapes: Soccer Fields as Sites of Urban Sociability in the Agglomeration of Dakar," *African Identities* 5, no. 2 (2007): 217–30.

11. Laura Fair, "Kickin' It: Leisure, Politics and Football in Colonial Zanzibar, 1900s–1950s," *Africa* 67, no. 2 (1997): 224–51.

12. Peter Alegi, *African Soccerscapes: How a Continent Changed the World's Game* (Athens: Ohio University Press, 2010), 14–35.

13. Couzens, "Introduction to the History of Football in South Africa"; Grant Farred, *Midfielder's Moment: Coloured Literature and Culture in Contemporary South Africa* (Boulder, CO: Westview Press, 2000); Peter Alegi, *Laduma! Soccer, Politics and Society in South Africa* (Scottsville, South Africa: University of KwaZulu-Natal Press, 2004); and John Clarke, "Football Hooliganism and the Skinheads" (Stenciled occasional paper, Department of Cultural Studies, University of Birmingham, January 1973).

14. Couzens, "Introduction to the History of Football in South Africa"; Ian Jeffrey, "Street Rivalry and Patron-Managers: Football in Sharpeville, 1943–1985," *African Studies* 51, no.1 (1992): 69–94; Sylvain Cubizolles, "Finding a New Identity for a Township Club—the Case of the Mighty 5 Star in Stellenbosch," *International Journal of the History of Sport* 28, no. 15 (October 2011): 2191–2205; and Worby, "Play of Race in a Field of Urban Desire."

15. Stephen Louw, "African Numbers Games and Gambler Motivation: 'Fahfee' in Contemporary South Africa," *African Affairs* 117, no. 466 (2018): 109–29.

16. Albert Grundlingh, "'Gone to the Dog': The Cultural Politics of Gambling—the Rise and Fall of British Greyhound Racing on the Witwatersrand, 1932–1949," *South African Historical Journal* 48, no. 1 (2003): 174–89; Detlef Krige, "'We Are Running for a Living': Work, Leisure and Speculative Accumulation in an Underground Numbers Lottery in Johannesburg," *African Studies* 70, no. 1 (2011): 3–24; and Louw, "African Numbers Games and Gambler Motivation."

17. Couzens, "Introduction to the History of Football in South Africa," 204.

18. Couzens, "Introduction to the History of Football in South Africa," 212.

19. Robert Archer and Antoine Bouillon, *The South African Game: Sport and Racism* (London: Zed Press; 1982).

20. Alegi, *Laduma!*

21. Worby, "Play of Race in a Field of Urban Desire," 120.

22. Vuyani Joni, "Banksie and the Gangster Soccer Academy," Supporters Club, October 10, 2014, http://www.soccerladuma.co.za/supporters_club /imbizo/article/428.

23. Beauregard Tromp, "Gangster Soccer League Luring Youngsters," IOL News, February 8, 2001, http://www.iol.co.za/news/south-africa/gangster -soccer-league-luring-youngsters-1.60509#.VRAE8ZWJjIU.

24. Tromp, "Gangster Soccer League Luring Youngsters."

25. Farred, *Midfielder's Moment*.

26. Jeffrey, "Street Rivalry and Patron-Managers," 71.

27. Cubizolles, "Finding a New Identity for a Township Club."

28. Sylvain Cubizolles, "Sports Dynamics and Informality in the Townships: The Case of Gambling Soccer in Kayamandi" (paper presented at Sports Africa Conference 2017, Bloemfontein, South Africa, April 10–12, 2017), http://sportinafrica.org/conference/?cr3ativspeaker=sylvain-cubizolles.

29. Andries du Toit, "Farm Workers and the 'Agrarian Question,'" *Review of African Political Economy* 21, no. 61 (1994): 375–88; and Tarminder Kaur, "(Un)Becoming Mountain Tigers Football Club: An Ethnography of Sports among the Western Cape's Farm Workers," *Anthropology Southern Africa* 40, no. 4 (2017): 290–302.

30. Sylvain Cubizolles. "Soccer in a Rugby Town: Restructuring Football in Stellenbosch," *Soccer & Society* 11, nos. 1–2 (2010): 105–17.

31. Kaur, "(Un)Becoming Mountain Tigers Football Club."

32. I was informed of spaces that were used by farmworkers to play soccer but were later plowed for farming purposes. Sometimes farmers made another piece of land available, other times they did not—a dynamic that depended on the relationship between the farmer and farmworkers in a given situation. For more details on the sporting landscape of Rawsonville, see Tarminder Kaur, "A Tale of Two Sports Fields: Contested Spaces, Histories and Identities at Play in Rural South Africa," in *Sport in African History, Politics, and Identity Formation*, ed. Michael Gennaro and Saheed Aderinto (New York: Routledge, 2019).

33. Tarminder Kaur, "Sporting Lives and "'Development'" Agendas: A Critical Analysis of Sport and "Development" Nexus in the context of Farm Workers of the Western Cape" (PhD diss., University of the Western Cape, 2016).

34. Kaur, "Sporting Lives and 'Development' Agendas."

35. Field notes, July 14, 2012.

36. Interview with male executive member of a local football club, Worcester, December 2012. The interviewee read an earlier draft of this chapter and chose to remain anonymous.

37. Interview with male executive member, December 2012.

38. Kaur, "(Un)Becoming Mountain Tigers Football Club."

39. Participation in sports just to "keep the guys busy" was a trope I heard repeatedly, and at times this reference was to adult men who worked as farm laborers (reflections recorded in the field notes; cf. 2012–13).

40. I have written about this dynamic in some detail elsewhere; see Kaur, "(Un)Becoming Mountain Tigers Football Club."

41. Tanduxolo "Kolly" Mkoboza (soccer coach/manager of the Rawsonville Gunners Football Club), WhatsApp interview, De Nova, Rawsonville, June 13, 2018.

42. Mkoboza interview, June 13, 2018.

43. Mkoboza interview, June 13, 2018.

44. Emmanuel Yolo Thoba, "Rawsonville Gunners Football Club: Story of a Winning Friendship" (paper presented at Sports Africa Conference 2017, Bloemfontein, South Africa, April 10–12, 2017), http://sportinafrica.org/conference/?cr3ativspeaker=emmanuel-t-yolo.

45. Grundlingh, "'Gone to the Dog,'" 181.

46. Leslie London, "The 'Dop' System, Alcohol Abuse and Social Control amongst Farm Workers in South Africa: A Public Health Challenge," *Social Science & Medicine* 48 (1999): 1411.

47. Louw, "African Numbers Games and Gambler Motivation," 21.

48. Farred, *Midfielder's Moment.*

49. Keith Hart, "Making Money with Money: Reflections of a Betting Man," in *Qualitative Research in Gambling: Exploring the Production and Consumption of Risk*, ed. Rebecca Cassidy, Andrea Pisac, and Claire Loussouarn (London: Routledge, 2013), 22.

SIX

African Sports Migration

European Dreams and Nightmares

ELEVEN

African Footballers' Migration to Europe

Shifting Perspectives and Practices

ERNEST YEBOAH ACHEAMPONG, MICHEL RASPAUD,
AND MALEK BOUHAOUALA

This chapter examines the ways that the migration of African footballers to Europe corresponded with African players' shifting perceptions regarding this opportunity and the development of the European
football (soccer) labor market since the 1980s. By exploring how these
patterns and perceptions have changed over time, we can better con-
textualize the migration processes and strategies of African players in
their pursuit of a professional football career in Europe. Since the 1980s,
shifts in African societies' perceptions of football, African football structures, and the European football labor market have changed the ways
that Africans engage in this form of migration. In order to reconstruct
these shifts in perspective, approach, and practice, we conducted dozens
of interviews with current and former African professional footballers,
which enabled us to identify key changes across three distinct periods:
the 1980s, 1990s, and 2000s. We argue that over these three decades,
shifting perspectives about the professional opportunities available in
Europe powerfully shaped the ways that Africans engaged with football
and, ultimately, pursued careers in the sport.

African Football and Migration Dynamics

Historically, African players have been migrating to other regions since the first Black professional footballer, Arthur Wharton, played in the English league from 1885 to 1902. The former Methodist minister came from a wealthy family from the Gold Coast (Ghana), in West Africa. He became a national celebrity in England as an all-round athlete and, in particular, in sprinting and football.[1] Subsequently, between the 1930s and 1950s, France recruited footballers from its colonies in North and West Africa to play in Leagues One and Two, and some of them later became French nationals.[2] Around this time, Belgium and Portugal also began recruiting African players from their colonies-cum-independent nations.[3]

The success of early professionals such as Arthur Wharton, Africa teams' performances in international competitions, and the evolution of the Union of European Football Associations (UEFA) leagues combined to trigger the migration of African footballers to Europe. Reinhilde Sotiria König and Marina de Regt have suggested that African migrants have historically engaged in this practice, and footballers often employ similar strategies, such as borrowing money to facilitate their travels.[4] Contributions from migrants' families, relatives, and members of their communities often play a central role in this facilitation. These contributions may be understood as collective investments in the development of human capital. Social networks also influence migratory flows, including the formal and informal channels through which migration occurs.[5] For example, John Bale identified networks involving "friends-of-friends," colleagues, and former and current players who passed on important information about migratory destinations and employment opportunities.[6] Migrants'"bridgeheads" and others may mobilize additional resources through their personal networks.[7]

Migration Strategies

This section discusses three periods—the 1980s, 1990s, and 2000s—within which shifts in African football migration are readily discernible, thereby highlighting change over time. The three periods capture Africans' shifting perspectives regarding professional soccer opportunities available in Europe. In general, the shifting perception from soccer as a social activity to an endeavor that generates professional opportunities is clear. There are overlaps in perception and corresponding migratory activity that transcend adjacent decades in our periodization, but the transition from one to the next generally creates clear divides in assessment and praxis, thereby facilitating our analysis.

THE 1980S: FOOTBALL VERSUS SCHOOL

> We had two stones for goalposts and played four against four. Sometimes, something sharp would cut your feet, but we played through our wounds, and didn't even think about them. We just loved to play.

—John Utaka[8]

In African communities, soccer is played virtually anywhere children can find space and a round object to use as a ball. Older children even walk kilometers to play after school or on weekends. Simply put, playing soccer is part of their social activity. For example, Annan, who earned sixty-seven caps for the Ghanaian national team, explained how his soccer career began, rather modestly: "I started from the community in my area where we used to play soccer with friends within the neighborhood. It was mostly in the backyards of people's houses with boys in the area, like the street soccer stuff because there was no organized 'colts' football."[9] At the time, the colts' system, roughly an early version of academy football, did not exist. As such, children played solely for the love of the game, with no professional objectives for which to strive.

Other informants shared similar experiences from the 1980s. For example, some indicated that they walked over five kilometers to play football with boys from different towns. In this manner, soccer constituted a special, inclusive practice for young people. The game kept young people active, deepened and expanded their social relations, and served as a strategy for integration into their communities. Annan added:

"Mum insisted we should make sure that we took our studies seriously, though we could play football alongside. She only got annoyed when we refused to do your house chores. All the same, she knew our dad was a footballer, and that she wasn't against us playing football at all."[10]

In school, boys played soccer because it was part of an assortment of extracurricular activities over which parents had less control. Indeed, informal soccer was seen by some adults, parents, and community members as a waste of time, and therefore they discouraged their children from playing. In short, they were against children playing soccer at the expense of their schooling. Interviewees, such as Ikpe, a former international soccer player from Nigeria who started his professional career in 1995 with AC Reggiana, in Italy, confirmed this attitude: "In those days, in the 1980s and 1990s, you didn't dare say you wanted to play soccer; even your neighbors will laugh at you, people will mock you. I knew a lot of friends who, by the time we went to play soccer and came back, had to sneak in or wash very well before they got home, otherwise they get serious beatings. In Africa, people saw soccer players to be hooligans, cowards, uneducated. So, playing soccer, it was like you are 'jobless,' you don't have a future, no plan, no career ambition."[11]

For most parents, soccer was not a socially endorsed activity and seemed to be a pastime for people who lacked vision. After decolonization, most African families adopted the European model of social ascension through education. Soccer supposedly was for "lazy" boys, which in some African countries is termed *kobolo*.[12] This term has existed since the 1960s. For example, Wilberforce Mfum, a prolific Ghanaian striker during the 1960s and 1970s who became one of the earliest African football migrants to the fledgling North American Soccer League (NASL) in 1968, recalled how the society perceived soccer players: "As people who were only interested in football-*kobolo*."[13] Boys who played soccer were presumed to be from low-income communities. As Mbvoumin, a former Cameroonian professional player who migrated to France in 1994 after returning from the 1993 FIFA U20 tournament in Australia, recalled: "In Cameroun, at that time a soccer player was sometimes from a very poor home and it was seen as an activity for 'bad guys' who are unsuccessful in life. Soccer was not a good example or model for the youth because of the kind of perception people had at that time."[14] Ikpe, who had over eighteen years of professional experience abroad, further explained: "There were times people were murmuring and gossiping about me in the street that, he was a 'hopeless guy always soccer, soccer.' So, it became obvious that sometimes I had to put my soccer shoes in a 'poly bag' pretending to buy something in the market or coming from the market but my soccer shoes were actually inside."[15]

In the 1980s, soccer was a contentious subject within African societies because it generally did not generate opportunities for social advancement, let alone provide incomes for its practitioners. For most Africans, little was known about the prospects for professionalism, in great part because at the time these were quite limited. In this context, few boys were scouted and integrated into formal teams. However, thanks to a few persistent soccer enthusiasts who tapped into their personal social relations and networks, opportunities began to materialize, even if only minimally. For example, Akunnor Charles, a Ghanaian soccer player and the first African player to captain a German club, in this case VfL Wolfsburg, from 2001 to 2002, explained how he was scouted as a young boy: "I was a young boy playing for fun. We used to meet as community boys to play in the area. I was spotted by someone who took me to Tema, the industrial city of Ghana."[16]

These small numbers of intrepid soccer players were undoubtedly passionate as they ventured into the realm of professional football. Some of their approaches were achieved through social negotiation, drawing upon strategies that they had learned from their various informal soccer experiences and events. As the soccer economy grew in Europe in the 1990s, the perception among Africans about the professional prospects of the game accordingly shifted. This perceptual change also coincided with improved performances of African teams at the Fédération Internationale de Football Association (FIFA) youth and senior competitions in the early 1990s, which further influenced the trajectory of African soccer migration.

THE 1990S: FOOTBALL STRUCTURES,
INTERNATIONAL COMPETITIONS, AND
SOCIOECONOMIC OPPORTUNITY

African perceptions of soccer improved with the growth of the UEFA leagues, which attracted deep-pocketed sponsors, increased media attention, and expanded broadcasts of games. Africans perceived this economic growth and the adjustment of labor rules within European soccer as positive developments. The performances of both youth and senior African national teams contributed to this shift in perspective and worked to expand viewership across the continent, which in turn enhanced the image of soccer players, many of whom became national heroes. This development was accompanied by the growth of formal and informal institutions and systems, such as academies, scouts, and intermediaries, which facilitated the recruitment of African players for the European labor market. Prince, a former Nigerian international who also played professionally in Italy, explained: "Soccer started to change people's perception in Africa after the FIFA World Cup in USA, in 1994, when Nigeria performed so well.... Then, people began to get an idea, but still, it was not rampant. And, that was when scouts began to come into Nigeria from Europe. Although I was very good at other sports and could have represented Nigeria in all [of them].... I quit handball because it was dividing my attention from soccer."[17] It was during this decade that soccer began to open up new economic opportunities for African players. And correspondingly, Africans increasingly recognized the new social status that could be attained via a professional career.

Through live broadcasts of international competitions and UEFA league matches, young boys began to identify role models or mentors. Local tournaments were newly organized to showcase the best young talent for foreign agents. This development demonstrates how African soccer has increasingly been organized around recruitment and training in preparation for the European soccer market. These opportunities provided more promising prospects for families as well, as they now weighed the advantages of school and soccer for young players. After the success that African teams experienced in the 1990s at the FIFA

World U17 championships—Ghana won the tournament in 1991 and 1995, as did Nigeria in 1993—foreign agents flooded the continent to recruit footballers to the European soccer market.[18]

Reflecting these developments, soccer in African schools was newly recognized as a positive form of physical education. Sports in secondary schools and colleges were quite competitive and served as fertile grounds for cultivating and unearthing talents. Through their secondary school exploits, some players earned invitations to their national teams. For example, Edema, who was a member of the Nigerian national team that qualified for its first World Cup in 1994, explained how he was selected: "They saw me as a school boy footballer, but with a lion's heart. I became the young, tireless midfielder in the Nigeria League. . . . In 1991, I played my first senior national team match against Burkina Faso."[19] Following this exposure, Edema was signed by a Turkish club, and he began his professional career with them in 1992. He finally became the "breadwinner" for his family, supporting it financially and covering his siblings' educational expenses.

Increasingly cognizant of these economic opportunities, parents and families began to permit their children to play soccer, recognizing its ability to facilitate educational opportunities. Indeed, our informants who were playing in Africa in the 1990s confirmed that their parents asked them to take their schooling seriously, while they were also permitted to play soccer. Players who had middle- or upper-class upbringings especially emphasized the importance their parents placed on education as the key to social success.[20] For their families, success was not limited to high income, but included social status and social recognition. Parents, continuing to value education even as they began to permit their children to play soccer, remained mindful of their children's education, insisting that any clubs for which they played should pay their school fees. Mbvoumin, a former Cameroonian professional player who is now the director of the Association Culture Foot Solidaire (CFS), an international nongovernmental organization (NGO) that works to protect young soccer players in general and African players in particular, recalled: "I was in school then . . . and my family didn't agree with me playing football. As I was very good player, my team, in the community of Yaoundé, was paying my school fees, buying books and everything for me. Later on, my family accepted me playing football because my team was helping to pay for my schooling."[21] As the social and economic benefits of soccer became increasingly evident to parents, family members, and even entire communities, these entities began supporting young boys by furnishing them with training kits and enrolling them in football academies.

This emerging notion that football could facilitate financial success was deepened by the media, which increasingly focused attention on the exploits and accomplishments of some of the African players who were drawing large salaries in Europe. The emergence of pay TV and live telecasts of international matches and European leagues, which featured successful African players, powerfully changed the perceptions of the game within African societies.

Meanwhile, the deregulation of the European football labor market via the landmark Bosman ruling in 1995 generated an opportunity for European clubs to attract highly skilled labor.[22] The trend of African players migrating to Europe had already intensified significantly, such that by the time of the ruling, an estimated 350 Africans were already playing in Europe.[23] This migration pattern subsequently accelerated; by 1998, 481 foreign-based players had participated in the African Cup of Nations (AFCON) tournaments.[24]

THE 2000S: MASSIVE FINANCIAL REWARDS, SOCIAL RECOGNITION, AND FURTHER IMPROVED FAMILY SUPPORT

Media rights, clubs' budgets, and international investment in the game rapidly increased the global soccer economy during the 2000s. Opportunities for African migrant footballers expanded exponentially, as did perceptions on the continent of the possibilities. Abedi Pele, a former Ghanaian international player who was the first to win a UEFA championship, in his case with Olympique de Marseille in 1993, and also the youngest player to win the AFCON (in 1982), recalled how the game was transformed during the decade: "We were enjoying it and having fun, but to see that such a thing can turn to the most lucrative business in the world is what amazes me, something that started like a joke became the most unique, powerful, influential business in the world, so that when you speak people listen. When you talk, you inspire millions of people, so you know that it's really incredible."[25] This transformation of the soccer economy continued to improve the social and economic status of African players beyond their communities. The allure contributed to the promotion of European soccer as a pathway to success for young men in Africa.[26] As such, between 2000 and 2010, 1,279 foreign-based players participated in AFCON tournaments.[27] These players were increasingly recognized as agents of social change in their home communities and countries.

Corresponding to these developments, parents and family members became more enlightened regarding professional soccer. The deepening of this professional dimension of the game fostered optimism among parents, family members, communities, and nations. As Ayarna, a Ghanaian international with over eleven years of professional experience who still plays in Europe, put it: *"Now every parent is open-minded so you can do everything, but back in the days, schooling was the only way you could be successful. So, every parent wanted their kids to go to school but now they watch football, other sports, and see what is going on around the world, that everybody could be successful anyway, not just by going to school. I don't blame them all. . . . [I]t was just that culture back then, so they had to do that to make their sons better people."*[28]

To this end, some parents even sold their properties to support their sons' professional careers abroad. From Togo comes the example of Zakaria, who started his professional career in Serbia in 2013 and is still playing actively in Europe. Zakaria indicated that his mother sacrificed her property to support his professional development, declaring: "My mum supported me to enter into football profession by selling her house to support me when I told her I had an opportunity[,] a chance to play in Serbia."[29] A development of this nature would have been inconceivable in the 1980s. Similarly, in their work, Nienke Van der Meij and Paul Darby have reconstructed the centrality of family members and relatives in decision-making processes regarding which soccer academy their budding players could join.[30] In the end, these players' success can translate into long-term financial reward for their families. These investment prospects have provided an incentive for players and even members of their communities to seek migration opportunities. Interviewees confirmed the immense contributions that their parents, families, and community members had made to their professional projects.

The investment in players became significant as they developed their human capital through formal training in football academies. These formal football structures provided a platform to prepare young people and integrate them into society through the remunerative opportunities they facilitated. The 2000s provided a new model for African footballers, who began to behave like rational economic agents, prudently utilizing the resources of their families and the football structures newly in place to achieve their professional aspirations.

Understanding Shifting Perspectives and Practices of African Footballers

In this chapter we have periodized African football based on shifts in the social, economic, and football infrastructure landscapes. In the first period, the 1980s, we considered the role of informal soccer and the tension between soccer and school. During this decade, players were forced to resourcefully pursue nascent strategies in order to become professionals in Europe. In the ensuing decade, soccer gained traction and experienced important economic and social growth, with formal structures emerging on the continent. African families and communities increasingly embraced these shifts and participated in players' migration strategies. New structures for training, selecting, and recruiting in Africa provided soccer prospects with opportunities to devise and explore novel strategies. Based on the expected return on investment, players and families began to take risks and adopted an entrepreneurial logic. The third period, the 2000s, ushered in an era of increasingly organized and rational labor markets in Europe and thus even created more opportunity and allure for African players. In turn, players became better managers of their careers, with enhanced abilities to negotiate and promote their economic worth. Yet clubs also gained more power during this period, as revenues increased their purchasing and negotiating capacities, generating often-protracted contract debates and player holdouts, with each side—mediated by player and club agents—trying to gain the upper hand.

This chapter has attempted to deepen understanding of African players' migration strategies, including the resources that these athletes mobilized to reach the European soccer market. The periodization of the African soccer landscapes enhances our knowledge of the ways that African footballers' migration strategies shifted over time and, we hope, will open up prospects for further, related research.

Notes

1. Phil Vasili, *The First Black Footballer—Arthur Wharton, 1865–1930: An Absence of Memory* (London: Cass, 1998); and Paul Darby, "Go Outside: The History, Economics and Geography of Ghanaian Football Labour Migration," *African Historical Review* 42, no. 1 (2010): 19–41.

2. Bill Murray, *Football: History of the World Game* (Aldershot, UK: Scholar Press, 1995); Wladimir Andreff, "Sport in Developing Countries," in *Handbook on the Economics of Sport,* ed. Wladimir Andreff and Stefan Szywanski (Cheltenham, UK: Edward Elgar, 2006), 308–15; Staniolao Frenkiel and Nicolas Bancel, "The Migration of Professional Algerian Footballers to the French Championship, 1956–82: The 'Desire for France' and the Prevailing National Contexts," *International Journal of the History of Sport* 25, no. 8 (2008): 1031–50; Darby, "Go Outside."

3. Raffaele Poli, "Africans' Status in the European Football Players' Labour Market," *Soccer and Society* 7, nos. 2–3 (2006): 278–91.

4. Reinhilde Sotiria König and Marina de Regt, "Family Dynamics in Transnational African Migration to Europe: An Introduction, African and Black Diaspora," *International Journal* 3, no. 1 (2010): 1–15.

5. Poli, "Africans' Status."

6. John Bale, *The Brawn Drain: Foreign Student-Athletes in American Universities* (Urbana: University of Illinois Press, 1991). See also Joseph Maguire and Mark Falcous, "Introduction: Borders, Boundaries and Crossings: Sport, Migration and Identities," in *Sport and Migration: Borders, Boundaries and Crossings,* ed. Joseph Maguire & Mark Falcous (Abingdon, UK: Routledge, 2011), 1–12.

7. Jean-Baptiste Meyer, "Network Approach versus Brain Drain: Lessons from the Diaspora," *International Migration* 39, no. 5 (2001): 91–110.

8. Quoted in Yaw W. Owusu, "Nigerian Soccer Star Visits Western Group," *Daily Guide Newspaper,* November 2011.

9. Anthony Annan, interview with authors, Finland, April 13, 2016.

10. Annan, interview, April 13, 2016.

11. Ikpe Prince, interview with authors, Europe, December 9, 2015.

12. James Esson, "Better Off at Home? Rethinking Responses to Traf-ficked West African Footballers in Europe," *Journal of Ethnic and Migration Studies* 41, no. 3 (2015): 512–30; and Ernest Y. Acheampong, "Socioeconomic Analysis of the Give Back Phenomenon: Professional Footballers in Europe and Their Assistance to the Communities of Origin in Africa" (PhD diss., Université Grenoble Alpes, 2017). *Kobolo* refers to supposedly lazy people who do not want to go to school and are aimless, only interested in playing soccer.

13. Wilberforce K. Mfum, interview with authors, Ghana, September 15, 2017.

14. Mbvoumin Jean-Claude, interview with authors, Europe, October 7, 2015.

15. Prince interview, December 9, 2015.

16. Akunnor Kwabla Charles (coach of Ghana's national team, the Black Stars), interview with authors, Ghana, September 12, 2015.

17. Prince interview, December 9, 2015.

18. Paul Darby, "Out of Africa: The Exodus of African Football Talent to Europe," *Working USA: The Journal of Labour and Society* 10, no. 4 (2007a): 443–56; Bente Ovèdie Skovgang, "African Footballers in Europe: Social and Cultural Diversity in a Sporting World," *Research in the Sociology of Sport* 5 (2008): 33–50.

19. Edema Fuludu, interview with authors, Nigeria, February 20, 2018.

20. Pierre Bourdieu, "The Forms of Capital," in *Handbook of Theory and Research for the Sociology of Education*, ed. John G. Richardson (New York: Greenwood Press, 1986), 125–37.

21. Jean-Claude interview, October 7, 2015.

22. The Bosman ruling was an important decision on the free movement of labor among the EU member states and had a deep impact on transfers of footballers within the EU territories. It freed soccer players at the end of a contract without any transfer fees being paid to their former clubs. Darby, "Out of Africa," 446.

23. Mark Gleeson, "The African Invasion," Kick-off: African Cup of Nations 1996, *Fans Guide* (January 1996): 106.

24. Acheampong, "Socioeconomic Analysis of the Give Back Phenom-enon." The African Cup of Nations (AFCON) tournament is the biggest soccer event on the Africa continent, showcasing the talents and quality of soccer players from participating countries. This biennial competition is organized and managed by the Confederation of African Football (CAF).

25. Abedi Pele, interview with authors, Ghana, March 9, 2016.

26. Raffaele Poli, "African Migrants in Asian and European Football: Hopes and Realities," *Sport in Society* 13, no. 6 (2010):1001–11.

27. Acheampong, "Socioeconomic Analysis of the Give Back Phenomenon."

28. Reuben Ayarna, interview with authors, Sweden, January 20, 2016.

29 Zakaria Isa, interview with authors, Europe, December 22, 2015.

30. Nienke van der Meij and Paul Darby, "'No One Would Burden the Sea and Then Never Get Any Benefit': Family Involvement in Players' Migration to Football Academies in Ghana," in *Football and Migration: Perspectives, Places, Players*, ed. Richard Elliott and John Harris (London: Routledge, 2014), 150–79.

TWELVE

Postcareer Precarity

Occupational Challenges among Former West African Footballers in Northern Europe

CHRISTIAN UNGRUHE AND SINE AGERGAARD

When Benoît Assou-Ekotto's former coach Harry Redknapp announced that the Cameroonian international had decided to end his professional football career and become an adult movie actor, the story generated astonishment and amusement in social media networks and received widespread attention from the mass media. Although the French-born footballer denied the story's validity shortly afterward, claiming Redknapp was joking, it entertained football fans and the wider public during the spring of 2017.[1] However, while this was one of the very few occasions on which an African footballer's postcareer trajectory was a matter of public debate, it also revealed that former African professional footballers' whereabouts, occupations, and living conditions are widely unknown and remain an underresearched topic.

In the realm of male African football migration, studies have presented glimpses into the postcareer trajectories of former football celebrities. Paul Darby, for example, has pointed out that successful players are able to transfer their accumulated intellectual, financial, and cultural capital after they have ended their careers.[2] Taking the case of the former Ghanaian international Abedi Pele as an example, Darby demonstrates that the postcareer trajectories of African athletes can serve as a node within a global value chain when a player retires from professional football, returns to an African country, and remains in the football business, for example by promoting transfers of local talent to Europe. Regarding footballers from the former Portuguese colonies in Africa, Todd Cleveland mentions that quite a number of them have embarked on professional careers in or outside of the game following their playing careers abroad, including Mário Wilson and Mário Coluna,[3] who were both successful coaches in Europe and Africa. In addition, although this is an unusual example, the case of George Weah, who has served as president of Liberia since early 2018, indicates the possibility for success potential outside the sports industry for former players. On the other hand, referring to Weah's initial unsuccessful run for the presidency in the 2005 elections, Gary Armstrong contends that the fame of African football celebrities is fragile upon reaching the conclusion of their careers and that their once-elite social status is newly subject to renegotiation.[4]

It remains to be seen how Assou-Ekotto's postcareer trajectory will evolve. Still, being a football celebrity and a top earner in Europe, he enjoys good prospects, and there is probably little to worry about regarding his football "afterlife." However, stories about transnational African football celebrities and their struggles to become presidents, movie stars, or promoters of professional football at home upon retirement overshadow the trajectories of the majority of professional African players in Europe, whose careers have been less successful and whose whereabouts are thus not a matter of public concern.

Thus far, research on African footballers' transnational migration has mainly focused on migrants' pre- and actual careers (e.g., their hopes and expectations and their paths into professional sports abroad), their migratory experiences, and political and economic conditions on a macro level, while widely neglecting players' postcareer trajectories.[5] Notwithstanding the handful of accounts of the glamourous worlds of (former) African football celebrities, recent research indicates that the majority of professional African players in Europe often face social and economic challenges after their careers end, particularly since many more have already experienced various risks, uncertainties, and hardships before and during their international careers.[6]

By examining the postcareer trajectories and experiences of former West African professional footballers in northern Europe, we aim to contribute to a more complex perspective on the phenomenon of transnational African football migration. This chapter is based on multisited ethnographic research, as well as twenty interviews with West African footballers who played in Denmark and Sweden between the mid-1990s and 2016.[7] In analyzing the trajectories of football "workers," rather than celebrities, we draw on the concept of precarity to link players' individual experiences with structural conditions in the global football industry.[8] This approach highlights the nuances and ambivalences that desirable careers in the neoliberal age may entail.[9] In particular, we focus on the reasons for and experiences of the occupational challenges and uncertainties that players face after their careers conclude.[10] Following a general discussion of precarious conditions in the global football industry, we highlight the impact of low salaries, the subordinate role of education, and the problem of limited job opportunities outside football for West African footballers in northern Europe. Here, we refer to selected testimony from our informants, who have ended their international football careers and are in the process of negotiating their future trajectories. While we illuminate their individual experiences, they are also exemplary of the wider group of transnational African players at the respective stages of their careers.

Postcareer Precarity among Former Footballers: General Observations

Entering a career's "afterlife" is a challenging turning point for many professional athletes. This has been observed in a number of studies that have traced postcareer trajectories among sportsmen and -women from European and North American countries. In general, a lack of alternative occupational opportunities, financial difficulties, and declining social status have been identified as crucial and (often interconnected) challenges.[11] Hence for many, transforming from athletes into other selves and transferring sporting capital into long-lasting forms of social, cultural, and economic capital appear to be difficult endeavors.

Several factors contribute to this challenge. First, many professional players already live on minimal salaries and face financial challenges during their careers. According to a study of the international players' association, Fifpro, of fourteen thousand professional footballers worldwide, three-quarters earn an average income of less than $400 per month.[12] Thus, many lack the possibility of accumulating sufficient financial means to secure a smooth transition into postcareers and to bridge times of unemployment and job seeking. Certainly the levels of wages and living costs differ in the various national environments of Fifpro's research. However, financial difficulties upon retirement are not restricted to players in low-income countries. For instance, a study in German professional football has shown that 20 to 25 percent of former players live on minimum social welfare at one time or another following their playing careers.[13]

Low salaries form only part of the transitional difficulties. The subordinate role of education and job training during professional careers leaves retiring athletes widely unqualified for jobs outside sports. As Fifpro's study reveals, only about a quarter of former athletes have obtained sufficient qualifications or job training to become employed. A reason for this deficiency may be that the professional football business—that is, clubs, (inter)national federations, players' associations, and agents—does not provide possibilities for job training or education and that players would rather choose professional contracts over educational opportunities. In the absence of adequate occupational alternatives, many former players attempt to remain in the football business, for example as coaches, with its very limited and competitive employment opportunities. Hence, low salaries and few opportunities to make financial preparations for the future, as well as low levels of education and insufficient job qualifications, often lead to precarious postcareer transitions and trajectories among players that may go beyond declining material conditions and affect former players' social status and identity.[14]

Although Fifpro's study provides an overview of problematic conditions in the business and highlights the challenges for professional footballers, in general the question of how and to what degree the specific group of transnational African players are particularly affected by these challenges and how they respond to them remains to be analyzed.[15]

Experiences of Occupational Precarity among Former Transnational African Footballers

Many of the professional African players we interviewed were ill prepared for their postcareer trajectories and were facing financial difficulties and declining social status. Apparently, higher social status acquired during one's career is difficult to maintain afterward. But why is this so?

According to Raffaele Poli, transnational African footballers are a particularly vulnerable group of athletes in Europe.[16] Above all, they are affected by underpayment and short contract lengths and often face economic hardships over the course of their careers. Hence, they appear to embody many of the general findings in Fifpro's study.

Indeed, providing for future lives is often impossible to do during their playing careers. This reality is illustrated by the case of Ibrahim.[17] He went to Denmark as an eighteen-year old, promising talent signed by an up-and-coming club. Despite his talent, he never experienced a breakthrough. During his career, he suffered from recurrent illness and a severe injury. Most of his contracts were not renewed, and he changed clubs frequently, spending most of his career in the lower-tier divisions of the country, in which salaries were minimal, roughly $2,000 a month before taxes. Following a second knee injury and the termination of his contract, he was unable to find a new club. After eight years in the country, he was forced to start thinking about life after football. Although he was in his midtwenties and did not want to give up the dream of playing professional football, he could not afford to only train to recover and look for a new club. Yet there were few alternatives. "I just wanted to work. I just wanted to earn money," he recalled, but "I didn't have [any] education. . . . [H]ow can you survive?"[18] Nevertheless, since he was entitled to social benefits, municipal authorities demanded further qualifications and sponsored his training to become an assistant nurse. He graduated after a fourteen-month course and now works full time as an ancillary nurse in the elderly care sector, a job in which salaries are rather low and which comes with particular challenges for him due to the injuries he incurred.

For African players, low salaries are only one aspect of the overall challenges. By investigating female African footballers' career transitions in Scandinavia, Sine Agergaard and Tatiana Ryba have shown that players originating from countries with limited educational possibilities or alternatives to sports are more vulnerable to postcareer challenges than local players.[19] Indeed, African players often lack the required qualifications or language skills necessary to enter educational programs in European countries.[20] For example, while playing for various Scandinavian clubs, Tony, a thirty-year-old former international for his West African home country, noticed the difference between local and African players. According to Tony, the local players have an advantage, building on a "social network and they have the qualifications already.... But we ... come from a different culture, a different place and then you need to have the qualifications to be able to compete with them. So, you need to be able to be on the same level with them, or even more, to be able to compete."[21] Moreover, African players lack information about the educational systems and the required qualifications for the job market, as Tony further revealed. "When I was playing, I didn't know there was one of my player friends ... studying at the same time [he] was playing.... But, I didn't know that I could be able to do that when I was [playing]. And, I didn't know that the club would allow me to do that. But this is the information I didn't get. That could have changed my decision. I could have done something.... So, it's about the information for you to be able to make better decisions."[22] Today, Tony has ended his professional career and is studying marketing, hoping to get a job with a Danish company. However, upon embarking on his studies, he found it difficult to switch from being a player to a student and to adjust to requirements and expectations within the university after several years away from an educational environment.

On the other hand, regulations and conditions in Europe may also specifically hinder African football migrants from preparing for postcareer job opportunities. For instance, support for dual career development, which is provided for domestic talent according to the EU Guidelines on Dual Career of Athletes (EU 2012), does not consider the specific challenges of non-European athletes. Moreover, clubs in European football do not usually support either education or job training for African players, often for a simple reason: while making use of the benefit of African labor at a comparatively low cost, investing in and promoting career alternatives for their African players would contradict their profit-driven approach.

Michael's case reveals this dilemma. Following a successful trial training with a Swedish club, he embarked on a one-year loan in early 2008. Although he only received a modest salary, his hope was to perform well and get a better deal with the club after the loan period. In the meantime, "the focus was only on football.... They [the Swedish club] didn't offer any education."[23] Michael, eighteen years old at that time, accepted these conditions. "Because if ... you sign the contract and you have [the] terms ... it's only about football.... You don't need to do anything. [You just] obey ... your club rules."[24] On the one hand, the club did not seem to have any interest in Michael's further educational or occupational trajectory beyond his actual sporting performance. On the other hand, Michael felt under pressure to meet the club's expectations and convince its coaching staff and officials to offer him a better and longer contract. "I know the game and it was like [going] from one place to the other and there was not ... much time to study or [to] go to school," he explained regarding the difficulties of pursuing occupational alternatives while being on loan.[25] Hence, without learning the language or other skills to prepare for his career after football, he placed his hope solely on succeeding in football. "Actually ... at that moment, it was all about football," he recalled. However, being a senior high school graduate in his home country, he would have considered further education in Sweden, "if I had the opportunity to stay."[26] His hope for a better contract did not materialize. Today, after several loans and short-term stays with different clubs on the European and northern African football periphery, he is back home in West Africa, playing for a Premier League club. Now in his late twenties, his international career is likely over. However, he still has not pursued any postcareer plans. Although he has some ideas about taking courses in information technology in the future, these remain vague.

Some African players do not want or do not see the need to promote their occupational opportunities beyond their football careers, particularly when young players make their first steps in professional football. It is common among African players at this stage to embrace opportunities to play football without thinking about alternatives in case of failure. Following in the footsteps of Michael Essien or Samuel Eto'o and living the dream of professional European football is what is on their minds. Referring to his first steps in northern European football, Ibrahim remembered how that period was characterized by a hopeful and enthusiastic sense: "'Now I can make it.' Now ... that they [a club in northern Europe] give me a contract, I can show them I can play football. Maybe [to] get [to] a higher level [and] to go somewhere [better]."[27] Nevertheless, since his dream of making it in football has not materialized, and he has had to embark on a precarious profession in the health sector instead, his trajectory underlines the need for professional footballers to consider alternative occupational strategies during their careers, rather than afterward.

Ibrahim's story is in line with earlier observations among ethnic minority athletes in other contexts. Pointing to Black athletes in North America, Harry Edwards argued in the 1980s that the majority of them do not have occupational strategies or even employment options for their postcareer lives.[28] Although unemployment and precarious labor are thus serious issues following the conclusion of their careers, they do not achieve the economic standing of their nonathlete peers over the course of their lives. Moreover, the importance of successful educational or occupational preparation during sporting careers for future livelihoods among African athletes is underlined by studies in southern and eastern African contexts.[29] Consequently, waiting until one's career has concluded before embarking on preparations for future occupational trajectories is a risky decision for African (migrant) athletes.

In the absence of support, motivation, or knowledge concerning adequate occupational alternatives, many former players realize their limited options very late and attempt to remain in the football business, for example as coaches or agents. Again, many lack sufficient qualifications for these careers and find it hard to compete in this highly competitive business. Often it is only when they reach the ends of their careers that players realize the difficulties and challenges associated with their occupational trajectories. Moreover, having reached the conclusion of their careers, it could already be too late to enter sports management or coaching. For example, despite his job in the health sector, Ibrahim's plan is to become a professional coach in Denmark. However, since he did not have the needed certificates or a network to embark on such a career on a professional level, he started to train some children in his neighborhood and a youth team of his former club. Nevertheless, because of his job training as an assistant nurse, he had to abandon this undertaking. "I have to train the kids three times a week and when they are playing a game on the weekend I have to follow them. But, I couldn't do it. I need to go to school. I need to work to support myself. So, I couldn't do it."[30]

Remaining in the football business and becoming a coach or player agent after retiring from active playing nevertheless remains an appealing option, and the experiences gained and networks built over the years in professional football abroad may serve as a ticket for some. In this way, football can be a door opener for making a living abroad following an active career. Yet there are only a few examples of African players who have made a career as a coach or player agent in Europe. Existing stereotypes in the European football business, such as an allegation that Black players are unable to coach, prevent many African players from embarking on professional football–related jobs after their careers end, with the result that only 1 percent of coaches are Black and ethnic minority.[31] Further, regulations in many European nation-states regarding immigration and citizenship often disadvantage non-European migrants. Instead, former African footballers have become coaches or player agents, or are otherwise occupied in the football industry only after returning to their countries of origin, even if their initial plan was to stay in Europe and pursue their postcareer livelihoods there. Hence, not being able to live and work in their country of choice (and in which they had probably stayed for years during a career) adds to players' occupational challenges and postcareer precarity.

Postcareer Precarity, Occupational Challenges, and Future Research

So far, the few accounts of postcareer trajectories (and rumors of certain postcareer occupations) of footballing celebrities have over-shadowed the precarious experiences of the many other, less success-ful players in the business. Although occupational challenges among retired players are a general observation in the football industry, they are especially significant among the majority of transnational African players. Facing various kinds of structural obstacles, and with a lack of knowledge and support to plan or provide for postcareer trajectories, they often face problematic livelihoods if their careers are not exception-ally successful. Hence, precarious experiences during one's active career often lead to occupational challenges afterward.

From an economic perspective, and considering our focus on north-ern Europe, playing football on a professional level (yet often in lower tier divisions) usually does not imply a salary that guarantees a well-off future for African football migrants. Hence, even in Denmark, Sweden, and other states with a higher degree of social welfare than other West-ern countries, many players face precarious postcareer trajectories when approaching the end of their professional sporting activity.

However, African football migrants are not just victims of an un-favorable global football industry. In addition to facing structural con-straints, migrant players often expend little effort on postcareer planning or have overly optimistic economic expectations connected to their active careers. Although their seemingly carefree approach adds to the ambiva-lence in the experience of precarity for African football migrants, it also leads the way to further questions in relation to the empirical scope of the concept. Whereas occupational challenges form only part of what pre-carity implies, future studies in the realm of African football migration need to take further dimensions into account. In order to consider how precarity plays out over time and space, it will be important to acknowledge the various and dynamic hopes, risks, and uncertainties that players face over their careers, from a transnational perspective that highlights the entanglement of these factors with players' social environments at home.[32] Overall, the inclusion of a focus on after-career experiences of migrant players contributes to a more comprehensive picture in the study of African football migration (and of sports migration from the so-called Global South more generally). This is because athletes' migration projects are not least a matter of complex transnational and long-term negotiations that affect their lifeworlds beyond the course of their active careers abroad.

Notes

1. Indeed, Assou-Ekotto extended his contract with the French-side FC Metz and continued his sporting career in the following season. See Matthew Smith, "Benoit Assou-Ekotto Laughs Off Suggestions He Could Quit Football to Become a Porn Star ... and Reveals What Happened When His Mother Found Out about His Supposed Career Change," *Daily Mail*, May 28, 2017, http://www.dailymail.co.uk/sport/football/article-4550052/Benoit-Assou-Ekotto-rejects-claim-porn-star.html.

2. Paul Darby, "Moving Players, Traversing Perspectives: Global Value Chains, Production Networks and Ghanaian Football Labour Migration," *Geoforum* 50 (2013): 46–47.

3. Todd Cleveland, *Following the Ball. The Migration of African Soccer Players across the Portuguese Empire, 1949–1975* (Athens: Ohio University Press, 2017), 211–13.

4. Gary Armstrong, "The Global Footballer and the Local War-zone: George Weah and Transnational Networks in Liberia, West Africa," *Global Networks* 7, no. 2 (2007): 231.

5. Darby, "Moving Players, Traversing Perspectives"; James Esson, "A Body and a Dream at a Vital Conjuncture: Ghanaian Youth, Uncertainty and the Allure of Football," *Geoforum* 47 (2013): 84–92; Christian Ungruhe, "'Natural Born Sportsmen': Processes of Othering and Self-Charismatization of African Professional Footballers in Germany," *African Diaspora* 6, no. 2 (2013): 196–217; Nienke van der Meij and Paul Darby, "'No One Would Burden the Sea and Then Never Get Any Benefit': Family Involvement in Players' Migration to Football Academies in Ghana," in *Football and Migration: Perspectives, Places, Players*, ed. Richard Elliott and John Harris (London: Routledge, 2014),

150–79; Christian Ungruhe, "Mobilities at Play: The Local Embedding of Transnational Connections in West African Football Migration," *International Journal of the History of Sport* 33, no. 15 (2016): 1767–85; and Christian Ungruhe and James Esson, "A Social Negotiation of Hope: Male West African Youth, 'Waithood' and the Pursuit of Social Becoming through Football," *Boyhood Studies* 10, no. 1 (2017): 22–43.

6. See Sine Agergaard and Christian Ungruhe, "Ambivalent Precarity: Career Trajectories and Temporalities in Highly Skilled Sports Labor Migration from West Africa to Northern Europe," *Anthropology of Work Review* 37, no. 2 (2016): 67–78; Raffaele Poli, "Migrations and Trade of African Football Players: Historic, Geographical and Cultural Aspects," *Afrika Spectrum* 41, no. 3 (2006): 393–414; Raffaele Poli, "African Migrants in Asian and European Football: Hopes and Realities," *Sport in Society* 13, no. 6 (2010): 1001–1011; and Christian Ungruhe, "Ein prekäres Spiel: Erfahrungen von Risiken und Unsicherheit unter afrikanischen Profifußballern in Deutschland," *Berliner Blätter—ethnographische und ethnologische Beiträge* 77 (2018): 94–114.

7. We would like to thank the Joint Committee for Nordic Research Councils in the Humanities and Social Sciences (NOS-HS) for financing our research. We are grateful to all participants and informants involved.

8. See Guy Standing, *The Precariat: The New Dangerous Class* (London: Bloomsbury Academic, 2011).

9. See Agergaard and Ungruhe, "Ambivalent Precarity."

10. The concept of precarity encompasses more dimensions than those related to occupational and economic uncertainty. See Standing, *The Precariat*; and Carl-Ulrik Schierup and Martin Bak Jørgensen, eds., *Politics of Precarity. Migrant Conditions, Struggles and Experiences* (Leiden: Brill, 2016.). While we have limited the analytical scope in this chapter for reasons of a more in-debt engagement with the occupational uncertainties in transnational footballers' postcareers, we have outlined the various dimensions of precarity at play in the realm of transnational African football migration in a previous publication (see Agergaard and Ungruhe "Ambivalent Precarity").

11. See Dorothee Alfermann and Natalia Stambulova, "Career Transitions and Career Termination," in *Handbook of Sport Psychology*, 3rd ed. ed. Gershon Tenenbaum and Robert C. Eklund (New York: Wiley, 2007), 712–36; and Sunghee Park, David Lavallee, and David Tod, "Athletes' Career Transition out of Sport: A Systematic Review," *International Review of Sport and Exercise Psychology* 6, no. 1 (2013): 22–53.

12. Fifpro 2016, "Global Employment Report: Working Conditions in Professional Football," https://www.fifpro.org/media/xdjhlwbo/working-conditions-in-professional-football.pdf.

13. Uwe Ritzer, "Ausgekickt, rausgekickt," 2011, http://www.sueddeutsche .de/geld/arbeitslose-fussballer-ausgekickt-rausgekickt-1.1128276.

14. J. Maseko and Jhalukpreya Surujlal, "Retirement Planning among South African Professional Soccer Players: A Qualitative Study of Players' Perceptions," *African Journal for Physical Health Education, Recreation and Dance* 17, no. 2 (2011): 157–71; and Elijah G. Rintaugu, Andanje Mwisukha, and M. A. Monyeki, "From Grace to Grass: Kenyan Soccer Players' Career Transition and Experiences in Retirement," *African Journal for Physical Activity and Health Sciences* 22, no. 1 (2016): 163–75.

15. See also Martin J. Roderick, *The Work of Professional Football: A Labour of Love?* (London: Routledge, 2006).

16. Poli, "Migrations and Trade of African Football Players"; and Poli, "African Migrants in Asia and European Football."

17. All the names of the informants have been changed by the authors to guarantee anonymity.

18. Ibrahim, interview with author, Copenhagen, Denmark, November 6, 2016.

19. Sine Agergaard and Tatiana V. Ryba, "Migration and Career Transitions in Professional Sports: Transnational Athletic Careers in a Psychological and Sociological Perspective," *Sociology of Sport Journal* 31, no. 2 (2014): 228–47.

20. Sine Agergaard, "When Globalisation and Migration Meet National and Local Talent Development," in *When Sport Meets Business: Capabilities, Challenges, Critiques,* ed. Ulrik Wagner, Rasmus K. Storm, and Klaus Nielsen (London: Sage, 2017), 30–42.

21. Tony, interview with author, Jutland, Denmark, September 25, 2016.

22. Tony interview, September 25, 2016.

23. Michael, interview with author, Accra, Ghana, April 20, 2016.

24. Michael interview, April 20, 2016.

25. Michael interview, April 20, 2016.

26. Michael interview, April 20, 2016.

27. Ibrahim interview, November 6, 2016.

28. Harry Edwards, "Race in Contemporary American Sports," *National Forum* 62, no. 1 (1982): 21.

29. See Maseko and Surujlal, "Retirement Planning among South African Professional Soccer Players"; Tshepang Tshube and Deborah L. Feltz, "The Relationship between Dual-Career and Post-sport Career Transition among Elite Athletes in South Africa, Botswana, Namibia and Zimbabwe," *Psychology of Sport and Exercise* 21 (2015): 109–14; and Rintaugu, Mwisukha, and Monyeki, "From Grace to Grass."

30. Ibrahim interview, November 6, 2016.

31. Steven Bradbury, "Institutional Racism, Whiteness and the Under-representation of Minorities in Leadership Positions in Football in Europe," *Soccer and Society* 14, no. 3 (2013): 296–314.

32. Ernest Y. Acheampong, "Giving Back to Society: Evidence from African Sports Migrants," *Sport in Society* 22, no. 12 (2019): 2045–64; and Christian Ungruhe and Sine Agergaard, "Cultural Transitions? Transcultural and Border-crossing Activities among Sport Labour Migrants," *Sport in Society* 23, no. 4 (2020): 717–33.

SEVEN

Sporting Biographies

THIRTEEN

Black Physical Culture and Weight Lifting in South Africa

FRANCOIS CLEOPHAS

A vast international body of literature exists on apartheid and sports. Yet there remains a virtual absence of scholarship that centers on South African Blacks in international sports developments from the 1930s to the 1950s. This chapter adds to this skeletal narrative by exploring the transition of physical culture to weight lifting in South Africa, primarily through the contributions of the South African–born, Indian physical culturalist, Coomerasamy Gauesa (Milo) Pillay. Pillay lived during a time when racial discrimination against South African Blacks was at its peak, affecting sports participation at local, national, and international levels. Through Pillay's efforts, however, which are outlined in this chapter, South African Blacks gained visibility in the outside world. In this chapter, I challenge the conventional conclusion that Oliver Clarence Oehley "can rightfully be described as the father of South African weight-lifting."[1] Instead, I demonstrate how Pillay promoted physical culture and weight lifting beginning in the 1920s. An exploration of Pillay's life also dispels the notion of strongmen as lacking political agency. Pillay was by all accounts the first Black sports administrator to officially engage the White South African Olympic authorities and exhibited a subtle, yet highly effective, brand of activism.

My reconstruction of Pillay's life, which was facilitated by means of a personal interview with his daughter, Jennifer Gelderbloem, and research in private and public archives, is significant in four particular ways. First, Dennis Brutus, an antiapartheid sports activist, has stated that it is possible that the much-lauded and -documented nonracial sports movement in South Africa, in fact, started with Pillay in 1936.[2] Second, Pillay facilitated the shift from physical culture to weight lifting by appearing on stage performing scientific lifts as well as feats of strength.[3] Whereas Hendrik Cornelius Tromp van Diggelen portrayed himself in the Eugen Sandow image of gladiator sandals and leopard skins, Pillay presented himself in the George Hackenschmidt portrayal of the champion all-round athlete.[4] However, he retained elements of a third-stream physical culturalist by being a "vegetarian, tee-totaller, a non-smoker, a believer in sun bathing and fresh air, trained in an open air gymnasium throughout the year and . . . a great lover of plunges into icy cold water for a swim."[5] Third, I challenge the White monopoly on weight-lifting history in South Africa. In this regard, Milo Pillay has heretofore not been recognized as a physical culturalist and weight lifter who contributed to the development of South African sports. Fourthly, Pillay's political actions shed a spotlight on the nuanced nature of Black resistance to institutionalized racism.

Physical Culture

Physical culture describes various activities in which people have engaged over the centuries to strengthen their bodies, enhance their physiques and health, increase their endurance, fight against aging, and become better athletes.[6] Traditionally, physical culture is associated with Western European classical history, with little impact on or connection to African society. This chapter strives to disrupt this notion.

Weight lifting grew out of physical culture, a concept that became popular during the late nineteenth century and developed in three overlapping streams.[7] The first of these streams was the "born strong man," which blossomed in Europe and America toward the end of the nineteenth century. These individuals were usually natural strongmen from working-class backgrounds, seeking fame and fortune. A misrepresentation about them that persists is that they often had bouts of overeating and drinking that matched their overweight physical appearance and thus did not contribute to the scientific development of physical culture.[8] On the contrary, these strongmen, and women, kept records of their performances and diets.[9] In turn, these records served the purpose of identifying the second stream, the "self-made strong man."

A few of these "strongmen" parlayed their experience of building large muscles into selling training services to the public, from which many made fortunes.[10] A well-known member of this group was the physically attractive Eugen Sandow, who popularized the use of dumbbells in 1887 at Queen Victoria's golden jubilee. Suddenly, however, the muscle-and-moustache strong man faded out of fashion, giving way to the third stream.[11] Characteristic of this stream was that strength and muscles were backgrounded, and the healing of illnesses, usually by means of natural medicines, became paramount.

These three streams consolidated in a physical culture "system" whose adherents "were particular about what they ate, were non-smokers, non-drinkers and abstained from tea and coffee."[12] Some of them, including Bernarr Macfadden, Charles Atlas, Tromp van Diggelen, and Eugen Sandow, made fortunes (and losses) out of selling physical culture programs. [13] After being prosecuted in England for publishing physique pictures in his magazine, *Physical Culture* (1892), Bernarr Macfadden restarted the magazine *Physical Culture* in New York in 1898. By then, the British version had become *Health and Strength*.[14]

Male physical culturists later specialized in weight training and became known as either weight lifters, bodybuilders, or powerlifters. Before women entered these areas, they initially organized beauty pageants or performed balancing acts. The term *physical culture* was applied to or used by those who viewed themselves as a cut above crass displays of strength and physique and who were, to varying degrees, trained specialists in the field.[15]

Physical culturalists deliberately intended to construct a relationship between physical activity and Greco-Roman heritage.[16] The use of the term *physical culture* suggests a way of life associated with various forms of exercise and other physical activities of the time. These systems of exercise and activities were embedded in beliefs, knowledge, and broader individual practices that are part of a series of transitions of continuity and change over time.[17]

Physical Culture and Weight Lifting in South Africa

Sandow toured South Africa in 1904, and according to the official South African version, this visit stimulated the sport.[18] Sometime during the second decade of the twentieth century, the natural-born strongman Herman Goerner was performing feats of strength in William Pagel's touring circus.[19] Van Diggelen, a third-stream South African physical culturalist, claimed he had advised Goerner to offer his services to this circus.[20] In South Africa, as elsewhere, physical culture evolved into weight lifting and bodybuilding, and in 1928, the South African Weight-Lifting Federation (SAWLF) was established, with the first national weight-lifting championships held in 1933.[21] By 1936, the SAWLF, headquartered in Port Elizabeth, had organized its championship meetings according to British Amateur Weight Lifting rules, inviting entries from the Union of South Africa, Northern Rhodesia (Zambia), and Southern Rhodesia (Zimbabwe), and had arranged a South African Men's and Women's Physical Excellence (Bodybuilding) Competition.[22] The SAWLF was the only recognized governing body south of Cairo that controlled both amateur and professional weight lifting on the African continent.[23] Various physical culture clubs and the efforts of strongmen like Van Diggelen, Matt October, Ron Eland, and Pillay subsequently facilitated a shift from feats of strength to scientific lifts, better known as weight lifting, in South Africa.[24] As mentioned previously, the focus in this chapter is on Pillay.

Milo Pillay

According to the *Sun*, Pillay was born in Queenstown on August 8, 1911, though in our interview his daughter, Jennifer Gelderbloem, stated that her father was born in 1910, and that that he died in Melbourne, Australia on December 15, 1994, from heart failure.[25] She also indicated that her paternal grandparents originated from Pondicherry, India, and immigrated first to Mauritius, then to Queenstown in the Eastern Cape, where Milo grew up as a Hindu boy playing football with Dutch Reformed boys. [26] The family moved to Port Elizabeth in 1929, at the beginning of the Great Depression, and Milo took up employment at Cuthbert's shoe factory.[27]

Because Pillay was classified Indian, he needed a permit to reside in Port Elizabeth and was not allowed to purchase fixed property. He married Christina Barendse, a Christian chambermaid in a local hotel, who was a keen tennis player and also organized the game among the residents in Gelvandale after the family was forcibly removed from their home in Salisbury Park owing to apartheid laws.[28] Gelderbloem recalled that the Pillay home was characterized by an atmosphere of religious tolerance; the mother was a baptized Dutch Reformer, the father was a Hindu who later converted to Catholicism in the 1960s, and the children were Anglican. Pillay endured criticism from sections of the non-White community who questioned why he stayed in the "Black" area of Gelvandale and not the Indian neighborhood of Malabar. Although the house in Gelvandale was a social headquarters for the community and was filled with rackets, clubs, and weights, the children did not share a passion for physical culture.

Yet. Pillay was inspired by Greek mythology and by 1938 was popularly known as "Young Hercules de Milo,"[29] also naming his son Hercules. He was part of a generation of strongmen who were shifting from Sandow's system of "building muscles of Iron" to Hackenschmidt's idea of "forging the iron into the finest steel."[30] Pillay indulged in a variety of sports, including but not limited to sprinting, cycling, shot putting, mountain climbing, and rugby.[31]

POLITICS

Politically, the South African weight-lifting fraternity pursued a path of moderation, and General James Barry Munnik Hertzog, the prime minister, was made patron of the SAWLF in 1937.[32] Pillay's particular approach, common among Black liberals, was to project an apolitical image and engage in protest via letter writing.[33] This was the case in 1945 when he attended a national weight-lifting conference in the Transvaal, organized by Whites, for which he attempted to have the color bar lifted.[34] By remaining on cordial terms with empathetic Whites, he was often able to win concessions. For example, through these relations, he managed to get Kudu Road in Gelvendale tarred, and other roads followed. He also received equipment from the all-White Collegiate Tennis Club.

In practice, Pillay's approach was consistent with political approaches strongly shaped and influenced by organized teachers. Until 1941, the "coloured" teachers organization, the Teachers' League of South Africa (TLSA), had a pro-establishment stance. However, its decision to affiliate with the anti-establishment Non-European Unity Movement (NEUM) that year drastically altered the political character of the organization.[35] Consequently, moderates in the TLSA left the organization to form the Teachers' Educational and Professional Association (TEPA).[36] These two camps formed irreconcilable binaries that reverberated throughout the "Black" community, with both camps extending their activities into physical culture.

Pillay was visible in the TEPA camp. In 1952, when the Goodwood branch of the TEPA presented a display of pyramid building on parallel bars, the judges were Danie Craven, the Springbok rugby coach, Tromp van Diggelen, Milo Pillay, Jack Lunz (a Jewish businessman who distributed bodybuilding products), Anne Ross (an American female diving champion), and Jean Brownlee (holder of the 1952 Ms. Cape Town title, for White women).[37] Owing to his affiliation to black weightlifting federations, Pillay drew the attention of the apartheid government, and he eventually emigrated to Australia in 1982, at the age of seventy. He left behind in Port Elizabeth the Toynbee Club, a physical culture club. Consistent with his actions in South Africa, once in Melbourne, he started a weight-lifting club, with the support of the National Credit Union.[38]

CAREER

According to Pillay, he started training on November 29, 1920, with train rails and two fifty-pound block weights used for scales, after he had witnessed Herman Goerner's feats of strength in the circus and watched Elmo Lincoln in the film, *Tarzan of the Apes*.[39] It is believed that he made his initial public appearance as a strongman at fifteen years of age at a school carnival.[40] He reportedly gained the title of the Strongest Youth in South Africa in 1928, which he retained until 1932.[41] The following year he established the Apollo School of Weight-Lifting, and according to the *Sun*, it was run on "an international basis."[42] By 1933 it had become known as the Herculean Weight-lifting and Physical Culture Club and was the first health and strength club in Port Elizabeth, as well as the first weight-lifting club in Port Elizabeth.[43] A manifestation of Pillay's growing stature, the following year the club was renamed The Milo Academy, and from it emerged the Eastern Province Weight-Lifting Union and the SAWLF.[44] Confirming the far-reaching effects that the Milo Academy had, some years later the Black press reported that it had been an "effective coaching and training centre . . . having trained over 400 young men of the South African Air Force, who were stationed in Port Elizabeth between 1929 and 1951 and over 7,000 men and women of all nationalities in physical culture, body-building and weight-lifting."[45]

Through Pillay, weight lifting became a popular sport in the Eastern Cape region, and a club was opened by M. R. Baderoon on Malay Street, Uitenhage, in 1936, while the East London Physical Culture Club existed under the secretary David Jones.[46] Although based in Port Elizabeth, the Milo Academy's influence was also evident elsewhere; in 1934, one of its members issued a challenge to a member of the Accro Club (established in 1933) in Cape Town to a weight-lifting or wrestling bout.[47]

In 1933 and 1934, Pillay won the national weight-lifting championships, and he was runner-up in 1935.[48] Although he retired from active weight lifting in 1935 with a torn leg muscle, he was appointed technical adviser to the Eastern Province Weightlifting Union, and reports indicate that he was selected to represent South Africa at an international weight-lifting contest in Lourenço Marques (present-day Maputo) as an official Springbok athlete in 1937.[49] As the decade neared its conclusion, in March 1938 he displayed his self-designed, three-inch grip barbell, nicknamed "Suicide Milo," which is still believed to be the thickest grip barbell ever employed by any weight lifter in the world at that time.[50]

Despite his personal success and the profile of the Milo Academy, Pillay and other non-White athletes nevertheless confronted various forms of racism that circumscribed their potential. For example, in 1947 officials from the Milo Academy wrote to the South African Olympic & British Empire Games Association (SAOEGA) informing them that, eager to showcase some of the talent centered at the club, they intended to send some Black amateur boxers, wrestlers, weight lifters, and athletes to participate in the Olympic Games in 1948 and pleaded for their recognition.[51] The SAOEGA's subsequent dismissal of Pillay's plea highlights the political impotence of these Black weight lifters.

This ineffectiveness was exacerbated by organizational incompetence. In 1952, for example, the Western Province Weight-Lifting and Body Building Association (a Black organization) was established. This association organized a physical excellence competition in the Salt River Railway Institute on December 12 of that year, with Tromp van Diggelen as one of the five judges. Yet the *Sun* described the program as "the dullest presented to a Cape Town audience for a long time, the comperé was boring, aspects ran late, there were long delays between events, and several changes were made in the program."[52] The audience apparently also booed decisions made by the judges.

His focus on domestic affairs notwithstanding, Pillay also had an international perspective. For example, the *Sun* reported in 1950 that he had negotiated with physical culture clubs in Ethiopia, Sudan, Liberia, Kenya, Uganda, Tanganyika (Tanzania), French Equatorial Africa (Chad, the Central African Republic, Cameroon, the Republic of the Congo, and Gabon), Nyasaland (Malawi), the Belgian Congo, and Portuguese East (Mozambique) and West Africa (Angola) to hold a conference in Lourenço Marques in June 1951 and to form the Pan-African Federation of Physical Education. The aim was to promote and encourage "physical culture, body building, athletics, gymnastics, and all other sports pertaining to physical education among individuals on the African continent for their physical, mental and moral upliftment."[53] The exact outcome of this initiative remains unclear, but Black bodybuilding and weight lifting undeniably grew organizationally from that time. The first South African Weight-Lifting and Bodybuilding

Federation (Non-European) championship was held in 1951.[54] The following year, the national body, the South African Weightlifters and Body Builders Association, devised an ambitious plan for a "coloured" Olympiad in 1953 to be staged in Port Elizabeth. Pillay contacted the Olympic Councils of Denmark, France, India, Sweden, Brazil, Argentina, and Pakistan, all of which indicated that they encouraged South African Black weight lifters and bodybuilders to seek representation as a team at the Olympic Games in Melbourne.[55] Unsurprisingly, this effort remained unrealized.

Pillay and other physical culturalists were products of their time and also part of a broader generation that had to work determinedly to demonstrate their fitness for inclusion as equal citizens in White South African society.[56] In order to understand their struggle for equal citizenry, it is necessary to understand how they responded to the constraints and possibilities generated by the sociocultural context in which they operated. Milo Pillay, and by implication the sport of weight lifting, operated largely apolitically in a period characterized by intense state racism, leaving Blacks with few political options other than seeking acceptance from White authorities. I have attempted to reconstruct this in this chapter, which is underscored by Pillay's absence in resistance politics. However, as Hendrik Snyders points out, "going against the popular grain of activism is not a sufficient excuse to marginalize, stereotype, or vilify individuals for their position at critical times during the course of history."[57] Pillay's struggle was for acceptance and recognition by White society, not a quest for power. That struggle would only come to fruition later, with the formation of the South African Council on Sport in 1973.

Notes

1. RGN-Sportondersoek, *Verslag van die Werkommitee: Sportgeskiedenis* (Pretoria: RGN, 1982), 54.

2. Cornelius Thomas, *Time with Dennis: Conversations, Quotations and Snapshots* (Selbourne, South Africa: Wendy's Book Lounge, 2012), 8.

3. E. H. Lawrence, "C.G. Pillay—South Africa's Superman," *Superman* 9, no. 3 (December 1938), 72.

4. Ina Zweiniger-Barielowska, *Managing the Body: Beauty, Health and Fitness in Britain, 1880–1939* (New York: Oxford University Press, 2011), 43.

5. Lawrence, "C. G. Pillay," 72.

6. Janice Todd, "Reflections on Physical Culture: Defining Our field and Protecting Its Integrity," *Iron Game History: The Journal of Physical Culture* 13, nos. 2–3 (November/December 2015): 5.

7. Benarr Macfadden, *Macfadden's Encyclopaedia of Physical Culture*, vol. 1 (New York: Macfadden, 1928), 3.

8. Francois Johannes Cleophas, "Physical Education and Physical Culture in the Coloured Community of the Western Cape" (PhD diss., Stellenbosch University, 2009), 13.

9. W. L. Parsley, "Famous Female Athletes of the Past: Including the Amazing French Actress Who Broke Horseshoes," *Health and Strength* 56, no. 13 (1935): 341; and Terence Colquitt Todd, "The History of Resistance Exercise and Its Role in United States Education" (PhD diss., University of Texas, 1966), 141.

10. Cleophas, "Physical Education and Physical Culture," 13.

11. Christopher Connolly and Hetty Einzig, *The Fitness Jungle, Stage 2 Fitness: The Exercise Survival Guide* (London: Century Hutchinson, 1986), 207.

12. Cleophas, "Physical Education and Physical Culture," 14.

13 Michael Fallon, "'Screwball' Macfadden (Holes in His Hat) Died a Millionaire," *Health and Strength* 84, no. 23 (1955): 11; Martinus Bart, "DC Boonzaier se Tromp van Diggelen haal R27 830," *Die Burger Veilings*, April 23, 2016, 1; and Zweiniger-Barielowska, *Managing the Body*, 9.

14. Fallon, "Screwball," 24.

15. David Kirk, "Physical Culture, Physical Education and Relational Analysis," *Sport, Education and Society* 4, no. 1 (1999): 65.

16. Kirk, "Physical Culture, Physical Education and Relational Analysis."

17. Kirk, "Physical Culture, Physical Education and Relational Analysis."

18. Zweiniger-Barielowska, *Managing the Body*, 96; and RGN-Sportondersoek, *Verslag van die Werkommitee*, 54.

19. Edward Ashton, "Herman Goerner, Enigma of Strength," *Health and Strength* 76, no. 6 (April 10, 1947): 232.

20. Tromp van Diggelen, *Worthwhile Journey* (London: William Heinemann, 1955), 218.

21. Lawrence, "C. G. Pillay," 54.

22. Anonymous, "South African Weight-lifting Championships," *Health and Strength* 59, no. 18 (October 31, 1936): 632.

23. Lawrence, "C. G. Pillay," 72.

24. Matt October first made a name for himself when he won the feath-erweight title at the South African Pageant in 1937, pejoratively dubbed the "Olympics of the slaves"; "South African Non-European Sports Pageant," *Sun*, January 8, 1937, 8. William Ronald Eland represented England in the 1948 Olympic Games after being shunned by the South African Olympic and British Empire Games Association because of a color bar; J. Matthews, "The Cinderella Sport Comes into Its Own," *Sun*, November 17, 1950, 7; and Lawrence, "C. G. Pillay," 72.

25. "Thirty-One Years Service to Weight-lifting in South Africa," *Sun*, November 23, 1951, 7. His daughter, Jennifer Gelderbloem, stated that he was born in 1910. Jennifer Gelderbloem, interview with author, Garden Court Hotel, Somerset-West, December 14, 2015.

26. Gelderbloem interview, December 14, 2015.

27. Gelderbloem interview, December 14, 2015.

28. An announcement in the press by P. W. Botha, then minister of "coloured" affairs, on May 1, 1965, that South End had to be cleared to make way for urban renewal resulted in the forced removal of Milo Pillay to a distant part of Port Elizabeth. This government act affected all "population groups." They were to be scattered to distant, desolate, cold, and isolated areas. "Coloureds" were to move to the northern areas of the metropole (Helenvale, Gelvandale, Gelvan Park, Salt Lake, Arcadia, and West End), Indians to Malabar, Chinese to Kabega Park, and Africans to New Brighton and Walmer Location. A limited number of Whites were dispersed throughout the city.

29. Lawrence, "C. G. Pillay," 71.

30. Zweiniger-Barielowska, *Managing the Body*, 43.

31. Lawrence, "C. G. Pillay," 71.

32. "Thirty-One Years Service," 7.

33. Gelderbloem interview, December 14, 2015; and Mohammed Adhikari, "*Let Us Live for Our Children*": *The Teachers' League of South Africa, 1913–1940* (Cape Town: Buchu Books, 1993), 57.

34. *Cape Standard*, February 6, 1945, 4.

35. Paul Ross Hendricks, "Engaging Apartheid: The Teachers' League of South Africa in the Western Cape, 1985–1989" (MEd thesis, University of Cape Town, 2002), 8.

36. Adhikari, "*Let Us Live for Our Children*", 71.

37. "Cavalcade of Health and Strength," *Sun*, October 24, 1952, 7.

38. Gelderbloem interview, December 14, 2015. During the nineteenth century Toynbee Hall, in England, had as its aim "to bring University culture into direct contact with the poorest of the people." See Charles Booth, *Labour and Life of the People* (London: Williams and Norgate, 1891), 122.

39. "Thirty-One Years Service," 7; and Lawrence, "C. G. Pillay," 71.

40. Lawrence, "C. G. Pillay," 71.

41. "Thirty-One Years Service," 7.

42. "Port Elizabeth Physical Educational Club," *Sun*, July 15, 1949, 4.

43. Lawrence, "C. G. Pillay," 72.

44. "Thirty-One Years Service," 7; and League Registrar, "Health & Strength League Gossip," *Health and Strength* 65, no. 5 (August 5, 1939): 196. The Milo Academy name was, however, used interchangeably with the Herculean Weight-lifting Club.

45. "Thirty-One Years Service," 7.

46. Anonymous, "We Hear," *Health and Strength* 59, no. 18 (October 31, 1936): 633.

47. "Annual Gymnastic Display," *Sun*, November 23, 1934, 8; and *Sun*, June 8, 1934, 2.

48. "Thirty-One Years Service," 7.

49. "Thirty-One Years Service," 7; and Lawrence, "C. G. Pillay," 72.

50. Lawrence, "C. G. Pillay," 72.

51. South African Olympic & British Empire Games Association, Minutes of the meeting of the Executive Committee of the South African Olympic & British Empire Games Association, held at the Carlton Hotel at 8 pm on Monday, January 13, 1947, 2, author's collection.

52. "Paul Abrahams Wins Another Physique Contest," *Sun*, December 19, 1952, 5.

53. "Pan-African Federation of Physical Education," *Sun*, November 3, 1950, 6.

54. "Weight-lifting News," *Sun*, July 4, 1952, 7.

55. "Coloured Olympiad!," *Sun*, November 14, 1952, 2.

56. Hendrik Snyders, "Subservient Jester? Gasant ('Gamat') Ederoos Behardien: Reinterpreting a Marginal Figure in South African Sport History" in *Exploring Decolonising Themes in SA Sport History: Issues and Challenges*, ed. Francois Johannes Cleophas (Stellenbosch: Sun Media, 2018), 23–34.

57. Snyders, "Subservient Jester?"

FOURTEEN

Sprinting Past the End of Empire

Seraphino Antao and the Promise of Sports in Kenya, 1960–64

MICHELLE SIKES

On December 12, 1963, the Union Jack came down in Kenya. Thousands witnessed a midnight flag ceremony in Nairobi in which the British flag was lowered and replaced by the black, red, green, and white flag of Kenya. Fireworks and shouts of "uhuru" greeted this symbol of nationhood unfurling over the capital. Sixty-eight years of British colonial rule in Kenya had come to an end. Ten months later, in October 1964, sprinter Seraphino Antao hoisted the Kenya flag and led the Kenya contingent into the giant Olympic stadium in Tokyo for the opening ceremony of the 18th Olympiad. His journey there is a story of one man's quest for athletic glory alongside one country's drive for independence.

"Uhuru," the Swahili word for freedom, was said to be the most popular word in East Africa the year that Kenya became independent.[1] The word peppered the pages of the local press and the speeches of politicians vying to control the state. Sporting competitions of various types, organized in Nairobi around the edges of the main flag ceremony in December 1963, also carried "uhuru" significance. Boxers from Kenya were put through several phases of an intensive training program before clashing with the Sudanese in a much-anticipated Uhuru boxing tournament.[2] The "Uhuru [football] competition" featured "the cream of Scotland's amateur talent," with Scotland, fresh from a shared victory at the 1963 British Home Championship, sending its best team to Nairobi for the event.[3] A Uhuru Cup volleyball tournament preceded the flag-raising ceremony.[4] Three days later, a full day of horse racing was held on the Ngong racetrack in Nairobi and dubbed the Uhuru Meeting. The winner of the main race of the day received £300 and the Uhuru Cup from Prime Minister Jomo Kenyatta.[5]

This extensive uhuru lineup also featured a track meet. Officially branded the Independence Celebrations International Athletics Meeting, the Uhuru Meeting, as it was more commonly called, drew athletes from the United States and Britain as well as countries in Europe and Africa. Kenya's best hope for glory was Seraphino "Seffie" Antao. Known as the "Flying Gazelle," Antao was one of the first athletes to put Kenya on the map of international athletics. Antao had, in the words of one journalist at the time, "stormed his way to the top of world athletics" the year before when he defeated the Commonwealth's best to win the 100 yards and the 220 yards at the 1962 Games held in Perth, Australia.[6] Antao also won the English Amateur Athletic Association championships that year at the same distances. For these sprinting successes, Antao was awarded the prestigious Helms Athletics Foundation award, given annually to the African continent's Sportsman of the Year.

By 1962 Kenya had only twice before participated in the British Empire and Commonwealth Games, as they were then called.[7] Its team in Perth included an athlete who would most prominently go on to strengthen the dynasty of Kenyan distance runners, Kipchoge "Kip" Keino. Yet at the 1962 Games, Keino finished eleventh in the three miles and failed to progress beyond his heat of the one mile.[8] It was, as a journalist at that time put it, Kenya's "smooth, panther-like sprinter," Antao, who claimed the spotlight when he became the first Kenyan to win gold at a major international track competition.[9] Two years later, "Antao Kenya!" was the roar of twelve thousand fans at the 1964 East African championships. They were delighted by his victory in the 220-yard dash, which equaled the Commonwealth Games record of 20.5 seconds set by Peter Radford of Britain.[10] Antao was intent on becoming the first athlete to win Olympic gold for newly independent Kenya, afterward declaring, "In Tokyo, I am going to be even faster!"[11]

This chapter aims both to introduce a little known yet very talented athlete and provide insights into the constraints and possibilities that faced Kenyans on the cusp of seizing nationhood. It does so by focusing on the Uhuru Athletics Meeting of December 1963, in which Antao was called upon to represent the newly independent Kenya against the best of Britain's sprinters. Colonial Kenya was a society fissured by racial discrimination, but with Kenya on the cusp of self-rule, Antao represented the possibilities of the era.

Seraphino: 1960s Super Sprinter

"Kenya's athletic fans will see star sprinter Seraphino Antao at his fabulous best at the Uhuru [Athletics] Meeting in Nairobi on December 10," Ray Batchelor promised the Kenyan press ahead of the track meet, one of a series of Uhuru events scattered around the date of Kenya's independence in 1963.[12] With the country in the midst of celebrating its imminent freedom from British colonial rule, the long-serving former Coast Sports Officer was being flown to Mombasa to prepare Antao for his "vital Uhuru clash" with one of Britain's best sprinters.[13]

For years, Batchelor had coached sprinters from Mombasa's Goan community, four of whom—Alcino Rodrigues, Joe Faria, Sylvano Pinto, and Antao—under his tutelage had run the 100 yards in under ten seconds. But Batchelor was best known for coaching Antao to the Empire and Commonwealth Games sprint double victory in 1962. At the Perth Games that year, Antao had become the first runner from Africa to win two gold medals, with victories in both the 100 and 220 yards.

Born in October 1937 in Mombasa, Antao was the oldest of the seven children born to Diego Manuel and Anna Maria. His father worked for the East African railways, and the family moved often. His parents had immigrated to Kenya from Chandor in Goa, a small area on the western coast of India. More than four centuries of Portuguese rule had brought to Goa Western institutions, laws, and religious beliefs. Recruited for the advantages conferred by this blend of cultures,

Goans diffused across the British and Portuguese empires. By the early twentieth century, drawn across the ocean to East Africa by economic opportunities in the railway, government administration, and business, the Goan community was firmly established in Kenya.[14]

Colonial Kenya was a divided society, highly structured by racial inequality, in which the tiny sliver of White settlers enjoyed significant political power and dominated the economy. Along with entrenched racial discrimination, the territory was marked by uneven regional variation and politicized ethnic cleavages, which in the 1950s erupted into the violent conflict known as the Mau Mau uprising.[15] The hostilities were followed in the early 1960s by rancorous constitutional negotiations, with trust difficult to build across ethnic, racial, and political lines.

Within this stratified society, Goans established their own churches, clubs, schools, and hospitals within the "Asian" sections of towns and cities. Politically and culturally, however, Goans in Kenya largely held themselves apart from other Asian groups.[16] According to one observer of the Goan community of Mombasa in the 1950s and 1960s, "Goa was all around—in the Konkani some of them spoke, in the smells from their kitchens, in their music, and in assorted cultural prescriptions, like crossing oneself in Catholic fashion when faced with uncertainty."[17] Sports contributed to this sense of Goan community, and Antao would become a celebrated son within it.

His was an athletic family. "The Antaos were quite sports minded," he said in an interview years later. "My cousin Effie Antao played football for Kenya. Pascoal Antao played for [football powerhouse in Goa] Salgaocars years back, and his son Trevor is also a good footballer."[18] His siblings also competed in track, with one sister, Ignaciana ("Iggy"), standing out as a sprinter, and his brother, Rosario, excelling as a long jumper.

Antao started his own athletics career relatively late, after graduating from Mombasa's Goan High School, where he played football. Antao's place of work, the Landing and Shipping Company, encouraged its employees to take part in various sports. In 1956, Antao decided to take part in athletics, where his talent for running was immediately apparent. Initially, his ambitions were modest: "All I was aiming for was to represent the Coast in the national championships."[19] By the following year, Antao had set new Kenyan and East African records in both the 100- and 200-yard events, and he earned selection for the Kenyan team at the 1958 Empire Games in Cardiff, Wales. Antao failed to advance beyond the heats, and he would later describe this first trip overseas as a "learning experience."[20]

In the first half of the century, sports in Kenya had been established, organized, and played along segregated lines, with the colony's de facto color bar separating athletes by race. Antao's emergence as a runner came just after athletics became desegregated, with national championships contested by athletes of all races. A representative Kenyan team first competed in the 1954 Empire Games held in Vancouver. Their debut failed to yield any medals, however. Nor were medals forthcoming at Kenya's first appearance at the Olympic games in Melbourne two years later. The first medals won by Kenyan athletes at a major track competition were claimed at the Empire and Commonwealth Games in Cardiff in 1958, when Arere Anentia and Bartonjo Rotich finished third in the 6 miles and in the 440-yard hurdles, respectively. As John Bale points out, Kenya by the mid-1950s "did not present an image of a nation of natural runners and potential champions."[21]

The 1960 Rome Olympic games were a turning point for Antao. According to press reports at the time, the Olympics "brought out the best in Kenya's runners," including Antao, who "conquered nerves in the fiery cauldron of the Olympic Stadium."[22] He "scorched home" to win the first heat of the 100 yards and ultimately reached the semifinals, finishing sixth. After the games, Antao was selected to join the Commonwealth relay team that raced against America's best in the 4-by-100 yards at the United States versus Commonwealth track meet held in London's White City stadium. The Commonwealth team tied with the Americans in a world record time of forty seconds.

Antao was by then training seriously under the supervision of Coach Batchelor, who was credited with transforming Antao "from a good footballer into one of the world's top sprinters," and alongside other Goan runners at the Mombasa Achilles Club. Athlete and coach reportedly practiced between two to three hours a day, seven days a week, moving between the Mombasa Municipal Stadium, the East African Railways Sports Club, and Mombasa's soft beaches.

Their efforts were rewarded in 1962. On the cinder track of Perry Lakes Stadium, the venue for the Perth Empire and Commonwealth Games, Antao ran the 100 yards in 9.5 seconds to finish a yard ahead of Tom Robinson of the Bahamas and Australia's Mike Cleary. A few days later, amid windy conditions, Antao finished 4 yards clear of David Jones of England to win the 220 yards. For Antao, the two races were the most memorable of his career. Speaking with the *East African Standard* in 2003, he reminisced: "Joy and pride engulfed my whole body when I hit the tape ahead of everybody else in the 100 yards event with a time of 9.5 secs. My joy was doubled when I bagged the 220 yards gold."[23]

Antao, "Africa's Greyhound"

Sports journalist Tom Clarke called the 1962 Antao-Batchelor pairing "the greatest partnership the Kenya sports world has ever known."[24] However, not long after the Perth Games, Batchelor was made coach of the national football team and transferred to Nakuru, four hundred miles from Mombasa, severing his partnership with the Goan sprinter.[25] Antao found it difficult to train on his own, and his confidence began to falter. When he traveled to Nairobi to receive the Helms Trophy as the athlete of the year for the African continent, his worries were reported by sports journalists, who closely monitored the athlete widely regarded as Kenya's best hope for victories in international athletics. Antao had last competed at the East African Championships in Kampala in August, and according to one *Daily Nation* reporter, he was worried that he would develop habits that could ruin his "chances of collecting a few more medals for Kenya."[26] The papers continued to publicize Antao's pleas for his coach's return to the Coast until, with Kenya's best hopes for uhuru victory resting on the sprinter, the minister for labour and social services, Ngala Mwendwa, at the last minute arranged for Batchelor's temporary transfer back to Mombasa.[27]

Batchelor was given a warm reception upon his return, with Antao reportedly racing down the Port Reitz Airport apron to welcome his coach.[28] Eyeing his star pupil, Batchelor thought Antao was in "good fettle" but underweight.[29] This, he declared, called for "the famous Batchelor diet of Guinness, raw eggs, milk and plenty of meat."[30] Building up Antao's stamina would demand "a lot of work on the seashore with the sea breeze," yet little time remained for athlete and coach to hone Antao's form.[31] With ten days left before the meet, the *Daily Nation* questioned, "Will Batchelor be able to beat this time limit?"[32]

Training began without delay. Antao was determined to reach peak form for the Uhuru Meeting on December 10.[33] His best shape was much anticipated, as it had previously brought Antao close to world record times.[34] Under Batchelor's supervision, he "pound[ed] the track" at Mombasa Stadium, according to press reports at the time.[35] Antao's confidence was also buoyed by his coach's return. The sprinter confided in *Daily Nation* journalist Cyprian Fernandes that he believed his coach's guidance would provide with the "extra something" that he needed to "stand a chance of winning the Uhuru double."[36]

December 10, 1963, dawned hot, windless, and dry in Nairobi: excellent conditions for sprinting.[37] The *Daily Nation* declared the weather just what Antao needed for "his world record bid at the Uhuru celebrations athletic meeting."[38] It also billed the competition as "Kenya's finest-ever gathering of athletes."[39] West Germany had sent athletes to compete in the field events, one of whom was expected to dominate the hammer throw.[40] Two Ethiopians had been invited to contend with Kenyan athletes in the distance events. Other runners from overseas, finding it difficult to adapt to the altitude of Kenya's capital city, were deemed little threat.

Attention was focused on the sprints, however, where "Africa's greyhound Antao" would measure up against British Olympian Ron Jones and other top athletes from Uganda and India.[41] Jones was regarded as Antao's foremost rival, having won bronze medals in sprint relays at the European Championships and at the British Empire and Commonwealth Games the previous year. Yet Antao was favored after besting the British sprinter in head-to-head competition in Perth. Even British team manager Pat Sage, who had seen the Kenyan sprinter compete on several occasions, conceded, "He is great; Antao is a natural."[42] Antao tried to contain everyone's expectations: "I am not saying I am going to win, but I certainly hope to beat Europe's fastest [sprinter] Ron Jones."[43]

Antao won both events. The papers proclaimed that he "slammed" Jones, the man regarded as "England's key hope for the Olympic gold medal."[44] Under the title "Seraphino Whips the Jones Boy," several photos published in the *Daily Nation* captured Antao in motion along the track. The captions explained: "Flying over the furlong . . . that's Seraphino Antao. He speeds to an easy victory in the 220 yards, and Ron Jones is well behind the 'Kenya Express.'"[45] Afterward, Jones pointed out that he had pulled his hamstring three months before the race. The Uhuru meet was the first in which he had competed since the injury. In his words: "I came to Kenya for two reasons, the first to get a crack at Antao and secondly to test the muscle in a very tough international competition. I got both my answers—Antao IS terrific and I have no need to worry about my injury."[46] Antao's racing earned this prediction from Jones: "Seraphino Antao will win the Olympic sprint double in October to become the world's fastest man."

The year of Kenya's independence from British colonial rule, 1963, would, according to one Kenyan paper, "go down in history as the year Kenya got off the mark in world sports."[47] In a roundup of the year's sports highlights, the Uhuru tournaments were noted as having been a success, with Kenya winning every major trophy. Kenya's football team had beaten Scotland's in a close 3–2 match, and its boxing team drubbed the fighters from Sudan. But for winning both the sprints and "slamming Europe's fastest man," the press singled out "Kenya's ace sprinter" as the "best bet to become the first to bring world honours to his country."[48]

Powerful leaders across the political spectrum also paid homage to their fastest countryman in the months leading up to Kenya's independence. When Antao received the Helms award in 1963 from the outgoing British governor, Malcolm McDonald, at Government House, the latter's imperialist position was well in keeping with the international nature of the award granted to the continent's best athlete. Prime Minister Jomo Kenyatta attached his appreciation of Antao's achievements to the national level when he sent Antao a telegram saying, "You have really become Kenya's priceless jewel in sports and shining athletic star. Please accept our profound appreciation of your tremendous success. Kenya shall always be proud of you." Zooming in further, Kenyatta's political rival Ronald Ngala, who hailed from the Coast, was appropriately on hand at the 1963 Coast Provincial Athletics Championships in Mombasa Stadium to present Antao with two awards for winning the Uhuru sprint double.[49]

Historian Mark Dyreson has described sports as an "arena in which Americans have searched for symbols of national identity."[50] Nor is the United States alone in this, as Dyreson points out. In Kenya, as calls for "uhuru" became increasingly loud, nationalist politicians looked to the symbolic plane, and to Kenya's first track champion, in their efforts to bring some sense of common purpose to the people of the colony. Antao's timely emergence as a sprinting great was as much an opportunity for Kenyan politicians as it was a source of local pride for Mombasa's Goan community.

∼

In a country that would come to be known for its dominance in distance running, the athlete first venerated for "putting Kenya on the map" was a Goan sprinter. His emergence as the fastest man in Africa, coinciding with the end of British colonial rule in Kenya, made salient a range of layers of his identity: Kenyan, Goan, and internationally connected athlete. To Kenyans in the early 1960s, Seraphino Antao would have been a well-known name. To the Goan community, he was a cherished son. To his peers, including British Olympian Chris Brasher, Antao was "one of the great sprinters of all time."[51]

Antao fell ill on the eve of the 1964 Tokyo Olympic Games and failed to reach the finals of either the 100 or the 220 yards. Disillusioned, not long after the 1964 Games he retired from running and left Kenya for good, eventually settling in London. Although it came to a disappointing finish, Antao's running career was a source of pride for the Goan community in Kenya and a symbol of unity for a divided society on the brink of nationhood. Many Kenyan athletes would conquer the Commonwealth Games in the coming years—Kip Keino in 1966, Ben Jipcho in 1974, and Henry Rono in 1978—but the first Kenyan to rule the track was a Goan sprinter.

Notes

1. Hugh Gloster, "'Uhuru' Is Ringing Out Across Land: It Means Freedom for the African," *New Journal and Guide*, October 14, 1961, 20.

2. Brian Marsden, "'Long Arm' Aims at the Sudan," *Daily Nation*, November 27, 1963, 23.

3. "Scots Will Send Top Players," *Daily Nation*, November 21, 1963, 19.

4. "Kenya ABA Just Can't Lose," *Daily Nation*, December 10, 1963, 23.

5. "Uhuru Meeting Attracts Big Field," *Sunday Nation*, December 1, 1963, 55.

6. Tom Clarke, "Remember Our Headline 3 Weeks Ago? Antao (Fastest-Yet 220 Yards) the Great and Now East Africa's Verdict Is—He's the Greatest," *Sunday Nation*, October 14, 1962, 3.

7. Kenya made its debut at the British Empire Games in 1954.

8. At the 1966 Commonwealth Games in Kingston, Jamaica, four years later, Keino would win both events.

9. Tom Clarke, "Antao Finds a New Fan," *Sunday Nation*, May 26, 1963, 34.

10. Cyprian Fernandes, "Five Records Broken—It's Smashing, Seraphino!," *Daily Nation*, October 7, 1964, 14.

11. Fernandes, "Five Records Broken."

12. Cyprian Fernandes, "Antao Will Be in Top Form, Promises Batchelor," *Daily Nation*, November 27, 1963, 23.

13. Fernandes, "Antao Will Be in Top Form."

14. Margret Frenz, "Transimperial Connections: East African Goan Perspectives on 'Goa 1961,'" *Contemporary South Asia* 22, no. 3 (2014): 240–54.

15. The literature on Mau Mau is vast, but see David Anderson, *Histories of the Hanged: Britain's Dirty War in Kenya and the End of Empire* (London: Weidenfeld & Nicolson, 2005); Caroline Elkins, *Imperial Reckoning: The Untold Story of Britain's Gulag in Kenya* (New York: Henry Holt, 2005); Daniel Branch, *Defeating Mau Mau, Creating Kenya: Counterinsurgency, Civil War, and Decolonization* (Cambridge, UK: Cambridge University Press, 2009); and Bruce Berman and John Lonsdale, *Unhappy Valley: Conflict in Kenya and Africa* (London: James Currey, 1992).

16. Mougo Nyaggah, "Asians in East Africa: The Case of Kenya," *Journal of African Studies* 1, no. 2 (1974): 205–33; Sana Aiyar, *Indians in Kenya: The Politics of Diaspora* (Cambridge, MA: Harvard University Press, 2015); and Cyprian Fernandes, *Yesterday in Paradise: 1950–1974* (Bloomington, IN: Balboa Press, 2016).

17. Klaus de Albuquerque, "Along the Colour Bar," *Transition* 73 (1997), 95.

18. Frederick Noronha, "The Gazelle Comes Homes for a Short Graze," *Herald*, November 26, 2004.

19. "This Man Antao," *Sunday Nation*, December 9, 1962, 45.

20. Archie Evans, "Seraphino Not the Only Kenya," *Sunday Nation*, December 23, 1962, 44.

21. John Bale, "Kenyan Running before the 1968 Mexico Olympics," in *East African Running: Toward a Cross-Disciplinary Perspective*, ed. Yannis Pitsiladis, John Bale, Craig Sharp, and Tim Noakes (Abdingdon, UK: Routledge, 2007), 18.

22. "A Jaunty Step through the Toughest Testing Ground—Our Athletes Shrugged Off World-Class Challengers," *Nation*, September 4, 1960, 36.

23. "Winning Two Gold in Perth Most Memorable," *East African Standard*, February 1, 2003, http://www.goanvoice.org.uk/supplement/SeraphinoAntao.htm.

24. Tom Clarke, "Our Greatest Track Team Is Broken," *Sunday Nation*, August 5, 1962.

25. Clarke, "Our Greatest Track Team Is Broken."

26. "Seraphino Says 'Thanks' to Minister," *Daily Nation*, November 21, 1963, 19.

27. Cyprian Fernandes, "Ray Batchelor Flies Off to Coach Antao," *Daily Nation*, November 26, 1963, 23.

28. Fernandes, "Ray Batchelor Flies Off to Coach Antao."

29. Fernandes, "Ray Batchelor Flies Off to Coach Antao."

30. Fernandes, "Ray Batchelor Flies Off to Coach Antao."

31. Fernandes, "Ray Batchelor Flies Off to Coach Antao."

32. Fernandes, "Ray Batchelor Flies Off to Coach Antao," 23.

33. *Sunday Nation*, December 1, 1963, 55.

34. Fernandes, "Antao Will Be in Top Form," 23.

35. *Sunday Nation*, December 1, 1963, 55.

36. Fernandes, "Ray Batchelor Flies Off to Coach Antao," 23.

37. Cyprian Fernandes, "Sun—Antao's Ally in World Title Bid," *Daily Nation*, December 10, 1963, 23.

38. Fernandes, "Sun—Antao's Ally."

39. Fernandes, "Sun—Antao's Ally."

40. Fernandes, "Sun—Antao's Ally."

41. Fernandes, "Sun—Antao's Ally."

42. Fernandes, "Sun—Antao's Ally."

43. Fernandes, "Ray Batchelor Flies Off to Coach Antao," 23.

44. Cyprian Fernandes, "Antao Is Set for Olympic Double—Ron," *Daily Nation*, December 12, 1963, 22.

45. Fernandes, "Antao Is Set for Olympic Double."

46. Fernandes, "Antao Is Set for Olympic Double" (emphasis in original).

47. Cyprian Fernandes, "Antao Best Hope for World Glory," *Daily Nation*, December 31, 1963, 14.

48. Fernandes, "Antao Best Hope for World Glory."

49. "Antao Returns to Coast in Triumph," *Sunday Nation*, August 18, 1963, 44.

50. Mark Dyreson, "The Playing Fields of Progress: American Athletic Nationalism and the 1904 Olympics," *Gateway Heritage* 14, no. 2 (1993): 4.

51. "This Man Antao," *Sunday Nation*, December 9, 1962, 45.

EIGHT

The Durable Impact of the Past:
Sporting Legacies and Heritage

FIFTEEN

Rugby Transformation as Alibi

Thoughts on Craven and Coetzee

DEREK CHARLES CATSAM

In 1988, Rhodes University history professor Julian Cobbing published a controversial and provocative article, "The Mfecane as Alibi: Thoughts on Dithakong and Mbolompo," in the *Journal of African History*. In that article he made a series of assertions that were so revisionist they led to a furor in South African historiographical circles, ultimately resulting in an entire book of essays refuting elements of his thesis. At the heart of the thesis was a complex argument that can best be reduced to the following. The well-known Mfecane, or "crushing," by which the Zulu kingdom expanded in the late eighteenth and well into the nineteenth centuries, absorbing or destroying all who stood in its path, was largely a creation of British colonialists, their sympathizers, and future architects of the apartheid state, in whose interest it was to depict the Zulu as warlike, ruthless, and violent. In Cobbing's telling, this was an "alibi" that justified colonial conquest and its own wave of violence on behalf of both the colonial metropole and the settler community.[1]

Independent of the merits of Cobbing's argument (and it was simultaneously provocative, important, and at times, simply wrong) the concern here is his use of the term *alibi*. Cobbing uses *alibi* in this sense as "excuse," a shallow and illegitimate justification, for colonial conquest and ultimately the apartheid project. And while an alibi can also be a legitimate explanation—an airtight and demonstrable argument of where one was when a crime or incident took place—in South African rugby there is a long history of alibis, usually of the "excuse" variety, that have justified what in contemporary terms is a "lack of transformation" across the sport—that is, a lack of inclusion of Black, "coloured," and Indian rugby players. This issue is especially prominent in public debate about the pinnacle of the South African game, the national side known as the Springboks. This chapter looks into the many alibis used over the past century to avoid integration in and transformation of South African rugby.

In April 2016, the African National Congress (ANC) government, in the person of sports minister Fikile Mbalula, decided to get tough with four sports bodies—cricket, netball, athletics, and rugby—for their lack of progress in achieving racial transformation, not only on the playing fields, courts, and tracks, but also in their higher structures. There had long been debates about various forms of transformation in sports, with the government part of the discussions. But this was the clearest gnashing of teeth on the part of the government, with Mbalula announcing that the four codes would be prohibited from bidding for hosting duties for international events for their respective codes.[2] Perhaps all sporting codes were equal in Mbalula's announcement, but rugby was quite clearly more equal than others. The South African Rugby Union (SARU) was in the process of preparing to bid to host the 2023 World Cup, a bid that it continued to pursue, putting forward an official offer in September 2016 in the face of Mbalula's (not rescinded) prohibition.[3]

In May 2016, former Stormers coach Allister Coetzee took the helm of the Springboks after months of the position being open. By the time of his appointment, his ascension was a poorly kept secret. Coetzee became South Africa's second "non-White" Springbok coach after Pieter De Villiers, who served a somewhat stormy tenure from 2008 to 2011, with some clear successes and a few failures, in keeping with the Springbok coaching experience since 1994.[4] Coetzee not only had success on the pitch as the headman in Cape Town; he also led the way in transformation at the Super Rugby level. The combination of success in the win column and his clear determination to help change the face of

Springbok rugby made him the ideal coach for the politicized cauldron (or, in former Bok coach Nick Mallet's words, the "poisoned chalice") that is the Springbok coaching position.[5] But Coetzee faced many of the same alibis pushing back against transformation that have endured for decades in a country where sports is deeply implicated in politics. Coetzee struggled in his tenure at the helm, and after achieving only a 47 percent winning percentage as headman of the Springboks, he was fired in early 2018 and was replaced by Rassie Erasmus (who, at the end of 2018, had won just under 54 percent of his matches as head coach).

Perhaps Erasmus's first significant decision was his choice for Springbok captain. After naming Pieter-Steph du Toit to that post for what amounted to a Springbok B team against Wales in Washington, DC, in June 2018, he announced that Siya Kolisi would be captain beginning with a three-test series against England that began a week after the Wales test. Kolisi would thus become the first Black Springbok captain, and as of December 2018 Kolisi had solidified his hold on the captain's armband.[6]

These snapshots perhaps tell us something about the state of Springbok *transformation*, the common term in South African society for the necessary reforms in the wake of apartheid. However, much of the dynamic of transformation in Springbok rugby has also led to significant opposition. Sports in South Africa are and always have been deeply implicated in politics. This chapter looks at transformation in current-day Springbok rugby in the context of the myriad alibis presented to resist change, alibis that have implications for South African society well beyond the playing fields.

Gaan Bokke! ("Blacks Are Not Rugby People" as Alibi)

The most enduring alibi promoted by (too many) White rugby people is the old "Blacks are not rugby people" canard, which is fairly easily refutable both by the presence of Black and "coloured" rugby cultures and by the simple fact that this particular alibi became something of a self-fulfilling prophecy: claim that Blacks are not rugby people and then do not allow them access to either facilities or competition, and you have Black South Africans who are not, in fact, rugby people.

Of course, there was also simple White supremacy—a crime that rarely required an alibi at all in certain circles—which said that Blacks and Whites should not mix in sports as in life, or that presupposed that Blacks were either not worthy or capable of playing a manly, honorable game such as rugby. This narrative has a long, transnational, transsporting lineage. White heavyweights refused to fight the great boxer Jack Johnson because Black fighters allegedly lacked courage and strength and manliness, yet when given a chance, Johnson pummeled the courageous and strong and manly Tommy Burns on December 26, 1908, to become the first Black heavyweight champion of the world, a title no Black fighter had earned only because no Black fighter had been allowed to compete for it, and that no Black fighter would be allowed to compete for over another generation.

Errol Tobias was the first Black Springbok, making his debut against Ireland at home in 1981, but he was just part of a generation of African and "coloured" players who approached the top level of rugby in the period from the late 1970s. In 1975, the SA Invitation XV was the first multiracial South African rugby side. The team faced a French team that had not lost on tour that year, in front of a capacity crowd at Newlands Stadium, and emerged with a comfortable 18–3 victory. Although the side was majority White, two players came from the Proteas, the representative side of the Coloured South African Rugby Football Federation (for which Tobias had made his international debut in 1971), right wing John Noble and prop Turkey Shields. The Leopards (or African XV) of the South African Rugby Board also contributed two players to the SA Invitation XV side, wing Toto Tsotsobe and flanker Morgan Cushe. As if to validate the mixed race squad, Noble scored what one observer has called the "try of the match" just before halftime. The architect of the squad was South African rugby legend Dr. Danie Craven.[7]

Much as Tobias would a few years later, Cushe faced criticism from his own Black community for his participation in the multiracial 1975 team. Cushe, who passed away in 2013, was a widely respected flank. He also played a conflicted role in a conflicted era. In the words of journalist Luke Alfred, "Depending on your politics, he was either the worst form of apartheid collaborator or a subsequently neglected trailblazer, unlucky not to have been awarded a Springbok blazer, as, say, Errol Tobias was," in 1981 and subsequently. Initially, Cushe preferred boxing to rugby, but eventually he took to the latter sport. Cushe rose through the ranks of Black rugby, including starring for the Leopards before making his appearance for the SA Invitation XV side against the French as well as against the mighty All Blacks.[8]

It is perhaps noteworthy that Tobias played a role in the next multiracial South African side to face international competition after the 1975 SA Invitation XV, when he starred for the South African Country Districts XV against a touring American side, the Cougars, at the Border Rugby Union Grounds in East London in August 1978. Predictably, the South African side crushed the Americans, 44–12, with Tobias scoring two tries and setting up two others as the side's fly half. Some observers mistakenly believed that the match against the Americans represented the first multiracial South African rugby team, revealing the extent to which many of these events were relatively sotto voce in what was still very much a closed society.[9]

Morgan Cushe and his cohort represented a generation born too soon to see the opportunities that a generation in the future would have, but soon enough to experience opportunities that had previously been denied generations of African, "coloured," and Indian rugby players, indeed, athletes from all sports. Tobias represented the best fruit from that poisoned vine, but he was far from alone in facing doubts from all sides, including his own community.[10] This transgression cut in multiple ways, so that Tobias was seen as problematic by both apartheid supporters and antiapartheid activists, while in his time he was celebrated by too few, a situation that has changed in recent years, with Tobias enjoying celebration and praise from within South Africa's rugby community for his pioneering status. And to be clear, there were dozens of other players from South Africa's excluded rugby traditions who also earned a name in rugby and should have had a chance to play in Currie Cups and on provincial sides and to play in national sides up to and including the Springboks. For a year and a half, in 2017 and 2018, *SA Rugby* magazine, a monthly publication, featured Black rugby players who have been overlooked in the larger rugby histories and chronicles, and even this welcome if belated coverage merely skims the surface of Black players who were outstanding rugby people.[11]

Craven (The Government as Alibi)

There are few figures in the long history of South Africa not named "Mandela" who have been subject to more unashamed hagiography than Danie Craven (usually referred to as "Doc" Craven by his admirers). After graduating from Stellenbosch, Craven taught at St. Andrews College in Grahamstown from 1936, coaching the school's rugby club even as he was selected for the Boks in 1937.

Craven was a Springbok hero as a player. He was a scrum half, mostly, with appearances as a fly half, center, and even number 8. But he also became a legendary manager, coach, strategist, selection authority, tactician, technician, administrator, and elder statesman. And he also, in his halting way, wanted to transform South African rugby, especially in his later years. Indeed, by most accounts, many of them admittedly from his hagiographers, Craven was the driving force behind integrating (or at least desegregating) the Springboks, and he certainly was central to Errol Tobias becoming the first Black Bok in 1981. Yet Craven had been involved in rugby for decades prior to 1981. His alibi was always reasonably good, though not airtight: that government interference, especially from the Vorster regime, prevented him from engaging in serious reform. Nonetheless, it hardly would have amounted to "Speech from the Dock"-style heroism for Craven to have frontally challenged the government, held mixed race trials, and announced Black Springboks in the 1960s or 1970s.[12] After all, Craven knew about great players such as Morgan Cushe, Toto Tsotsobe, "Turkey" Shields, and Johnny Noble, and he had helped bring those players together for the South African Invitation XV, that first mixed South African team, in 1975. Craven deserves credit for this, to be sure, but the Select XV was not the Springboks, and after all, Errol Tobias was a scintillating fly half in the 1970s, reaching the end of his career by the time of his selection in 1981, and a sprightly but aged thirty-four when he starred for the Boks against England in 1984.

Furthermore, Craven's motivation quite clearly seemed to be all about rugby; his goal was to maintain South Africa's standing in global rugby, not to bring about change within South African society. Black rugby players would benefit the Springboks. We have little sense that University of Stellenbosch physical education professor Craven cared much about how the larger integration of Black South Africans would be good for his country, and in the high-water-mark years of apartheid, the 1950s and 1960s, Craven had long asserted that the Springboks would never see a Black player on his watch.

There is no sense coming to either bury or praise Craven. He did more than most rugby people but less than many, and certainly less than he could have from the 1950s through the 1970s. One could simply assert that as a White South African of Afrikaner descent, he was "a man of his time," but that is its own alibi. Bayers Naude and Bram Fischer, after all, were Afrikaner men from almost precisely Craven's time. They had all of the possible alibis at their disposal and chose to forsake alibi altogether. Perhaps, then, the belated discovery that Blacks were, in fact, rugby people warrants a little less hagiography and a little more scrutiny, and the excuse that the government would not have allowed integration is not sufficient reason not to have tested that government well before Craven did.

Tobias (as Alibi)

Errol Tobias and "coloured" assistant manager Abe Williams (who accompanied the Springboks during Tobias's time on the national side) themselves became a form of alibi for South African sports. During the infamous 1981 Springbok tours to New Zealand and the United States, manager Johan Claassen (who was at a minimum not sympathetic to racial issues) and Coach Nelie Smith (who passed away recently) were willing to have Tobias on the squad, but could not find fit to play him in any of the test matches in New Zealand or in the peculiar test played near Albany, New York, in 1981. Tobias faced criticism from many sides—certainly among Whites who resented his presence, but also among "coloured" and Black players and supporters, who painted him as a traitor and an Uncle Tom—and yet was used like a shield by promoters of the tours in 1981.

Tobias would be the sole Black Springbok until he played alongside Avril Williams in 1984 against England. The third Black Springbok would be Chester Williams, Avril's nephew, on the 1995 squad. These three players from the rich South African "coloured" community became the thin reed of alibi on which to hang the argument that Springbok rugby was changing, something that events as late as the early 1990s revealed to be quite false. Throughout the controversies of 1981, defenders of the tours across New Zealand and America held Tobias (and to a lesser extent Williams) up as shields to claim that South African rugby was not segregated, that it was not subject to apartheid. This was not merely an alibi; it was either a gross misunderstanding of South African society, a naïve acceptance of tokenism, or an outright lie.

Invictus (Nelson Mandela, Francois Pienaar, and Chester Williams as Alibi)

To have Nelson Mandela on one's side provides one hell of an alibi, especially when the alibi is filmed by Clint Eastwood and voiced by Morgan Freeman. (A historical footnote: in the film *Invictus*, Chester Williams was played by McNeil Hendricks, who earned two caps and scored one try as a wing in Bok colors in 1997–1998.) In seemingly every bar, pub, or tavern in any South African dorpie, stad, city, or suburb (though perhaps not all shebeens and villages), there is a framed photograph of Ellis Park from June 24, 1995. On that date, Joel Stransky kicked the team into history, or at least into legend, by providing the winning kick of the 1995 IRB World Cup, propelling the Springboks to victory over the mighty All Blacks of New Zealand. From that moment emerged perhaps the most pernicious of all alibis, the *Invictus* myth, which was that Nelson Mandela, by embracing the Springboks in 1995 and donning Captain Francois Pienaar's number 6 jersey during the William Webb Ellis trophy presentation, also established South African rugby as a force for good in the New South African Rainbow Nation.

Nelson Mandela, Francois Pienaar, Chester Williams, and the rest of the 1995 Springboks thus provide perhaps the most pernicious of these alibis, because the feel-good narrative, the feel-good alibi, may well have made transformation harder, not easier, substituting the story we like to tell for the story we need to hear. Plus, invoking Mandela on your side in an argument is always a good argument-ender. Just as Gideon Nieuwoudt, the apartheid security force policeman who engaged in countless acts of murder and mayhem on behalf of the apartheid state, was shocked when he went expecting easy forgiveness from the family of Siphiwo Mthimkulu, an activist Niuwoudt had murdered while an apartheid security force policeman, many White South Africans seem to think that Mandela absolved them from rugby sins past, present, and future.

Coetzee (Merit as Alibi)

Perhaps the most common alibi used today is "merit." But this alibi is built on a false dichotomy, whereby merit and transformation are somehow opposing forces rather than mutually reinforcing forces. Even as astute an observer of the South African scene as the political cartoonist Zapiro fell victim to this particular misconception.

Yet why do we conceptualize transformation and merit as being oppositional forces? Only if we assume that Black must be inferior and White superior, only by assuming that *merit* is an objective rather than a subjective term, only if we believe that merit operates independent of human failings and biases, and only if we believe that merit exists as a fixed empirical category with clear and measurable lines of demarcation, can we buy into this false, and pernicious dichotomy pitting two concepts against each other that should buttress one another.

This is the alibi that Allister Coetzee, the new Springbok coach, faced. Many believed he was well equipped to do so. Not only was he was front and center in transforming the Stormers as their coach, but he did so while maintaining a record of the Stormers not only as the best South African Super Rugby (and Currie Cup) side, but also as a top challenger in Super Rugby, a competition in which, like the Rugby Championship and the last two World Cups, South Africa tends to be, at best, a distant second place to New Zealand. The Stormers flew in the face of the false dichotomy. Coetzee and his staff (including his assistant coach, Mzwandile Stick) seemed to be well equipped to deal with merit-based transformation. And yet with each loss, rather than look into the myriad reasons why a sports team fails, too many critics pointed to "politics," by which they meant "transformation," by which they meant "race" as the reason for the team's failings, even though virtually none of the Springbok losses during Coetzee's difficult tenure can reasonably be traced to failings that had anything to do with transformation. Indeed, the biggest issues Coetzee faced were that he was appointed far later than he should have been, that he was hamstrung by rules about using foreign-based players (who could earn far more money playing in Europe or Japan than in South Africa), and that South African rugby was in an ongoing trough on the field and in the national administrative structures. In the end, Coetzee ended up gulping from the poisoned chalice that has been toxic to nearly every other postisolation Springbok coach. Yet this also, unfairly, created another antitransformation alibi.

This is as good a place as any to address the most vacuous argument in a South African dialogue full of vacuous arguments: "Why don't we have transformation for Whites in soccer?" This reveals such a woeful ignorance of the intertwined histories of apartheid and sports that one has to assume that it is an intentionally obtuse argument rather than one born merely of ignorance.

Back to the Government (Rugby as Alibi?)

Of course, this all has largely been a one-way street of White resentment and alibi-making against transformation. But let us be clear: Isn't rugby transformation, and transformation in sports more broadly, possibly something of an alibi for the government? For if rugby has not transformed satisfactorily—indeed, if South African society has not transformed satisfactorily, which it has not—nor has the government always satisfactorily addressed issues like service delivery, unemployment, infrastructure, sexual violence and violent crime more generally, corruption, and state capture. Is it not possible for two things, then, to be true: that sports in South Africa generally, and rugby in particular, have not adequately transformed, AND that this lack of transformation has itself become an alibi for the government and the ANC tripartite alliance? Minister Fikile Mbalula surely believed that he was doing his job in attacking a lack of transformation in South African sports. His declarations might not have drawn so much attention if so many of his colleagues were not falling down in doing their jobs. Rugby has thus become an excuse in some circles for failings in areas far more important than rugby, or even worse, in areas such as education and providing safe public recreation and sporting facilities, where the government could be providing services, pushing transformation across society, and creating the conditions for not only South African rugby, but South African sports more broadly, to succeed.

No More Alibis

The most ardent critics of transformation talk about how politics and sports ought to be separate, how nation building ought to play no role in rugby, how transformation belies merit. The original Springbok touring party certainly would have found these criticisms to be puzzling. In 1906, the South African national rugby team, which would officially adopt the name "Springboks" before they took the pitch at Crystal Palace to take on the English, had intentionally been chosen to include a balance of both English- and Afrikaans-speaking White South African players. The captain was Paul Roos, an Afrikaner. The vice captain, Harold "Paddy" Carolin, was an English speaker. Coming together as a team had, according to Roos, "united" the newly anointed Springboks, and South Africa "was one, all differences had been forgotten." The players, and possibly the country's White denizens, "understand one another better, and if that is going to be one of the results of our tour, we shall be more than satisfied."[13] Rugby had become a tool for nation building, while politics had been a consideration in building the team. Yet none of the era's White observers complained about merit. If such considerations were good enough for the original Springbok tourists, why should the modern era's far more diverse inheritors of the green and gold not be granted comparable latitude?

Afrikaner and White nationalists want to maintain rugby as their one remaining symbol of dominance and supremacy. Meanwhile, there are many who see a different form of nationalism developing in South Africa. This form of nationalism is nonracial, or multiracial. They advocate for South Africa as the "Rainbow Nation," with sports as a microcosm of this new nationalism both inside the country and in international competitions.

At this point, it is unclear which nationalism will win out on the pitch. On the one hand, there is the image of the Springboks, including burly, blonde Afrikaners, singing the national anthem, "Nkosi Sikelel iAfrika," before every game. This picture, like Mandela's donning a Springbok jersey in 1995, and like *The Sowetan* paying homage to *Amabokoboko*, is largely symbolic. Some might say that so too is the use of sports-cum-nationalism. But symbolism and nationalism go hand in hand. Perhaps all nationalism is symbolism writ large. In South Africa, sports in general, but especially rugby and the struggle over it, looms as a symbol with significant ramifications for the country's continuing transformation.[14]

During a 1992 Springbok match, officials called for a moment of silence to mark the Boipatong Massacre. Breaking the silence, some Afrikaners in the crowd sang aggressive choruses of *Die Stem* to express their disdain for the changes under way. So let there be no mistake: things have changed in South African rugby. After all, the leading try scorer in Springbok history is Brian Habana, a "coloured" player whose presence on the Boks would have been impossible as recently as 1980 and would have been perfunctory into the 1990s, and who recently earned his one-hundredth Springbok cap. And arguably two of the most popular Springboks today are Tendai "The Beast" Mtawariri, whose presence on the pitch is met with rousing chants of "Beast" from the still overwhelmingly White throngs before which the Boks play in South Africa, and Siya Kolisi, whose captaincy has been hailed across South Africa as a galvanizing development.

Yet are things changing quickly enough? And how should rugby officials, politicians, and others address the pace of transformation in the country? The country continues to debate these questions, with a return to a quota system announced in 2013, to considerable discussion and disagreement.[15] The legacies of apartheid sports continue and are likely to continue well into the future. In March 2017, Mbalula appeared to have slackened his ban on the Springboks' hosting international tournaments, though no official announcement accompanied the government's backing off from its most rigorous pronouncements.[16]

It is perhaps telling that the revival of South Africa's national cricket teams in the last couple of years in all three formats of the game (test, one-day, and T20) has come about during a time when they are also fielding the most transformed teams in the country's cricketing history. It is also telling that the merit argument—which is to say, the presupposition that Black, "coloured," Indian, and Muslim players must of necessity be first and foremost political appointees—has slurred and libeled some of the best players in South Africa's recent history, including Hashim Amla, Makhaya Ntini, Vernon Philander, and Kagiso Rabada.[17]

When it comes to the vexing, connected issues of race, politics, and sports in South Africa, the words of William Faulkner ring true. "The past is never dead. It's not even past."[18]

Epilogue

I had a conversation over lunch at an African restaurant in Grahamstown in June 2016 with then Rhodes development officer and the university's head rugby coach, Qondakele Sompondo. Sompondo, one of the vital movers and shakers in rugby's transformation in the Eastern Cape and nationwide, argued that the team that was to take the pitch that month against Ireland was not only a team taken on merit, but was in fact the first Springbok rugby team ever chosen on merit. This turned one of the alibis neatly on its head.

In 2019 the Springboks won the Rugby World Cup. Against long odds after the grim days in 2016 and 2017, the Springboks won their third world championship. They were led by their widely respected captain, flanker Siya Kolisi from Zwide township outside of Port Elizabeth. Kolisi became the first Black captain of the Springboks in May 2018, and apart from times when he was injured, he maintained that position into 2020. The 2019 Springboks were led by Black players all across the pitch. But that hardly absolves the country's rugby authorities of past sins, nor does it make them immune to future ones. Indeed, if officials learn the wrong lesson, the 2019 Springboks could provide yet another alibi for a country whose rugby structures need to actively pursue change and not simply rest on the laurels of Siya Kolisi and his teammates, and which certainly has not earned the right to complacency.[19]

It is taking a long time for South African rugby to transform. And it's about time to dispense with the alibis.

Notes

1. Julian Cobbing, "The Mfecane as Alibi: Thoughts on Dithakong and Mbolompo," *Journal of African History* 29, no. 3 (1988): 487–519; for the many responses see Carolyn Hamilton, ed., *The Mfecane Aftermath: Reconstructive Debates in Southern African History* (Johannesburg: Witwatersrand University Press; Pietermaritzburg: University of Natal Press, 1995). It is perhaps worth noting that Cobbing's article is a good example of what a bad idea it is to try to measure scholarship based on metrics like citations, references, downloads, or "hits." "The Mfecane as Alibi" may be the most cited and referenced article in all of South African historiography, but virtually all of those citations and references are for the purpose of showing why Cobbing was so very, very wrong. Cobbing was secure enough in his professional standing (and his reputation as a provocateur was, if anything, enhanced) that he was largely unaffected professionally by the response to his article, but most of us would not encourage our junior colleagues or graduate students to take such an approach.

2. Sbu Mjikeliso, "Mbalula Gets Tough on Transformation," *Herald* (Port Elizabeth), April 26, 2016.

3. South Africa quite controversially lost that bid to France despite having a bid nearly universally recognized as superior.

4. De Villiers pulled no punches in recounting his own experience in *Politically Incorrect: The Autobiography* (Cape Town: Zebra, 2012).

5. On the mixed post-1994 history of Springbok coaches see Gavin Rich, *The Poisoned Chalice: The Rise and Fall of the Post-isolation Springbok Coaches* (Cape Town: Zebra Press, 2013).

6. See Jon Cardinelli, "Unifying Force," *SA Rugby*, August 2018, 37–41. *Rugby World* magazine included Kolisi at number 6 in its feature article "The 50 Most Influential People in World Rugby—2018," September 2018, 57–87.

7. John Griffiths, "Ask John" column, ESPNscrum, April 26, 2010, http://en.espn.co.uk/scrum/rugby/story/114664.html.

8. Susan Njanji, "Tackling Race Issues in White-Dominated Cricket, Rugby," *Mail & Guardian*, October 24, 2013, https://mg.co.za/article/2013-10-29-tackling-quota-issues-in-white-dominated-cricket-rugby/.

9. "South Africans Down Americans," *Charleston News and Courier*, August 13, 1978. See also "Sports at a Glance," *Charleston News and Courier*, August 27, 1978.

10. South African athletes were not alone in facing these dilemmas. Black athletes in the United States during the Jim Crow era sometimes faced accusations of being "sellouts" when they became pioneers in integrated sport. For just one example of this see Charles H. Martin, *Benching Jim Crow: The Rise and Fall of the Color Line in Southern College Sports, 1890–1980* (Urbana: University of Illinois Press, 2010), 213.

11. In addition to the relevant articles in the 2017–2018 issues of *SA Rugby*, most written by former SARU player Gary Boshoff, see also Boshoff's article "Rugby's Freedom Fighters," *SA Sports Illustrated*, July 2011.

12. "The Speech from the Dock" was Nelson Mandela's speech presented from the defendant's dock on April 20, 1964, during the Rivonia trial, in which he declared, "*During my lifetime I have dedicated myself to this struggle of the African people. I have fought against White domination, and I have fought against Black domination. I have cherished the ideal of a democratic and free society in which all persons live together in harmony and with equal opportunities. It is an ideal which I hope to live for and to achieve. But if needs be, it is an ideal for which I am prepared to die.*"

13. F. N. Piggott, *The Springboks: History of the Tour, 1906–1907* (Cape Town: Dawson, 1907), 96.

14. See, for example, the essays in Ashwin Desai, *The Race to Transform: Sports in Post-Apartheid South Africa* (Cape Town: HSRC, 2010).

15. Following is a sampling of the news stories and analysis on this issue in recent years: Lloyd Gedye, "Why Are the Boks So White?," *Mail & Guardian*, November 16, 2012; Gedye, "Is South African Rugby Racist?," *Mail & Guardian*, November 22, 2012, https://mg.co.za/article/2012-11-22-is-south-african-rugby-racist/; Gedye, "Does Saru Care about Transformation?—The Southern Kings as Case Study," *The Con*, May 3, 2013; Murray Williams, "Race Quotas Return to SA Rugby," *IOL Sport*, August 14, 2013, https://www.iol.co.za/sport/rugby/race-quotas-return-to-sa-rugby-1562241; Williams, "Reverting to Quotas 'Backed by All,'" *IOL Sport*, August 15, 2013, https://www.iol.co.za/sport/rugby/reverting-to-quotas-backed-by-all-1562545; Sihle Mlambo and Aphiwe Ngwenya, "'I Want to Be Picked on Merit,'" *Daily News*, August 16, 2013, https://www.iol.co.za/dailynews/i-want-to-be-picked-on-merit-1563562; Mlambo, "Afriforum:

Quotas Like 'Child Labour,'" *IOL Sport*, August 16, 2013, https://www.iol.co
.za/sport/rugby/afriforum-quotas-like-child-labour-1563651; Kallie Kriel and
Vata Ngobeni, "Are Quotas Taking Rugby Backwards?," *Sunday Independent*,
September 1, 2013, https://www.iol.co.za/sundayindependent/are-quotas
-taking-rugby-backwards-1571242; Gedye, "Race Quotas in SA Rugby: How
Afriforum Will Have You Believe That They Care about Black Players,"
The Con, September 14, 2013; Gedye, "It Isn't Rugby: On White Springbok
Rugby Fans and Quotas," Africa Is a Country, September 14, 2013, https://
africasacountry.com/2013/09/its-not-rugby; Susan Njanji, "SA Hopes Quotas
Can Unearth Black Stars," *IOL Sport*, October 29, 2013, https://www.iol.co.za
/sport/cricket/domestic/sa-hopes-quotas-can-unearth-black-stars-1598993;
Luke Alfred, "Community Rugby: Legends on the Field," *Mail & Guardian*,
March 14, 2014, https://mg.co.za/article/2014-03-13-community-rugby-clubs
-legends-on-the-field/; Malusi Mlambo, "Wanted: Whites Trust for Black
Players," *The Con*, April 18, 2014; Andy Capostagno, "Rugby Teeters on the
Cutting Edge," *Mail & Guardian*, April 25, 2014, https://mg.co.za/article/2014
-04-24-rugby-teeters-on-the-cutting-edge/; and Gedye, "Heyneke Meyer and
the All Whites," *The Con*, September 5, 2014, https://menzikulati.wordpress
.com/2014/09/07/heyneke-meyer-and-the-all-whites-by-lloyd-gedye-on
-september-5-2014/.

16. See Andy Capostagno, "Keep Your Eye on the Rugby Ball," *Mail &
Guardian*, March 17–23, 2017.

17. See Dileep Premachandran, "'Quota' Players? What a Joke," and "Young,
Black, Beautiful," *Mail & Guardian*, January 12–18, 2018; see also Niren Tolsi,
"The Rainbow Beauty of Hashim Amla," *Cricket Monthly*, ESPNCricInfo,
January 4, 2018.

18. William Faulker, *Requiem for a Nun* (New York: Vintage International,
2011), 73.

19. In both the lead-up to and the aftermath of the 2019 World Cup, I
wrote a series of articles on South African sports and race for *Africa Is a Country*, several of which also appeared in the *Mail & Guardian*. They can be ac-
cessed at https://africasacountry.com/author/derek-catsam.

SIXTEEN

No Place of Honor

*The Erosion of Historical Space and Place
within the Kimberley Rugby Narrative*

MARK FREDERICKS

The A. R. Abass Stadium stands on the corner of Stockroos Street
and Philel Road in Kimberley at what once used to be the heart of sporting activity within the nonracial fold of Kimberley and the Northern
Cape. Flanked by the derelict spaces of the hockey grounds, the hal-
lowed but by now pockmarked cricket field known as the Eddie Williams Oval[1] and the Squarehill Park tennis courts, the A.R. Abass
Stadium stands alone as a silent monument from the past. (See figure
16.2.) A sign behind securely locked steel gates declares: "AR Abass Stadium—Home of Universal RFC." The Universal Rugby Football Club
celebrated 130 years of service to the community of Kimberley and the
game of rugby in 2016, and is the lone survivor from the South African
Council on Sport (SACOS) era.[2] The post-1990 period ushered in the
era of unity and the "'normalization'" of sports in South Africa (1991–
1992), during which many township clubs and structures were physically
dismantled and historically obliterated[3] in the rush to have the sports
moratorium lifted.[4] In 1991, by the time Clive Rice led a South African
cricket team out of isolation on a tour of India, the National Sports

Congress (NSC) had usurped SACOS as the official sports wing of the liberation movement.[5] Aligned with the African National Congress (ANC), the NSC received its full support and was recognized by the National Party and establishment sports representatives as the key player in lifting the sports boycott.

Unification of the various sports bodies in South Africa during the 1990s was preceded by the rejection of SACOS by various sports code affiliates after the SACOS meeting of November 26, 1989, in Kimberley, at which the "dual membership resolution" was adopted.[6] Overnight SACOS lost rugby, cricket, soccer, table tennis, squash, and other affiliates to the NSC. This hemorrhage climaxed in the unification of rugby at the Kimberley Hotel in 1992, heralding a new beginning for establishment sports, while the sports structures that had struggled against apartheid were evaporated upward into the more powerful and better resourced establishment and elite sporting bodies, diverting social energy away from the communities that had supported them during apartheid. Community sports effectively ceased to exist with the coming of sports unity in South Africa. The very powerful sports bodies that were connected to the apartheid sports social system continued to function, albeit with the added "burden" of having to accept a smattering of Black members in the aftermath of sports unity.[7] In the biography of NSC frontman Bill Jardine, author Chris Van Wyk notes:

> In an ironic twist, however, the rise of the NSC and the quest for equality had a negative impact on sport in some communities. When SACOS was the only game in town, sport was encouraged and nurtured. But now that clubs were encouraged to compete against those in other communities—in White, coloured and Indian suburbs—teams that had once belonged to SACOS and were now affiliated to the NSC were weakened. Even Bill's old Newtonians club did not escape the problem. All the Transvaal Independent Rugby Football Union teams, including Newtonians, reacted by forming themselves into one club which they called the Transvaal Independent Rugby Football Union (Tirfu). Tirfu, previously a union, now became a club.[8]

Once vibrant centers of social activity, community sports facilities fell into silence and dereliction, and the energy of the sporting social common dissipated as the triumph of the mega-sporting event overpowered the senses.[9] Ironically, SA Rugby routinely presents the face of a unified South Africa through the game of rugby and its interconnectedness to the grassroots base of the game through carefully crafted and highly stylized television commercials.[10] The visuals tie South Africans to the game and its unifying power by often including the iconic images from the 1995 Rugby World Cup final, with visuals of a smiling and triumphant Nelson Mandela in his Springbok attire. In Kimberley, the once-vibrant sports center known as the A.R. Abass Stadium stands as an unheralded, silent monument to a history rarely acknowledged in mainstream sports narratives. Kimberley, in this sense, serves as a microcosm of the larger collapse of social sports and social activism through sports in South Africa. This chapter examines aspects of the collapse of social interaction as embodied by the SACOS-affiliated communities in the physical and geographical spaces around the A.R. Abass Stadium and the sociopolitical education that took place through sports and recreation (figure 16.1).[11]

Figure 16.1. Members of the Universal RFC at practice outside of the A.R. Abass stadium, February 1, 2018. The club has been locked out of its traditional rugby home by a postunity deal struck between the GWRU and the Northern Cape Department of Sport. *Image courtesy of Universal RFC chairperson Bryan Pietersen.*

Playing on Holy Ground

Saturdays were magical days during the hard, biting Kimberley winters. Titanic struggles would take place at the Union Grounds, which in 1986 became known as the A.R. Abass Stadium, in honor of Mr. Abdullah Abass, a founding member of the nonracial South African Rugby Union. Rugby was also played at the stadium during the week, with schools battling it out in front of capacity crowds on Thursdays. The city of Kimberley, despite its diminutive size, embraced the rugby-loving community, and the few high schools in the city attracted large crowds. Every match was a derby, and the rivalries were fierce. But it was on Saturdays that the stadium buzzed and heaved with athletic and social energy. Duties were rotated among the clubs, and fundraising for clubs as well as for the rugby union depended on the support of the spectators, who came in droves to socialize around the game of rugby. A sports report in the newspaper[12] does little justice to the memory of the atmosphere and the excitement generated by a day at the Union Grounds:

> Rugby of a high standard was seen at the Union Grounds on Saturday afternoon. Showing excellent form, Collegians, the Griqualand West Coloured Rugby Champions, outclassed Arabian College to win 15—0. In the early game, Dennis Jacobs, the Collegians flyhalf, played magnificently. Not only did he scheme most of his side's moves in the first half, but he scored six of Collegians nine points before half time. A Knee injury just before half-time forced Jacobs to leave the field for the remaining half of the match. Collegians fully deserved their victory. They handled the ball well and their back line showed penetration. The Arabian College backs disappointed.[13]

Of course the same excitement and social energy was generated around the other sports codes, such as cricket, hockey, and soccer, and all the codes that men and women participated in. It was a system that can best be described as a social ecosystem[14] that revolved around the life of the sports codes and clubs that descended on the A.R. Abass Stadium during the rugby season and gave many young people hope and, in a sense, political purpose during the bleakest years of apartheid.

This social ecosystem flourished in spite of the downward pressures of apartheid because of the support networks within the system, and the enjoyment that sports delivered did not cloud the broader issues that apartheid thrust upon the communities who supported the sports and the businesses within the group areas. Duncan Greene, in his book on the struggles of poverty-stricken communities and their efforts to raise themselves up from their situations, describes the sociopolitical energy released around social soccer matches in Bolivia: "Organising themselves at first under the guise of a soccer league—the only way they could meet and talk with Chiquitanos from other villages—the indigenous activists of Monteverde fought for things that mattered to them: land, education, rights, a political voice."[15] The clubs were fierce rivals on the field, and very often the rivalries would hinder off-field relationships, at times even hampering cooperation in the running and maintenance of the stadium facility. Mostly, however, it was a labor of shared love and the understanding that the clubs were all involved in more than just sports. The messages on the political situation, while not overtly intrusive within the festive atmosphere, reached the ears of those in the changing rooms as well as the stands (bleachers), and this was how the issues of social justice remained at the forefront of the sports struggle. Sports, along with religious gatherings and funerals, was one of the few ways that large groups of Black people could gather during apartheid. Because of the energy generated by sports, the organizational planning thereof, and the passions involved, the politicization process posed a real danger to the apartheid regime to such an extent that the apartheid minister of sport, F. W. De Klerk, declared SACOS the most dangerous rebel grouping in South Africa.[16]

Unity, in effect, gave De Klerk his wish, as sports and social resistance through sports ended with sports unity in 1992. It was a multipronged attack on the vibrancy of political social cohesion,[17] which finally saw silence descend on the A.R. Abass Stadium and centers like it across the country. Flag-waving and jersey-wearing spectatorism is a poor substitute for the social energy that was liberated on game days at the A.R. Abass Stadium.

Unity and Destruction

In a comical revelation of the level of deception exercised by key players within the NSC in their efforts to cripple SACOS, Bill Jardine describes how he masterminded a plot to vote out of power a "trouble-maker" who sat at the head of Athletics South Africa in 1991.[18] At the time of the incident, the NSC was so new that it had virtually no functioning structures within townships in the country:

> Bill had thought of this. And when he presented the solution to the problem, they all thought he was joking. So bizarre was the plan that even Bill had to smile as he explained it. "You go as the representative of the Johannesburg Athletics Congress" he told one of them, "you represent the Kangwane Athletics Association, you represent Kwandabele, you represent Pietersburg, Germiston, Pretoria...." "Uncle Bill, you can't be serious! None of these associations exists!" Motoring down to Cape Town, Banele and his gang of hoaxers almost lost their nerve as they kept arguing: "No, you are Kangwane, I am Pieterburg...." But they pulled off the ploy and September was ousted.[19]

The mass exodus of codes from SACOS to the NSC had crippled the administration of community sports bodies, and the scramble for positions in the newly formed NSC took precedence over the management and cultivation of sports in townships.[20] On March 28, 1998, seven years after Bill Jardine and his merry band of "hoaxers" had pulled off their plot, Jardine, in an address to the NSC Council, asked: "What has unity meant for us? Where are the 22 Saru union affiliates today? What happened to the more than 200 volunteer rugby administrators and technical personnel? Our school rugby programme, the building blocks of Saru—where has it gone? Our rugby culture in the Black community has been destroyed in the wave of euphoria of nation-building and reconciliation. Our desire to negotiate and to work in the interest of the nation has once again been interpreted as a weakness to be exploited."[21] Having pushed hard for the unity of sports before any political settlement had been reached, the NSC stood by while community sports collapsed.[22] Rugby unity devastated social rugby in Kimberley, as elsewhere in the country. Though a very small city, Kimberley had been home to a vibrant nonracial rugby community affiliated with SACOS. Today, only the Universal Rugby Football Club remains from the nonracial era. The Arabian College RFC, which was established in 1903, unified with Hoffe Park in 1992; sadly it was a union that was not to survive long. Arabian College was a club with a very strong Muslim culture and ethos, birthed out of the squalor of the early days of Malay Camp, yielding many Kimberley legends; its union with a White club in an area far from its community roots was a recipe for disaster, and today neither club exists.

No Space or Place for Celebration

The story of rugby within the exclusive and well-resourced enclave of elite, establishment sports receives more historical and media attention than the story of the rugby that existed in the shadow of racial, social, and economic oppression. Unity has not seen the amplification of the voices silenced by apartheid; on the contrary, a new form of silence has descended on the heritage, cultures, and histories of marginalized sports communities. This silence has been evident in the absence of literature, visual, and aural outputs, and by the shutting down of sports centers such as the A.R. Abass Stadium. The physical spaces of self-expression and identity have also fallen into silence, because the oral vibrancy has also been silenced. Christopher Merrett writes that not only were playing and organizing sports under the hostility of apartheid systems expressions of identity, but "[t]o play cricket in this context meant acknowledgement of the well-known laws, traditions and spirit of the game positioned alongside commitment to social and political justice."[23]

In a commemorative booklet celebrating 125 years of Griqualand West's rugby heritage, there is scant mention of Kimberley's rich history of Black rugby.[24] In response to criticism regarding the lack of Black history in the booklet, van der Berg has responded: "In all my books there is little about the Blacks' contribution as it did not form part of the history and development of the union I was writing on."[25] Van der Berg's attitude toward Black rugby history in Kimberley is supported by the custodians of the game in the area, the Griqualand West Rugby Union (GWRU). In their eagerness to cash in on the FIFA 2010 Soccer World Cup windfall, the GWRU relinquished all social and developmental responsibility to the rugby communities they had "unified" with in 1992 by declaring the nonracial GWRFU, with whom unity was "achieved" in 1992, defunct. The cold and decontextualized wording in an extract from the memorandum of agreement between the Northern Cape provincial government and the GWRU states:

> The Stadium Company is irrevocably committed to letting GWK Park Stadium to the Northern Cape Provincial Government for its use as a training venue for the Uruguay national team and for other purposes as described in this agreement. In accordance with its plan, the Government is committed to upgrading the training venue to FIFA specifications. The Rugby Union warrants that it is borne of a merger of several now-defunct rugby unions that included the Griqualand West Rugby Football Union. The Rugby Union is the successor in right and title to the defunct Griqualand West Rugby Football Union. As the successor in right and title of Griqualand West Rugby Football Union, the Rugby Union is entitled to Erf 6377, Kimberley known as the AR Abass Stadium. As a consideration for the upgrade of the upgrade of the training venue, the Rugby Union is irrevocably committed to transferring its rights and title to the AR Abass Stadium to the Government at no extra consideration to the Government.[26]

In return for their relinquishing of the A.R. Abass Stadium, the GWRU would see the Griqualand West Rugby Stadium, known as GWK Park, receive upgrades paid for by the provincial government (in other words the taxpayers) to suit the needs of the touring Uruguayan football team, as well as receive hire income for the use of the stadium as a training

Figure 16.2. The barren space that once was home to a thriving and vibrant sports culture: the Eddie Williams Oval that was bordered by the A. R. Abass Stadium in Kimberley. *Image courtesy of Lance Fredericks © 2011.*

venue. The sporting community around the A.R. Abass Stadium received nothing from this agreement and nothing in return for the stadium itself. The memorandum of agreement between the GWRU and the Northern Cape government declares: "The Government and the Uruguay Football Association have identified GWK Park as a training venue for the Uruguay national team. The Stadium Company is irrevocably committed to letting GWK Park Stadium to the Northern Cape Government for its use as a training venue for the Uruguay national team and for other purposes as are described in this agreement. In accordance with its Plan, the Government is committed to upgrading the training venue to FIFA specifications."[27] The irony of the A.R. Abass Stadium saga is that GWK Rugby Park stands on the very ground from which the community that gave birth to the A.R. Abass Stadium was removed as a result of the apartheid era Group Areas Act in the 1950s. The community that benefited from the racially motivated forced removals has never been called to account, and sports unity has privileged those very communities who were well served by apartheid laws and legislation (figure 16.2).

There Is No Wall on Which to Hang Our Photographs

In the preface to *Beyond a Boundary* by C. L. R. James, he poses a wonderfully simple and equally complex question: "What do they know of cricket who only cricket know?"[28] With the collapse of rugby as embodied by the A.R. Abass Stadium and what it represented in terms of the struggle for justice and equality during apartheid, much the same question could be posed to the custodians of the game in Kimberley today: "What do you know of rugby who only rugby know?" What is it that the current rugby situation in Kimberley can teach marginalized communities about social cohesion? What can they teach us about the struggle for social justice through sports? The A.R. Abass Stadium and the space around the stadium enabled people across the age, class, and educational spectrums as well as those holding different religious beliefs to intersect within a space where sports was the common language in articulating the struggle for social justice.

The post-apartheid rugby structures are rooted within the cultural, ideological, and physical boundaries of apartheid. Apartheid's socioeconomic geography is still largely in force because of the unequal economic structure of South African society. The same spaces that now hold custodianship of the game of rugby gave birth to the racial laws that led to apartheid. In Kimberley, Universal RFC play their games in limbo, often having to pay a hire fee to schools or clubs in traditional White areas for a suitable rugby facility, because there are no facilities other than the A. R. Abass Stadium in the community where Universal RFC resides. The lack of access to a facility that has been home to nonracial rugby in Kimberley since being removed from the GWK Park area in the 1950s has seen rugby slowly die out in the Black community of Kimberley.

This lack of physical space is also reflected in publications and other media products within the mainstream. In 2011, an official publication of the GWRU, *Diamonds in the Rough: 125 Years of Griqua Rugby, 1886–2011*, made scant mention of the contribution of Black rugby to the development and cultural history of the game in Kimberley. Three pages in the booklet hint at the existence of Black rugby outside of the accepted enclave of White rugby.[29] On page 30 there is a photograph of the 1992 SACOS-affiliated GWRU executive, with no names. This was the executive in charge of the GWRU during the year of unification![30] Pages 30 to 34 are dedicated to the "biggest moments" in GWRU history, and yet unification is not mentioned. On page 39 there are two photographs of the 1947 Griqua team Rhodes Cup holders, and below that the 1953 Wilfred Orr Shield winners, Young Collegians. Mr. A. R. Abass, the man whose name adorns the nearly derelict space on the corner of Stockroos Street and Pniel Road, is not mentioned in any context relating to his contribution to the game of rugby, except on page 59, where it is mentioned that the old GWRU grounds was renamed the A. R. Abass Stadium.

The socialization and politicization of the youth and the communities who were actively involved in sports are also important. Mr. A. R. Abass is but one of the figures involved in the fight for social justice through sports, and in Kimberley alone many other names could be added to an honor role dedicated to those who fought the injustices of racism and apartheid through sports.

Thistle RFC, which celebrated its centenary in 2008, does not exist anymore, and even efforts by community members to start rugby clinics in the community have been thwarted by lack of access to the A. R. Abass Stadium. Moreover, the community that supports Universal RFC has received no compensation for a stadium in which its members are heavily invested emotionally, politically, and historically.[31] The Baby Richards Hall, which is at the A. R. Abass Stadium, is named after the first president of the "unified" GWRU. On the walls of the hall are scattered photographs of past rugby greats, a display that does no justice to the epic rugby dramas that played out at the stadium. Many sports images are stored at the Afrikana Library in Kimberley, an underutilized repository of social and historical materials relating to Kimberley and its past—a place that very few residents around the A. R. Abass Stadium would ever conceive of visiting.[32]

The work done by community leaders through sports during the apartheid era cannot be discounted. Sports was, in essence, the lifeblood of structured and disciplined community resistance and defiance against apartheid. Through sports, apartheid was shown to be a destructive social policy, and as the sports boycott denied apartheid South Africa a place among the nations of the world on the playing fields, community centers such as A. R. Abass Stadium were beacons of hope and sites of political and social education during an era of extreme violence and repression. Today no such center exists in Kimberley, because the A. R. Abass Stadium has locked out the community for which it sprang into existence in the first place. The decline of the fortunes of the

Springboks and the South African Super Rugby teams was preceded by the decline of community clubs within the historical areas of apartheid repression, as epitomized by the saga of the A. R. Abass Stadium. The visuals of Nelson Mandela and Francois Pienaar celebrating the Springbok victory in 1995 are hollow when contrasted with the histories that these images downplay or obliterate. The bitter struggle against apartheid through sports has resulted in the liberation of White sporting honor and the suppression of Black sporting honor, as epitomized by the antiapartheid sports struggle in and through sports.

There are no spaces of honor for the heroes of anti-apartheid sports in the new South Africa. The apartheid sporting structures that were legitimized through the processes of unity remain intact, far removed in terms of sociopolitical ideology and social distance from the communities that bore the brunt of apartheid viciousness. In Kimberley, the A. R. Abass Stadium and the Eddie Williams Sports Complex are a testament to the continued marginalization of Black sporting communities in South Africa.

The ceding of the A. R. Abass Stadium to the Northern Cape provincial government has removed a space within which the heroes of the nonracial struggle can be honored in Kimberley. The removal of the A. R. Abass Stadium from the center of the rugby community in Squarehill Park is an insult to the memory of people who are not honored by the current system. Clubs such as Arabian College (1903–1992), Thistle RFC (1908–2010), Young Collegians (1953–1993), and Universal RFC (est. 1886) have no place of honor within the spaces created by the current GWRU structures, as illustrated by the omissions in *Diamonds in the Rough*.[33]

The nature of the current sporting system in South Africa, specifically pertaining to rugby, serves to decontextualize the broad framework of apartheid and its constrictive hold over Black communities in all areas of public life. Through sports, apartheid has become little more than a footnote, as references are made not to the apartheid era, but rather to the era of isolation, without framing the latter era within the sociopolitical context of apartheid and the preceding eras of conquest and racial segregation. Slick marketing and public relations campaigns such as the

2023 SARU bid video[34] can only divert attention from the truth about our sporting and social realities for a limited time. George Orwell wrote that sports, once removed from the social common, become "bound up in with the rise of nationalism—that is, with the lunatic modern habit of identifying oneself with large power units and seeing everything in terms of competitive prestige."[35] We need to return to the energized space of the "village green," where, as Orwell wrote: "It is possible to play simply for the fun and the exercise."[36]

Notes

1. Mine dumps surrounded the Eddie Williams Cricket Oval. The blue-gray mounds encircled the field and formed a sort of amphitheater, with the sound of bat against ball echoing around the ground. The Northern Cape government issued mining concessions, and the dumps have been reworked, completely destroying the playing field and obliterating the mounds of tailings dumps.

2. SACOS was established in 1973. It was widely recognized as the official sports wing of the liberation movement within South Africa. It was replaced by the ANC–aligned National Sports Congress (NSC) in stages between 1989 and 1991/1992.

3. In Kimberley, as in the rest of South Africa, the effects of apartheid intruded deeper than just skin color, and the sports experience revealed how reconciliation on unequal terms was destined to be problematic for an indeterminate period. Clubs in poor communities were encouraged to combine in order to compete on financial terms with the financially stronger White clubs. The individual histories of the clubs were considered to be inconsequential or were not considered at all, and much was lost in terms of social history during this period of unification.

4. Cornelius Thomas, ed., *Sport and Liberation in South Africa—Suggestions and Reflections* (Alice, South Africa: National Heritage and Cultural Studies Centre: 2006), 143, 149.

5. Chris van Wyk, *Now Listen Here—The Biography of Bill Jardine* (Johannesburg: STE, 2003).

6. Thomas, *Sport and Liberation in South Africa*, 143.

7. Ashwin Desai, *The Race to Transform Sport in Post Apartheid South Africa* (Cape Town: HSRC, 2010), 61–62. Due to "transformation" and development requirements of the new unified rugby (sports) bodies, White clubs were encouraged to field Black athletes as part of their quota requirements.

Socioeconomic disparities limited the Black rugby footprint in White suburbs, leading to the practice of poaching and/or importing of Black rugby talent to meet quotas.

8. Van Wyk, *Now Listen Here*, 217.

9. Thomas, *Sport and Liberation in South Africa*, 143, 149.

10. Official Springbok YouTube, "#2023 RWC Bid Video," October 25, 2017, https://www.youtube.com/watch?v=LVMk4UoZjBo.

11. Thomas, *Sport and Liberation in South Africa*, 121.

12. The *Diamond Fields Advertiser* (DFA) was founded in Kimberley in 1878 and is official evidence of the existence of rugby specifically and sports generally in the Black communities of Kimberley prior to unity in 1992.

13. K. Duminy, *McAnda's Sport—A Photographic Collection* (Kimberley, South Africa: Kimberley Africana Library, 2009), 7.

14. The Hotel Kemo, which is just down the road from the A.R. Abass Stadium, served as home to official club meetings as well as official Griqualand West Rugby Union meetings. The hotel was also home to a nightclub—Moon-flower—that donated some of its takings to the various clubs by prearrangement. Mr. Noor Moosagee, son-in-law of Mr. A. R. Abass, owned the hotel. The butcher shop of Mr. Joey Bezuidenhout was just around the corner and provided meat products to clubs for their various fund-raising efforts; in turn the communities supported the butcher shop. The area was also home to the Lyric Cinema, and clubs would book the cinema from time to time and sell tickets to the community at slightly inflated prices in order to raise funds. All codes and schools affiliated with SACOS made use of the goodwill of the businesses in the area in their fund-raising efforts; the businesses donated goods, services, or cash. Many other businesses formed part of this network, including pharmacies, clothing stores, and hardware stores. It was virtually impossible to escape sports talk when visiting these businesses, as the owners as well as community members were heavily invested in their shared passion for sports.

15. Duncan Green, *From Poverty to Power* (Oxford: Oxfam International, 2008), 18.

16. New Unity Movement (NUM), *50th Year of Struggle: 1943–1993* (Wynberg, South Africa: New Unity Movement, 1993), 63–64.

17. Thomas, *Sport and Liberation in South Africa*, 148, 149.

18. The biography of Bill Jardine is a highly entertaining read, but it is very thin on the details that would be of interest to academic researchers. It is nonetheless an important book for sports researchers.

19. Van Wyk, *Now Listen Here*, 213.

20. Thomas, *Sport and Liberation in South Africa*, 143. For various reasons, primarily SACOS's staunch opposition to the permit system and strict adherence to the "'double standards'" resolution, the footprint in Black African

townships was very limited. The NSC's promise of spreading sports to these barren areas was mere lip service to hasten the processes of unity and the lifting of the sports moratorium. The lack of organized mass-based sports in townships today is a testament to the failure of this promise by the NSC.

21. Van Wyk, *Now Listen Here*, 230.

22. Thomas, *Sport and Liberation in South Africa*, 150.

23. Christopher Merrett, *Sport, Space and Segregation* (Scottsville, South Africa: University of KwaZulu Natal Press, 2009), xv.

24. Wim van der Berg, *Diamonds in the Rough—125 Years of Griqua Rugby* (Johannesburg: Online Publishing, 2011).

25. Wim van der Berg, email to GWRU's Nadia Louw, August 18, 2014 (in response to my emails regarding the lack of Black historical representation in the 2011 *Diamonds in the Rough* commemorative booklet).

26. Memorandum of Agreement between the Northern Cape Provincial Government and the Griqualand West Rugby Stadium (PTY) Limited, February 6, 2010 (author's collection).

27. Memorandum of Agreement, February 6, 2010.

28. C. L. R. James, *Beyond a Boundary* (London: Yellow Jersey Press, 1963), preface.

29. Van der Berg, *Diamonds in the Rough*, 30, 39, 59.

30. By 1992 SACOS had all but lost all code affiliates. At the special general meeting held in Kimberley on November 26, 1989, the "dual membership" resolution was adopted, which prohibited affiliates from belonging to both SACOS and the NSC; this resolution resulted in many code affiliates terminating their membership in SACOS and moving over to the NSC.

31. All documents relating to the purchase of the A.R. Abass Stadium have been located, and verified copies have been obtained. The local deeds office in Kimberley, however, has been unable to grant permission for the use of the documents in this chapter for reasons that are unclear. Verbal permission has been repeatedly granted, but the permission to publish form has not been signed, apparently because no one has the authority to grant such permission.

32. Since the community was shut out of the stadium, it is unclear whether these items are still on display in the hall.

33. Van der Berg, *Diamonds in the Rough*.

34. Official Springbok YouTube, "#2023 RWC Bid Video."

35. George Orwell, *Seeing Things as They Are: Selected Journalism and Other Writings* London: Penguin Random House UK, 2016), 348.

36. Orwell, *Seeing Things as They Are*, 347.

SEVENTEEN

The Gift of a Running Shoe

Heritage and the Comrades Marathon House

MARIZANNE GRUNDLINGH

Every year, thousands of road runners flock to KwaZulu-Natal to take part in the Comrades Marathon, the world's oldest and largest ultramarathon event. Those who have completed the race can proudly associate with the distinguished group of people who can claim that they have a 90-kilometer road race as part of their running repertoire. The ritualistic and symbolic elements of the Comrades Marathon have been explored by anthropologist Christo van Vuuren, but scholars have otherwise largely neglected the dynamics of heritage associated with the race.[1] Drawing on interviews with the curator of the Comrades Marathon House (the museum dedicated to the race) and prominent runners who have completed the Comrades Marathon, this chapter analyzes how the dynamics of heritage play out in both tangible and transient ways. The concept of *topophilia*, as applied by John Bale, is used to argue that the Comrades Marathon House and those runners who frequent it have developed a distinct "love of place."[2] The "relationship" runners have with the museum and the race itself is reciprocal, and I show how the practice of gift giving is central to the survival of the museum.

The interpretive and experiential qualities of heritage have increasingly become the focus of contemporary studies on heritage production.[3]

Sports as a form of heritage has been considered an especially relevant social setting in which the experiential qualities associated with heritage can manifest, whether through intangible means (e.g., songs, rituals, or superstitions associated with a sports team or venue) or more tangible means (e.g., visiting sports stadiums, sports museums, and sports halls of fame). Trends in "new museology" have focused on museums as spaces where objects on display are not fixed but shift with changing contexts. Visitors' perceptions of displays are also malleable, and museums have become places of "edutainment," with interactive displays becoming key to the visitor's experience.

History of the Comrades Marathon

The Comrades Marathon House is a museum dedicated to preserving the heritage associated with the Comrades Marathon. The histories of the race and the museum are intertwined. This section of the chapter provides a brief history of the Comrades Marathon, highlighting significant events and memorable moments.

The founder of the Comrades Marathon was Vic Clapham, a South African soldier who returned home after World War I. His vision was to pay tribute to those soldiers who had died during the conflict. The first race took place in 1921. The founders of the Comrades Marathon consciously considered the race to be for the "ordinary man," not the athlete—the infantryman, not the officer.[4] The Comrades Marathon is until this day considered to be a race that is inclusive of all.

In the 1930s the Comrades Marathon was dominated by four-time Comrades Marathon winner Hardy Ballington, and it was in this decade that Wally Hayward, who was to become a legend of the race in his own right, won his first title (in 1930). This decade also witnessed the first Black man completing the Comrades Marathon, albeit unofficially. It was not until 1975 that people of all races, as well as women, were officially able to participate in the race. World War II interrupted the organization of the Comrades Marathon, as no race was held between 1941 and 1945.

The second half of the twentieth century saw the race undergo significant changes. The number of entrants grew significantly, and by 1969, eight hundred runners had entered the race. The Comrades Marathon grew substantially in the 1970s, both of the number of participants and who was allowed to compete. The race numbers increased from 865 entrants in 1970 to 3,410 at the close of the decade, in 1979. The marked increase in the popularity of the race can be traced to broader political and societal concerns regarding sports at the time. South African sports had been boycotted because of the country's apartheid policies. Considering that there was little outside the country in terms of sporting events, local events like the Currie Cup and the Comrades became fortunate beneficiaries of this period.[5] It was also during this decade, in 1975, that television was introduced in South Africa, which offered the race organizers an opportunity to cover the race live and reach broader audiences.

The 1980s stand out as a significant decade in the history of the race. This was a result of the increased media coverage and publicity that the race received, but also because of the blond, long-haired Wits University running machine, Bruce Fordyce. Fordyce won the Comrades for eight consecutive years (1981–1988), and with his humble nature and dogmatic political stance against apartheid, he won the hearts of millions of South African liberals. The 1981 Comrades Marathon was especially laden with political significance, as the uneasy relationship between sports and politics became a public spectacle. The apartheid government had announced that the 1981 Comrades Marathon would form part of the celebration of Republic Day. Many students at English-speaking universities, who traditionally opposed apartheid, disapproved of being associated with nationalistic celebrations through their participation in the race. Many decided to boycott the race, while others made a visible protest by wearing a black armband, a symbol broadcasting their antiapartheid stance.[6] Fordyce, in solidarity with his fellow runners, also wore a black armband, showcasing his political disapproval of the apartheid regime.

Despite these distractions, Fordyce won the 1981 Comrades Marathon and would cement his place as one of the Comrades Greats over the course of the 1980s. By the early 1990s, South Africa's political landscape had changed drastically. On February 2, 1990, President F. W. de Klerk announced that Nelson Mandela would be freed, and the ban on the African National Congress was lifted. This shift in politics would inevitably affect all sectors of society, including sports. South Africa was readmitted to the international sporting scene, and this meant that a wave of international athletes ventured to compete in the Comrades Marathon. South Africa started its route toward transformation, and by April 1994, the country had held its first democratic election.

The Comrades Marathon would also adapt to the drastically chang-ing South African society. Sam Tshabalala became the first Black South African to win the Comrades Marathon, in 1989, in the down run (the route direction from Pietermaritzburg to Durban), and he paved the way for the race in the new dispensation. It was during this decade that athletics in South Africa became fully professional. Athletes were now lured to compete for monetary rewards.

In the twenty-first century the Comrades Marathon has witnessed an increase in professional and elite athletes competing for top honors. The race itself has undergone significant changes, as sponsorship of the race and athletes has become a major contributing factor in organizing the race, luring athletes with lucrative prize money. The winner of the 2018 Comrades Marathon (for both men and women) earned R425,000. The date on which the race is held has also changed, from June 16 to the first weekend in June, after the ANC Youth League complained that the race distracted attention from Youth Day celebrations.[7]

The Comrades Marathon House

The Comrades Marathon House, located at 18 Connaught Road, Pietermaritzburg, is both the venue at which the race is organized and a museum that exhibits the race's history. It is the only museum in the country that is dedicated solely to road running. Entrance to the mu-seum is free. The museum is registered as a nongovernmental organi-zation (NGO), and the contents are determined by the Heritage and Traditions Committee of the Comrades Marathon Association. The running artifacts in the museum were collected by a group of well-known runners, in particular Alan Robb, who traveled across the coun-try to obtain memorabilia. The museum has a wide selection of personal memorabilia associated with the Comrades, as well as a comprehensive set of pictorial boards covering the history of the race from its inception.

Topophilia and Heritage at the Comrades Marathon House

The Comrades Museum's only interactive display is the scale model. Most of the exhibits rely on the visitor's existing knowledge of road running in South Africa. The curator of the Comrades Marathon museum, Sian Theron, elaborated on the fairly "traditional" nature of the exhibits: "You'll see that the displays haven't changed much at all for the last 30 years, since the museum was conceived. So, it is very old school. And it does focus on legends. The guys who have won five to nine times, who've really done amazing things in the race."[8]

There has been a shift in the conceptualization of South African sports museums to meet consumer and commercial demands. This is particularly apparent at the Springbok Experience Museum at the Victoria and Alfred Waterfront in Cape Town, as well as the planned Blue Bulls rugby museum in Pretoria. The Comrades Museum has not, however, become overly commercialized, and the use of technology is minimal.

As an NGO, the museum's aim is not necessarily to make a profit by selling regalia associated with the Comrades. There is, however, a "Comrades Wall of Honour" situated at a point on the race route, overlooking the Valley of a Thousand Hills. The wall serves as a permanent landmark at which runners who have completed the race can purchase spaces where their names will be enshrined. Plaques are bought by runners, family members, or friends on their behalf to be presented as gifts for special birthdays, anniversaries, Comrades milestones, or other occasions. Many of the blocks commemorate deceased Comrades runners, and several feature religious relics and mini-memorial gardens. The Wall of Honour memorial blocks cost R450 each, which includes the block, plaque, and engraving, as well as maintenance and upkeep of the block and site for posterity. Heritage in this instance is manufactured and of personal significance to the athlete or his or her family.

What then is the relationship between those who have run the Comrades and the Comrades Marathon museum? Sports geographer

John Bale has used the term *topophilia* to describe the affective ties that people develop with the material environment, to capture their distinctive "love of place."[9] He uses five metaphors to explore the public meanings of football stadiums. First, the stadium is a "sacred place," where a sense of spirituality is experienced by those fans who frequent it. Second, the stadium may be a place that is visually pleasurable and therefore one of "scenic" qualities. Third, the idea of the stadium as a "home" for players offers a psychological advantage to visiting teams. Fourth, the stadium may be a "tourist place," a form of heritage where visitors can learn about the history of the stadium and memorable events, through stadium tours. Fifth, the stadium may represent local pride; the team constitutes "a focus for community bonding and the source for 'reconstruction' of some former Gemeinschaft."[10]

With reference to Bale's use of the concept topophilia, I argue that the Comrades Marathon House elicits similar positive affiliations with a sporting place to those indicated in Bale's analysis of football stadiums. First, the Comrades Marathon House is a "sacred place" where revered memorabilia of the race are preserved, and where particular rituals take place prior to the race. For example, at the official opening of the Comrades House in 1988, one of the coveted artifacts was the bullhorn that Vic Clapham used to start the first Comrades Marathon in 1921. Vic Clapham's son, Doug, was photographed posing with the bullhorn at the museum's official opening. This gesture is indicative of how the history and the material culture associated with the race are preserved by an intimate group of people whose personal histories are intertwined with the race. It also points to the significance of preserving material artifacts that are of sacred value in terms of the race's history. The words of the current curator of the Comrades House museum highlight how some of the superstitious beliefs of runners play out at the Comrades Marathon House:

> Many runners make a point of it to come register at the Comrades
> Marathon House (rather than any of the other registration
> venues). They believe that by visiting the museum and having a
> chance to look around at the significance of the race over a long

history gives them that drive to become one of the many who have finished the race. The ritual of coming to registration and going through the routine of waiting in line to collect the race number, chatting to the fellow runners, and reminiscing about past races all contributes to their preparation for the race. It is almost like a sacred space that they need to enter, and for some, that superstition will determine the success of their run.[11]

Several scholars have extended the idea of a sacred sports place to include traveling to sporting events as a form of secular pilgrimage.[12] Sean Gammon argues that "some sport sites (whatever the category) will provoke intense feelings of awe and wonderment, similar to those experienced by pilgrims at religious sites. However, it would be misleading to propose sport as a new form of religion. It would be safer to conclude that sport can (especially with regard to fandom) offer similar functions to religion such as invoking a sense of belonging, purpose and consolation."[13] This tentative proposition that sports and religion have commonalities, espousing a sense of belonging, can be attributed to the Comrades museum as a "pilgrimage" site. Furthermore, the nature of the actual race—running from one city to the other—also resonates with the idea of pilgrimage, which in its simplest form can be understood as a journey to visit a destination that holds some form of personal or collective meaning (however profane) for the traveler.[14] Van Vuuren's work on the ritualistic dimension of the Comrades exemplifies this point: "The Comrades is also a ritual of transition, a transfer into a new order, and simultaneously a rite of incorporation into the order of Comrades medallists, the Comrades legacy and the mythological past. Running the Comrades repetitively comprise a rite of intensification. The notion of territorial passage through real and symbolic portals and gates features prominent during the Comrades passage."[15] Several runners I spoke to referred to their desire to run the Comrades as a feat they wanted to achieve for specific emotive and symbolic reasons. The physical, emotional, and mental aptitude required to complete the race is often supported by a desire to complete the race for "something bigger than themselves."

The second factor contributing to a sense of affiliation with a sporting place, according to Bale, is its visual attractiveness. In this regard, the Comrades Marathon Association took great pains to ensure that the Comrades House would be visually appealing. The restoration of the Victorian-style building was done by Wynand Claassen, an ex-Springbok rugby player and himself a Comrades runner. To ensure its aesthetic appeal, the restorers went to the trouble of acquiring one of the last old-fashioned lampposts from the Pietermaritzburg municipality. The property has been formally listed as a national monument.

As for the third element that Bale mentions, from the layout of the museum and the social events that are organized there, it is evident that the Comrades House acts as a "home" for runners. A pub area was established on the ground floor and was initially used for monthly social evenings. Although the Comrades House does not offer a distinct advantage for local runners, it does serve as a beacon of familiarity for those who return to it prior to a race.

In the fourth place, the idea of a sports museum as a "tourist place" is particularly applicable to the Comrades Marathon House. The museum is affiliated with the provincial KwaZulu-Natal Museum Services and receives a subsidy from the province every year. Foreign athletes who compete in the Comrades Marathon are taken on a tour of the actual running route and of the museum prior to the race. Barbara Kirshenblatt-Gimblett argues that museums have become "destinations" within the tourist industry: "Tourism needs destinations and museums are premier attractions. Museums are not only destinations on an itinerary; they are also nodes in a network of attractions that form the recreational geography of a region and, increasingly, the globe. Heritage and tourism are collaborative industries, heritage converting locations into destinations, and tourism making them economically viable as exhibits of themselves. Locations become museums of themselves within a tourist economy."[16]

The Comrades museum as a "location" at which the race is organized and a physical place where memorabilia associated with the race are displayed has become one of the many tourist destinations in Pietermaritzburg. The influx of runners to the museum, especially building up to the race, is apparent. Approximately 5,000 visitors frequent the museum annually, 4,000 of whom come to the museum over the race weekend. The economic injection that the region receives as a result of hosting the race is remarkable. The 2000 Comrades Marathon had a record 24,800 entries, and it is estimated that Comrades runners and their supporters poured R300 million into the economy that year.[17]

Regarding the fifth element that inspires a love of place, the museum elicits local pride and a form of communal bonding in the week leading up to the race, as an estimated four thousand runners gather at the museum. With international athletes dominating the Comrades in the past decade, the museum serves as a reminder to South African prospects of what can be achieved and in turn is a space for communal affiliation around nationhood. The spectatorship of up to 502,000 people at the 2000 race, mostly from the local community, substantiates the local support that runners have from the fans who line the route.[18]

Most of the running memorabilia in the museum were donated by athletes or family members of athletes. An "agreement of donation" contract is signed between the Comrades Marathon Association and the donor. The next part of the chapter considers how the anthropological concept of gift giving may inform an understanding of the significance of gifting race-running memorabilia.

The Individual and the Gift of the Running Shoe

Sports museums often exhibit items related to sports stars who have cemented their place in sporting history. Balthi du Plessis, the heritage consultant and exhibition designer for the planned Blue Bull rugby museum at Loftus, explained the importance of building an exhibition around a sporting icon:

> You can't sell a sport. One can try to sell soccer, or rugby, or athletics. But no one is really interested in the sport. People are interested in sport through an association with a person or a team. Interest is stimulated if you can attract attention to an individual who excelled in sport, heroes from the past. As one

delves deeper into that specific heroic figure from the past, one can create new sport heroes and that can trigger a nostalgic attachment to that person. That is actually what you sell. You don't sell Loftus museum as the stadium's museum. You sell it as the field that Frik du Preez scored a try on, or the field that Victor Matfield won the Super 14 on. That is what you sell. It is all connected to the individual. A successful museum experience is always on a personal level, never on a generic level. The most important common denominator is the association with an individual.[19]

Many sports museums use the sporting apparel of sports stars to generate an association with the individual athlete. The exhibition dedicated to Bruce Fordyce highlights how his memorabilia are used to represent the symbolism and ethos of the race's association with the individual. In an interview with Fordyce, he explained that he considers himself a form of living heritage, embodying the values of the Comrades. It is for this reason that he is still actively involved in organizing races around the country as well as commentating on the race every year.

The context in which Bruce Fordyce rose to fame in the 1980s is important to understand why he has achieved legendary status. Fordyce has completed thirty Comrades Marathons, winning the event every year between 1981 and 1988 and again in 1990. The exhibition dedicated to him in the museum has two pairs of running shoes. The caption reads: "The vest and shoes worn by Bruce Fordyce from 1980–1984, when he ran for Wits." The caption for the second pair of running shoes on display reads: "Running shoe worn by Bruce Fordyce during the 1983 Comrades Marathon. He lost a toenail during the race, hence the front cut away."

The running memorabilia of legendary athletes are not the only mode of heritage. Gammon argues that the significance of their achievement is often socially determined: "Heroes, then, are culturally formed and situated. The interpretation of courage, skill, achievement and any other related criteria is socially determined, as is the extent that such achievements are valued and nurtured. They represent a cultural ideal that people wish to protect, celebrate, and ultimately emulate.... The living hero, then, is a conduit to the past; one who embodies the extraordinary achievements and experiences that so many admire and look up to."[20] These artifacts and the detailed description of the shoe Fordyce wore in the 1984 race all point to how the exhibition at the museum uses an individual to celebrate the race's heritage. The detailed description of the loss of Fordyce's toenail enables the visitor to associate with him, not as an immortal running machine, but as a human, a person who shares characteristics with the "ordinary" man. The Comrades is therefore not a generic event with faceless people; rather, the museum has used specific icons to create an association with the race through an individual, in this case Bruce Fordyce.

The curator of the museum explained that the museum is for many athletes an embodiment of the race and the ethos of the race. They therefore want to contribute to the legacy of preserving the material culture of the race by donating many of their personal running memorabilia. The gifting of sports memorabilia allows for an analysis of the social dynamics of giving and receiving sports memorabilia for museum purposes.

Exchange relations have historically been a core interest for anthropologists. One of the earliest classical studies on exchange was Bronislaw Malinowski's work on the Trobriand Islands and his discussion of the Kula ring in *Argonauts of the Western Pacific*.[21] Malinowski was concerned with showing how Trobriand Islanders engaged in exchange in recognizable and sensible ways, as independent, calculating transactors. Another prominent theorist, Marcel Mauss, has examined social identifications and understandings of people, objects, and social relations. The Maussian view of gift relations considers exchange in terms of (1) the obligatory transfer of (2) inalienable objects or services between (3) related and mutually obligated transactors.[22]

Inalienable objects refers to the idea that gifts are to some extent part of people.[23] The gift generates and regenerates the relationship between the giver and the recipient. The inalienable object as a gift is particularly relevant to the donating of sports memorabilia as gifts. For example, the value of the running vest and shoes that Fordyce wore in the Comrades is determined by the person who wore them and the context in which he achieved fame. The memorabilia are therefore an extension of his persona, his achievements, and how he as an individual has become representative of the Comrades Marathon. For Mauss, the object given possesses a "personality," and therefore a person presented with an object receives part of the giver's personality. This *Hau* or "spirit of the gift" demands a form of reciprocity.

Mauss's theory can be applied to the giving, receiving, and reciprocating of running memorabilia. First, the running shoe, vest, or medal is an extension of the athlete, and the giving of it is the first step to building social relationships. Second, considering that the Comrades museum is dependent on donations of sporting artifacts, it is obliged to receive the gift, thereby accepting the social bond. In return, and as a form of reciprocation, the museum exhibits contribute to the veneration of past athletes for their achievements, and they in turn become symbolically immortal through the artifacts on display. The *symbolic capital* that is bestowed on the athlete is therefore an extension of his or her achievement and fixed in public memory.

The donation of running memorabilia to the Comrades museum occurs within a group of runners who share a particular collective status and have cemented relations based on their involvement and achievements in the Comrades Marathon. The symbolic capital that these artifacts reflect contributes to athletes of the past being cemented in public memory, and through this gesture they achieve a sense of symbolic immortality through their exhibits. The reciprocity of the gift is therefore able to promote the legacy of these athletes for generations to come.

This chapter has probed both the intangible and tangible aspects of heritage associated with the Comrades Marathon. The shifting dynamics of the preservation of the race's heritage point to the role that community sports museums can play in an era in which heritage has become overtly commercialized. The Comrades Marathon House as a sacred space and the ritualistic dimension of the heritage of the race have been explored here. By drawing on Bale's notion of topophilia, I have shown how the museum carries significant meaning to those who have completed the race. The living form of heritage and the idea of "heroes as heritage" contribute to the legacy of the race, which thrives outside of the confines of the actual museum. The practice of gift giving of memorabilia associated with the Comrades has been interrogated. The museum is dependent on memorabilia that are donated, and this transaction carries significant intangible consequences. The symbolism associated with sporting artifacts ensures that the legacy of athletes remains ingrained in public memory.

Notes

1. Christo van Vuuren, "A Ritual Perspective on the Comrades Marathon," *South African Journal for Research in Sport, Physical Education and Recreation* 36, no. 2 (2014): 211–24.

2. John Bale, "Playing at Home," in *British Football and Social Change*, ed. John Williams and Stephen Wagg (Leicester, UK: Leicester University Press, 1991).

3. See Sean Gammon, "Sporting New Attractions? The Commodification of the Sleeping Stadium," in *Sport Experiences: Contemporary Perspectives*, ed. Sean Gammon and Joseph Kurtzman (London: Routledge, 2010), 115–26; Sean Gammon, "Heroes as Heritage: The Commoditization of Sporting Achievement," *Journal of Heritage Tourism* 9, no. 3 (2014): 1–11; Gregory Ramshaw, "Living Heritage and the Sport Museum: Athletes, Legacy and the Olympic Hall of Fame and Museum, Canada Olympic Park," *Journal of Sport and Tourism* 15, no. 1 (2010): 45–70; Gregory Ramshaw, "The Construction of Sport Heritage Attractions," *Journal of Tourism Consumption and Practice* 3, no. 1 (2011): 1–25; Laurajane Smith, *The Uses of Heritage* (London: Routledge, 2006); and Hyung yu Park, *Heritage Tourism* (London: Routledge, 2014).

4. D. Williams, "The Comrades Marathon: A Historical Perspective," in *Comrades Marathon: Highlights and Heroes, 1921–1999*, ed. I. Laxton, T. Cotterel, and D. Williams (Johannesburg: Jonathan Ball, 2000).

5. Williams, "The Comrades Marathon."

6. John Cameron-Dow, *Comrades Marathon: The Ultimate Human Race* (Johannesburg: Penguin Books, 2011).

7. From 1963 to 1994, the race was run on May 31, Republic day. This public holiday was scrapped in 1995 by the newly elected ANC government, and the race date was changed to June 16, Youth Day. In 2007 the race organizers

controversially changed the race date, after political pressure enforced by the ANC Youth League, which argued that the race distracted attention from the actual meaning and significance of the day, which was to commemorate the youth who died in the 1976 Soweto Uprising.

8. Sian Theron (Comrades Marathon House curator), interview with author, January 7, 2014.

9. John Bale, *Landscapes of Modern Sport* (London: Leicester University Press, 1994).

10. John Bale, "Playing at Home."

11. Theron interview, January 7, 2014.

12. Sean Gammon, "Secular Pilgrimage and Sport Tourism," in *Sport Tourism: Interrelationships, Impacts and Issues*, ed. Brent W. Ritchie and Daryl Adair (Clevedon, UK: Channel View Publications, 2004); Sheranne Fairley, "In Search of Relived Social Experience: Group-Based Nostalgia Sport Tourism," *Journal of Sport Management* 17 (2003): 284–301; Gerald Redmond, "A Plethora of Shrines: Sport in the Museums and Hall of Fame," *Quest* 19 (1973): 41–48; and Eldon Snyder, "Sociology of Nostalgia: Halls of Fame and Museums in America," *Sociology of Sport Journal* 8 (1991): 228–38.

13. Gammon, "Secular Pilgrimage and Sport Tourism."

14. Gammon, "Secular Pilgrimage and Sport Tourism."

15. Van Vuuren, "Ritual Perspective on the Comrades Marathon."

16. Barbara Kirshenblatt-Gimblett, *Destination Culture: Tourism; Museums and Heritage* (Berkeley: University of California Press, 1998).

17. "Economy Gets R300 Million Boost from the Comrades," *Business Day*, June 19, 2000, 5.

18. "Comrades a Huge Economic Boost," *Natal Witness*, June 19, 2000, 8.

19. Balthi Du Plessis (Blue Bulls Rugby Museum Heritage Consultant and Exhibition designer), interview with author, August 4, 2014.

20. Gammon, "Heroes as Heritage."

21. Bronislaw Malownoski, *Argonauts of the Western Pacific* (London: Routledge and Kegan Paul, 1922).

22. Marcel Mauss, *The Gift* (London: Routledge and Kegan Paul, 1965).

23. Mauss, *The Gift*.

ABOUT THE EDITORS AND CONTRIBUTORS

Ernest Yeboah Acheampong is a lecturer in the Department of Health, Physical Education, Recreation and Sports (HPERS) at the University of Education, Winneba, Ghana, and an associate researcher in the Laboratory of Sport and Social Environment at Université Grenoble Alpes, France. His research interests are African football, footballers' migration and mobility, football management and coaching, youth football and education, sports for development, and the giving back phenomenon. He has recently published (with Malek Bouhaouala and Michel Raspaud) *African Footballers in Europe: Migration, Community and Give Back Behaviours* (Routledge, 2019). He has published articles in a number of academic journals, chapters in forthcoming books, and articles in sports newspapers and magazines. He is a reviewer for some scientific journals and a member of several scientific societies (e.g., EASS, ISSA, EASM, 3SLF).

Sine Agergaard is a social anthropologist and a professor with specific responsibilities in humanistic and social sports science at Aalborg University, Denmark. Her research focuses on migration issues within sport and is published in a wide range of peer-reviewed journals and books, including *Women, Soccer and Transnational Migration* (Routledge, 2014) and *Rethinking Sport and Integration* (Routledge, 2018). Agergaard is a cofounder and manager of the International Network for Research in Sport and Migration Issues.

Gerard Akindes is currently working for the Josoor Institute in Doha, Qatar. His roles with the Josoor Institute consist of organizing training and coordinating research projects in sports and events sports management. He is one of the cofounders and coordinator at the Sports in Africa Conferences and the electronic interdisciplinary journal of African sports, *Impumelelo*. Akindes has an extensive sports background of active engagement in both playing and coaching. He played international basketball in Benin, Togo, and Cote d'Ivoire and coached youth, women's, and men's basketball in Belgium. His research interests include political economy of sports broadcasting, elite and young athletes' migration, sports development, and sports for development.

Peter Alegi is a professor of history at Michigan State University and a research associate at the University of KwaZulu-Natal in South Africa. His books include *Laduma! Soccer, Politics and Society in South Africa* (University of KwaZulu-Natal Press, 2004), *African Soccerscapes: How a Continent Changed the World's Game* (Ohio University Press, 2010), and (coedited with Chris Bolsmann) *Africa's World Cup: Critical Reflections on Play, Patriotism, Spectatorship, and Space* (University of Michigan Press, 2013). He hosts the *Africa Past and Present* podcast (afripod .aodl.org) and convenes the Football Scholars Forum (footballscholars .org). Alegi is founding editor of Michigan State University Press's African History and Culture book series and is an editor of *African Studies Review*, the journal of the US African Studies Association.

Malek Bouhaouala is an associate professor of socioeconomics of sport at the University of Grenoble Alpes. His research interests concern socioeconomics of sport, entrepreneurs' behaviors, and ecosystem innovation in sports and sports tourism. He has published a book on the management of small business in sports recreation and numerous articles on entrepreneurs' behaviors in the sports sector and sports consumers' socioeconomic behaviors. Currently, he coordinates a research program on ecosystem innovation in the mountain sports industry. He serves on many scientific boards of international conferences and is a reviewer for several scientific journals. He supervised a thesis on the give back behavior of African footballers in Europe.

Matt Carotenuto is a professor of African history at St. Lawrence University in Canton, New York. He is also chair of the board of directors of Africa Network, an organization focused on promoting the study of Africa within the undergraduate curriculum. His research has long focused on Kenyan history, sports, and the politics of identity. At St. Lawrence he works closely with the university's long-standing Kenya Semester Program, and with Katherine Luongo he is the author of *Obama and Kenya: Contested Histories and the Politics of Belonging in Kenya* (Ohio University Press, 2016).

Derek Charles Catsam is a professor of history and the Kathlyn Cosper Dunagan Professor in the Humanities at the University of Texas-Permian Basin and is a senior research associate at Rhodes University in Grahamstown, South Africa, where he spent 2016 as the Hugh Le May Fellow in the Humanities. He is the author of *Freedom's Main Line: the Journey of Reconciliation and the Freedom Rides* (University Press of Kentucky, 2009), *Beyond the Pitch: The Spirit, Culture, and Politics of Brazil's 2014 World Cup* (Amazon, 2014), and *Bleeding Red: A Red Sox Fan's Diary of the 2004 Season* (New Academia, 2005). He is currently working on books on bus boycotts in the United States and South Africa in the 1940s and 1950s and on the 1981 South African national rugby team's tour of the United States.

Francois Cleophas is a senior lecturer in sports history at Stellenbosch University. His research interests are concentrated on sports practices in historically marginalized communities of the Western Cape. His most recent works include the edited volumes *Exploring Decolonizing Themes in SA Sport History: Issues and Challenges* (2018) and *Physical Culture at the Edges of Empire* (2020). Decolonization themes, particularly related to physical education and sports in local contexts, feature prominently in his work.

Todd Cleveland is an associate professor of African history at the University of Arkansas. His research interests are broadly concentrated around the interactions between Europeans and sub-Saharan Africans during the colonial period and, in particular, labor and social relations between the Portuguese and the indigenous populations in the former's assortment of African territories. This research features in three books: *Stones of Contention: A History of Africa's Diamonds* (Ohio University Press, 2014); *Diamonds in the Rough: Corporate Paternalism and African Professionalism on the Mines of Colonial Angola, 1917–75* (Ohio University Press, 2015); and *Following the Ball: The Migration of African Soccer Players across the Portuguese Colonial Empire, 1949–1975* (Ohio University Press, 2017), as well as in a number of articles and chapters in edited volumes.

David Drengk is an Africanist with a focus on African history who currently works at the History Department at the Technical University of Darmstadt in Germany. As a doctoral research fellow, he is part of the wider interdisciplinary research group (A Global History of Technology, 1850–2000) at the Technical University of Darmstadt (funded by the European Research Council). In his current PhD project, he focuses on the technological landscape of the forest in colonial Ivory Coast and aims at building a bridge between African history, anthropology, environmental history, and history of technology to write a West African history of technology that is informed by methodological pluralism. He has graduated from the Humboldt University in Berlin and Leiden University/the African Studies Centre Leiden (ASC). He holds a diploma in area studies Asia/Africa, agricultural sciences (BA) as well as African studies (MA research). His special interests are social and oral history in a Southern and Western African context, and his research projects have led him to Malawi, South Africa, Togo, Ghana, and Ivory Coast.

Mark Fredericks is a video-lab assistant at Walter Sisulu University in East London, fulfilling the role of technical assistant to the broadcast lecturer in the Journalism Department and assisting third-year journalism students with their final-year video documentary productions.

He also teaches photojournalism as part of the broadcast course at the first-year level. His research interests are concentrated on the omission of social narratives in postapartheid sporting discourses. Mark has presented on the relationship between sports, society, and politics locally and abroad, using mainly audiovisual presentation methods. Mark has completed his master's degree at the University of the Free State.

Jasmin M. Goodman is a communication consultant, scholar, and professor who completed her PhD in communication, culture and media studies at Howard University. A critical race, gender, and media scholar, her research focuses primarily on TV/film, social media, digital streaming, and Black popular culture. Her dissertation examines the gender and cultural dynamics that shape the experiences of professional TV writers and influence the images and stories seen on television. The study also investigates the processes for creating television narratives for women characters and characters of color. Her goal is to continue analyzing how Black women—and other marginalized groups—use traditional and new media to engage in discourse about social justice and activism. The ultimate goal of her work is to move beyond the privileged walls of the academy to spark much-needed discourse within communities.

Albert Grundlingh is a graduate of the University of the Free State and was appointed at the University of South Africa in 1973, where he obtained MA and DLitt et Phil degrees. In 2001 he moved to Stellenbosch University as head of the History Department and served in that capacity until 2015. Grundlingh is the author, coauthor, and editor of several books as well as numerous academic articles published locally and internationally. He specializes in social and cultural history, with a particular interest in war and society. His major work deals with the "Handsuppers" and "Joiners" during the Anglo-Boer War of 1899–1902, and he followed this up with publications on Black and "coloured" South African troops during the First World War. He has also written extensively on sports and society, published as "Potent Pastimes." His work on rugby and South African society, he likes to argue, is akin to dealing with the phenomenon of war in a different format.

Marizanne Grundlingh is a lecturer at the IIE's Varsity College, Cape Town. She obtained her BA (international studies) from Southern Methodist University, Dallas, Texas. She completed her BA (HONS) cum laude in social anthropology at Stellenbosch University and then went on to complete her MA in social anthropology at the same institution. Her dissertation for her PhD in anthropology from the University of the Free State was titled "'After the Triumph': An Anthropological Study into the Lives of Elite Athletes after Competitive Sport." Her research interests include the anthropology of sports, sports and symbolic immortality, and the dynamics of sports and heritage in the South African context. Her current research is exploring the intangible heritage associated with rugby stadiums in South Africa.

Tarminder Kaur is a postdoctoral research fellow in the Department of Anthropology and Development Studies at the University of Johannesburg, South Africa. Her research interests are broadly sports among working people and how they negotiate their subaltern identities in southern Africa. For her doctoral thesis, she wrote an ethnography of the sporting lives of farmworkers of the Western Cape. Her research is published in a number of articles and book chapters. She coedited two special issues: "Becoming and Unbecoming Farm Workers in Southern Africa," *Anthropology Southern Africa* 40, no. 4 (2017) and "Sporting Subalternities and Social Justice: Rethinking South African Sports Studies," *Acta Academica* 50, no. 2 (2018). In 2017 she co-organized the 11th Sports Africa Conference, hosted by the University of the Free State, Bloemfontein. She continues to serve on the board of Sports Africa Network.

Todd H. Leedy is associate director and senior lecturer in the Center for African Studies at the University of Florida. His previous work has appeared in *History in Africa, Agricultural History,* and *History of Education Quarterly.* He started racing bicycles in 1982.

Chuka Onwumechili is a professor of communications at Howard University in Washington, DC. He serves as a member of the executive boards of the International Association for Communication and Sport (IACS) and ex-Enugu Rangers International Players Association (ERIPA), USA. His recent research focuses on sports, communication, and Africa in the areas of labor, identity, and image crisis. His most recent work is a textbook, *Sport Communication: An International Approach* (Routledge, 2018). He has published widely, including more than ten books, book chapters, and journal articles, including *Identity and Nation in African Football: Fans, Community, and Clubs* (with Akindes) (Routledge, 2020) and "Analysis of FIFA's Attempt at Image Repair: (with Bedeau) in the journal *Communication and Sport*. He also has published sports articles in *Soccer and Society*, *Critical African Studies*, *International Journal of Sport Communication*, and *International Journal of the History of Sport*. In addition, he helps former international players write memoirs. A recent memoir he has helped with is by Nigeria's former international star Francis Moniedafe, *Moniedafe: My Life and Glory Years of Bendel Insurance FC*.

Trishula Patel is a PhD candidate at Georgetown University in Washington, DC. She specializes in the history of Southern Africa and South Asia, with a particular focus on racial segregation in Rhodesia/Zimbabwe. Her dissertation is tentatively titled "Becoming Zimbabwean: A History of Indians in Rhodesia, 1890–1980." She is originally from Zimbabwe and holds a BA and MA in history from the University of Pennsylvania, as well as an MS in journalism from Columbia University. She has worked as a photographer, journalist, and high school teacher.

Sebastian Potgieter is a senior PhD candidate at the University of Otago, New Zealand. His research centers on apartheid-era sports, deconstructionist historical method, and the narrative and literary composition of textual historical representations. Currently he is working on a deconstructionist approach to the shifting narrative representations of the 1981 Springbok rugby tour of New Zealand.

Michel Raspaud is emeritus professor of sociology of sports at the University of Grenoble Alpes. His research interests cover the history of sports, European and African soccer, sports and leisure, stadium facilities management, and Brazilian soccer. He has published several papers and edited books on African and Brazilian soccer. He is member of several scientific boards and a reviewer for journals. He was dean of the Faculty of Sport Sciences and director of the Social Environment of Sport Research Centre at the University of Grenoble Alpes. His most recent book (with Ernest Yeboah Acheampong and Malek Bouhaouala) is *African Footballers in Europe. Migration, Community and Give Back Behaviours* (Routledge, 2019).

Michelle Sikes is an assistant professor of kinesiology, African studies, and history at Penn State University. She previously held academic posts at Stellenbosch University and the University of Cape Town in South Africa. Dr. Sikes earned her PhD from Oxford University, where she began her studies as a Rhodes scholar. In addition to her academic achievements, Dr. Sikes is an accomplished distance runner. Competing for Wake Forest University as an undergraduate, she won the 2007 NCAA Division I national championships in the 5000 meters. She earned All-American honors in both track-and-field and cross-country and represented the United States in the 5000 meters at the 2007 World Track-and-Field Championships in Osaka, Japan.

Christian Ungruhe is a social anthropologist and Marie S. Curie Fellow at Erasmus University Rotterdam, the Netherlands. His research interests are issues of spatial and social mobility in the realm of youth, work, and sports in West Africa. He previously held positions at Bayreuth University, Germany, and Aarhus University, Denmark, where his work centered on the career imaginations, trajectories, and postcareer experiences of African athletes. Currently he leads a research project in which he investigates the longitudinal processes of West African footballers' social and geographical mobilities and subjectivities en route to and in Southeast Asia.

Solomon Waliaula is a senior lecturer in literature and cultural studies at Maasai Mara University, Department of Languages, Linguistics and

Culture & Research Associate at University of Witwatersrand, Department of Afridan Literature, Kenya. His research interests are the areas of electronic audiences and popular cultures as they manifest in football and African cinemas. He has also studied and published on the oral literature and cultural productions of the Bukusu of western Kenya. He has been involved in a long-term ethnographic study of the spectatorship of both stadium and "televisual football" on the one hand and Nollywood cinema on the other hand. This study has produced a number of publications in the form of journal articles and book chapter contributions. He has been an Alexander Von Humboldt Fellow and is currently an African Oxford Research Initiative Fellow, working on a book project on electronic media audiences and sociocultural identification in Eldoret, Kenya.

INDEX

Figures are indicated by page numbers followed by *fig.* Notes are indicated by page numbers followed by n.